The Forgiving Path to the City of Springs

By

James J. Hill III

This story is a work of fiction. The characters were all created using the author's imagination. Any similarities in the characters to anyone are purely coincidental.

ISBN paperback-978-1-7367105-7-9

ISBN hardback-978-1-7367105-6-2

Also available on eBook

Contact the Author at:
Jameshillsellshomes@gmail.com

Instagram @GirlDadof5

Facebook-Author James J Hill III

James has also published other novels, including "When the Dandelions Sing," along with "Phoebe's Heart of Stone," and "The Gift of Life, Plus One".

This story is dedicated to anyone who has been placed in a world of uncertainty, and yet smiled through it all.

Special thanks to the following people who continue to help with my editing:

Flora Poloway

Amy McCormick

Contents

"Tell me something and be honest with me, Von. What exactly happened to you? I mean, why are you here, with all these other, well, you know. All these people that have nowhere else to go? What did you do that forced you to end up here, in this place where no man or woman, nor child for that matter, should ever end up? You don't seem as if you belong here as much as they do," I said.

He looked down at the rough, dry, clay ground just beneath the worn out soles of the shoes on his feet and smiled ever so slightly while shaking his head humbly with a sort of personal gratification. His demeanor was as it always had been since the moment we first met. The coarse, dirty-blonde hair on the top of his head is a knotty mess, and through the strands of hair dancing in all directions on his cheekbones, I can see they are lined with fine fibers of dirt from at least a week ago. The clothes he wears are raggedy at best, and torn at the ends, but that mind of his. Oh that brilliant mind of his is as sharp as anything I've ever heard, and it shares thoughts of something, anything other than the state he is in now.

"Well, it's a tale filled with triumphs before sadness and of great loss before a new, impossible gain. But let me tell you this first; I belong here more than most of these folks do. That much I am sure of. It's as clear as the blue sky above us is now. How much time do you have?" He says with a smirk upon his face, as he looks back to where I am, willing to give me that which I am searching for most.

I first met Von while doing some court-required

community service after a terrible day. Drinking and me, well, let's just agree that we didn't mix too well on a few occasions. I had an evening out with some boys of mine where I lost my temper, and to put a long story short, the judge gave me an option of serving jail time or serving the community. I decided jail in the city was not for me, and quickly agreed to the community service without a need for thought, although at the time, I had no idea the impact that would have on my life.

When presented with the different options lined up in front of me, I took several, seemingly long minutes to decide the fate I was about to endure. At first glance, I was bored and entirely unfocused with the task at hand. I tried desperately to avoid anything, but here I was, trying to figure out which one of the services I had to pick between that would be the quickest and easiest, and one that would not make my days any more of a chore than this entire mess already seemed to be.

While skimming through the lines of unfamiliar names of the groups and glancing at the requirements each would require of me, I was stopped abruptly by one. One name jumped out more than the others, as if it was calling me by name. It just sounded as if I could and more so, *should* choose this one over any others, even the ones I had not even arrived at yet. My eyes were locked tightly and I had no need to check any further.

The Mudflaps Homeless Community Interaction.

What was this about? I had never heard of the Mudflaps

before, and although I knew our city had a revolting homeless problem like no other place I had heard of, I had never known there to exist an entire community of homeless bums all in the same area. There were always filthy dirty beggars with the same old smelly clothing worn day in and day out, and vagrants wandering helplessly around the city streets, either with handmade signs claiming that they were veterans and needed money for food, or that they had families on the street as well, because they had lost their jobs and their kids were homeless because of the mistakes of others, never theirs. Some, though, were honest enough to make signs saying, "Money for alcohol. Why lie?"

I never gave my money to any of them when presented with their pleas. If I could work a normal work week, coming from the horrid, miserable background I had been forced to accept in my younger life, then so could all of these people. I use people lightly to describe them. They are more a drain on a decent society. That is what they are when it comes right down to it. People who would rather beg for money from mostly honest, hard working people with dignity instead of just getting jobs of their own and earning a paycheck. It wasn't hard to find work really, but they still sat around on poorly lit street corners covered in trash and smelling like something out of a sewage plant, making you feel bad for minding your business and simply walking by them without acknowledging their useless existence.

Not for me, though. I couldn't care less what they think of me. They gave nothing back to our society, and in fact, created a stench for the city with the clothes they never washed, and their disgusting bodies that were never cleaned and reeked of dreadful odors I could never forget even if I tried. Who would want to live like that? Not any human I knew, and that is where I had trouble finding human in them.

No, these people were desperate losers who could not find a decent thing to offer those that they begged from shamelessly. Not a single thing. I wondered why they even bothered staying alive? Why live in a world with so much potential right at your fingertips, so many opportunities if you would just open your eyes and look around, if you could not enjoy life? I never understood that about them.

"What's this one?" I asked the miserable woman behind the other side of the desk who seemed just as excited to be there as I was. As much as I hated the homeless, I felt the urge to learn more about this Mudflaps place, figuring that I could breeze through whatever they required of me.

"You never heard of the Mudflaps? That figures", she said with a look of disdain on her face.

"It's down by the river, the far end, where the trail the joggers use in the warmer months of the year ends, and the homeless folks live in makeshift tents made from anything they can find. The city has tried to remove them a few times over the years I've been here, but there are always a few people who stand up for them people and fight to keep them there. You want to work down there with them, do you?" she said as if to tell me, trust me, you are not the right fit for that place and those people.

I sat back in the cheap, half-broken chair across the desk from this feisty, but almost cold as ice woman, rocking back and forth a few times as it squeaked steadily with each motion I made, and then looked quickly at the list once more. Nothing else seemed to be anything that interesting to me. I did not want to remove graffiti from the brick walls downtown where those I work with travel during both the week and the weekends. I had no interest in kneeling all day in the dirt, weeding the flower beds of City Hall or picking garbage up from the side of the highways in a bright orange suit with a stick in one hand and a trash bag in the other, while everyone drove by looking to see if they recognized anyone. This all seemed like bullshit work to me, so my options were thin from the start. For a split second, I even considered going back in front of the magistrate and explaining to him that I had made a mistake and changed my mind, but I knew that would be a terribly bad decision.

"Well, it's not as if you have anything that appeals to me, so yea, this one. This is the one I choose."

I pushed the chair back some more, looking dead at her and asked,

"So are we done here?"

The older woman behind the desk just laughed under her breath. She could see I was cocky, bored, and just looking for an easy way out, but she also knew without telling me, I had picked one of the hardest of the options available to me. She knew that I could not fully understand what would be expected of me, but she was more than happy to comply with my request. She probably figured I deserved this for whatever it was I had done, but what she did not count on was what this was going to do to, and for me. That she did not count on, and neither did I.

"Well, I'm sorry our menu of options leaves you such a perplexed young man. You are all signed up. You will meet the man in charge at this address first thing next Saturday morning, and don't be late. Marcus will show you around and trust me on this; you don't want to piss off Mr. Marcus. He's the one person you will want to keep happy. He can make this manageable for you, or incredibly difficult, if that is the way you play this," she said.

And as she said that, she had a shit-eating grin on her face that told me she knew something I did not.

I didn't care, though. Mr. Marcus, the homeless drains on society, the magistrate judge, all of this was temporary for me anyway. I had to bide my time there and just suck it up long enough to finish what I was forced to, and then it was back to my life and my way of making my own decisions, where I just needed to be a bit more careful from now on.

They can all make this as difficult as they like but in the end, I am the one that will win. I go back to the life that I created for myself. My well-paying full time job and my beautiful girlfriend. I go back to doing what I do best and for me, and these people are stuck in their miserable lives, doing whatever it is they do. And I don't give a rat's ass what that entails.

As I stood up to grab the loose paper that she wrote the address on off her desk, I smiled right back at her, letting her know she was not going to change the course of my day with her attitude. I was not going to allow her to intimidate me, but something inside that I didn't share with her makes me wonder. What is going to happen down there that she knows and I don't? What are the Mudflaps truly, and how the hell am I going to help these people that I loathe, and that can't even help themselves off the ground?

I'm not going to dress nicely for this. I'll wear the oldest, most worn clothes I can find in the bottom of my closet. With a name like The Mudflaps, I'm bound to get dirty and disgusting just as they are on the daily. Only, I have a lesson coming that I never thought would. One I needed more than I cared to admit, but eventually may have to. A lesson, for all lessons.

Chapter 1

* * *

Bourbon is my drink of choice when given the option. Well, it was my drink of choice, but not anymore. Not ever since that early morning where I was forced roughly into the rear of a police cruiser, taken to the station, and placed in a small, damp cell with other drunks laying around on the cold floor, cuddled up in fetal positions just waiting to go home. Or maybe not.

The wretched smell of that miserable place, and the smell I must have had on me after vomiting in the back of that police car and down the front of my new shirt and pants, was enough to make anyone sick, even a bunch of drunks.

I sat there on the cool, pale gray concrete floor, nursing my bruised knuckles that were still bleeding from the fight I had had earlier in the early evening, and I tried to remember exactly what had happened. It was a blur for the most part, but I remember accidentally bumping into someone, then one of the people they were within their group said something stupid to me they should not have, and I just blindly reacted. Obviously, not in the way I should have reacted mind you, but it was still how I was. How I am, really. Reactive with little thought process behind those actions.

I don't usually think through chaotic situations well, instead opting to handle things with ferocious speed and without calculated thoughts. It has served me well in many situations, but there are those other times, like that night, where it does more harm than good to be so quick and reactive.

It's all I know how to do, really. I don't think I intend to be a quick, reactive individual, but my past has dictated my present. My childhood upbringing was one that you would most aptly categorize as rough and miserable almost daily. My birth parents were not easy to deal with most of the time. They both drank heavily, and more often than not, I was the center of their frustration and deliverance of said frustrations..

When they would argue irrationally after a full afternoon of day-drinking, it would turn to one of two things that always caused their issues and frustrations to come to a head: money or the lack of, or my brother and me. We would be at the short end of a leather-belt whipping, or if my father could stand straight up long enough, a wrap across the mouth or a black eye or two, depending on the size of his frustration. And of course the strength he had to throw those blows before falling down on his own face and busting his lip, usually caused him to pass right out where he landed and snore.

We were young kids, and although you always love your family, you don't always *love* your family. What I mean is, you want to love your mother and father unconditionally despite their flaws and shortcomings, and you find yourself praying Hail Marys at the end of those long nights, through warm salty tears that trickle down your red cheeks, to please make them love you more tomorrow. But when you realize those prayers are never going to be answered, and you realize that love was misplaced, you grow to even hate the person you are for having even loved someone who could be so brutal to begin with.

My brother was a year and a half younger than I was, so I felt the need to take the bulk of the punishment they dished out for him. I somehow saw that as the "right thing to do," but who knows. Was it honorable? Maybe all those extra blows made me into this vulgar person I am today. With little care for other people's feelings or emotions that I encounter in the real world. Because if I had to go through a sickening hell, they should have to as well. Fair is fair in my mind. They should have to fight for their well-being as much as I had to.

My mom didn't work much, and I think that was the cause for most of their issues. She would have a small job at a diner or more often at a corner bar in some terrible part of the city, serving other drunk adults who more often than not had their own bad intentions, but half the time she would be so inebriated herself that she would never make it in. Then my dad would scream holy hell at her and ask how the hell he was supposed to deal with her crap over and over, but nothing ever changed.

My dad, for his part, at least made it into work, even if he was hung over from the slosh-fest of drinking the night before. His job was working at construction sites in and around the city, and he could do his work with a full-on buzz, no matter how bad he felt the morning of. He could never understand why my mother could not, but I always wondered why they had to drink to begin with. It never seemed to make either of them feel good about their lives, yet they continued doing so as if it was all they had in this world. I think they were searching for a feeling that would allow them to escape what they knew, but they always ended right back to what they had.

Eventually, it caught up with the both of them at the same moment in time. My mother had enough of his screaming and pounding on her one evening, and although her driver's license had been revoked so long ago that I can no longer remember, she took the car keys off the Formica counter, slid carefully into the driver seat of their old run-down car, and with my father screaming feverishly at her to get the hell out of his damn car, she backed up and over top of him in one jerking motion.

My dad laid there motionless for several passing minutes until the paramedics arrived, but by the time those agonizing moments passed, the damage was already done. My drunk of a father passed away at some point before they could revive him, while my brother and I sat inside the family living room on the one decent couch we owned, peering out through the dusty, cracked window my father had broken last summer and never fixed, as we wondered which one my dad was going to blame when he came back in. He never came back in though.

My mother is still incarcerated in North Oakmont Penitentiary, at least she was the last time I asked. I haven't visited her since I was a kid and was forced to, and even then I hated it. My foster parents took me a few times, but they ended up being mostly worthless role models to me and stopped completely.

My brother, though, ended up with a decent Catholic family in a different city altogether. His foster parents formally adopted him, and he went on to do well in school and has a really good job in Seattle at a decent sized law firm. I speak to him once in a while, but not a lot. I'm genuinely happy for him, but mostly sad for me so it's hard to talk with him for any length of time. I took those extra beatings from my parents so that he didn't have to suffer, and he ended up with the better family life, while I was given the shitty end of the stick for my noble actions. Life isn't fair that way, but who cares anyway?

So when I started drinking at an early age, it just made sense to me. It's all I ever knew, so I felt I had an excuse to be a loser just like my parents were. My foster parents, Dale and Emma, didn't drink a drop of liquor. They were church-going Christians, one day a week, but after Sunday ended, they were bastards. They argued a lot, and Dale would spend the night God knows where, leaving Emma crying late into the morning until he returned, pretending as if it were all her fault.

I was expected to go to church with them and two other kids who lived with us. Those kids seemed to fit right into their roles, but me, I just never grasped the idea of going to church to praise someone who let me take those beatings and allowed me to watch as my mother ran down my father, tearing my already fragile family further from where it was. They wanted me to praise someone for allowing all that? No thanks. I had better things to do with my Sundays than to pray to someone who didn't give a shit about me and my life.

So after a while, I started to sneak out of their perfect home, and found myself growing up much quicker than I should have. I saw things I wish I never had, and found myself getting chased by the police a little more than I ever wanted, but what else was there to do for me in the monastery they called home?

When I reached the age of eighteen, Dale and Emma sat me down in their kitchen, and told me they had given me all they could as a start for my adulthood. They said that through sacrifice and prayer, they ensured that I had a roof over my head, a full belly at night, and a purpose in life, although I never felt I had any.

Once I graduated from high school, I was expected to leave *their* home by the end of the summer, and to find my own way in life. That was it. Just throw me away like I was never anything to them but a check they got from the state. Now that those checks would stop? I was no longer needed or useful for them, and that home they told me was just as much mine, was no longer ours.

Screw them Sunday Christians. They probably thought I would fail, but they were wrong. Dead wrong. I started working my summers for a landscape company when I was fifteen, and each summer, I went back. I had saved some money from doing that and a few side hustles I had set up, so now I just needed a place to crash until I could get my own.

Rather than wait out the entire summer before leaving their commune, I talked with Randy, who was a kid I went to school with, and the kid who's uncle owned the landscape business we both worked for. He had an extra room in his parent's basement that he said I could use until I got on my feet. His parents were cool, so it was set.

I didn't even tell my foster parents that I had found a place. I just packed a few bags when they were out one Sunday at church and raided their refrigerator and junk drawers for anything I could use, and I was off. You would think they would have looked for me to make sure I was all right, but that never happened. At least not that I knew of. I never talked with those people again, and it was for the best really. Anyone that was a drain on my life, and I was not required to keep in it, I deleted from my world like removing a contact from your phone. I preferred it that way.

Randy was a good kid with a big heart, and for some reason or another, took a genuine liking to me. Maybe he just felt bad for me and the cards I had been dealt during the past decade or longer. We got along really well for the most part, and anytime I was in a funk of any kind, he always had my back. Even though his upbringing was much more normal than mine, he never looked to make me feel any different than anyone else or that I was a charity case. He understood that we didn't get to choose our families, so why penalize someone who didn't have the same opportunities?

In the early fall, Randy would be heading off to college, and I was not. Once again, I was proud of Randy and certainly happy for him, but damn it, why? Why was I again being left alone to pick up the minuscule scraps of life, while those who were small boys and young men just like I am, had all these opportunities handed to them? Life didn't seem fair or balanced in that sense. I just wanted a break for a change, but it wasn't to be and that is just how it goes sometimes.

So it would be more landscaping for me in the sweltering summer months, and then who knows what I would find to do in the fall and for that matter, the rest of my life. I was no doubt a hard worker, so I wasn't worried about finding something to make my living. I knew I could hustle my way into just about anything I wanted to, but I had no clue as to what I actually wanted to do with my life from this point on. Not yet, anyway.

By this time I had no family, other than my younger brother who was still in high school with his perfect, ready-made family and his nice name-brand clothing that looked brand new all the time instead of the second-hand clothes I had. I stopped calling him, but he would call me to check in here and there anyway. He's a good kid, don't get me wrong, but I wanted more family in my life than he could provide on his own. I never knew my grandparents and even though my parents had siblings on each side, they had long lost contact with them and in turn, with us, probably because of the heavy drinking my parents did. No one wanted to be around that shitshow for any length of time, not even a kid. But I had no choice, and so here I was, a product of my environment. Feeling sorry for myself year after year, barely hanging on to what sanity I had left, and wondering if I would end up a terrible, useless drunk like they had.

I received a short letter from my mom, though. She sent it to my little brother because she knew where he was living, but had no way of contacting me directly. He said he would keep it and all the others she was writing to me safely stored away, but that eventually I was going to need to open them and let go of my past.

Easy for him to say. His past did not define him the way my past had done for me. Let go of my past? Why did people always tell me to do that when it was not the past they had to live in? Besides, I didn't care to hear anything my birth mom had to say to me. No amount of heartfelt apologizing or sorrowful tears were going to change any of the things she took from me and from my childhood that I should have enjoyed. So why waste my time pretending it would somehow?

Chapter 2

* * *

I ended up doing fairly well those first few years after I left my foster care situation. While I didn't get to experience the rite of passage to college immediately. Like most kids I knew, I did eventually find a way to manage that part of my life over time.

After working some prosaic construction gigs, just like my own dad had for all those years he was alive, and doing some minuscule janitorial work late at night where I could earn some extra cash, I eventually managed to save enough money to get a small place with a guy named Jose who worked with me from time to time. He was a cool dude overall, and always full of tantalizing wisdom and indisputable happiness about his life, even though he came from a more humble background than I had, that seemed to be filled with shambles of a life more than an actual life.

He came from some small hilly town in central Mexico, but I honestly do not remember the name of it. Doesn't matter, because it wasn't like I was going to visit it anytime soon or would need to recite the name in my life.

Jose would work long, arduous hours, and send half of his take home pay back to his hometown, no matter how much or how little he earned that week. It was religious for him to never miss sending that half, and he took that with an insane type of pride.

I asked him once why he would send so much of his hard-earned money back when he was living here in the city where he could buy whatever he needed, and he would assure me that his family back home needed it much more than he ever would. His hometown was poor. "Muy pobre", which meant dirt poor, he said, and so he wanted to give his parents, grandparents and siblings a better way of life, for which this became the vessel for doing so. I remember telling him that those people back home simply needed to work a little harder, or search longer hours for better paying jobs, and he would just smile at me, and nod in what seemed to be an agreeing motion, but was truly not. It was almost as if he knew more about that than I did and just wanted to let me believe what I was going to regardless.

He wasn't a citizen, coming across the southern Texas border illegally through tunnels dug out over years of backbreaking labor, and at first, it pissed me off something fierce, but as I got to know and understand him better over time, I realized he was just doing what anyone else would in his shoes. He was providing a better means to life for those he loved unconditionally, and to be honest, I admired his honorability. I never had anyone, other than my younger brother that is, that I wanted to give a better life to from the one I was building for myself.

Jose was simple, never purchasing anything he didn't need immediately, and always packed a brown-bagged lunch each morning for the day of work ahead. When the other guys we worked with would go out after work to have a few drinks with the guys, Jose would always politely decline, and head back home, or off to a side job he had lined up the week before. He was always working, and always striving for a better life that was not just for him, but others he didn't live with, and I had to admire that ethic he possessed.

Not me, though. I was always out with the boys, and drinking more than my fair share, which always left me feeling horrible and exhausted the following morning. I was trying to take night classes for school, while working a full-time construction job during the days, all while managing awful hangovers which were growing almost daily.

I think that is why I built such a disdain for homeless people. I hated that I would wake up at the crack of dawn, day after repeated day, no matter how my body felt drained of life or did not want to react to what I told it to do, and I still went to work. And after that? I headed to classes late in the evening and wash and repeat. It was my cycle, one I accepted for now, and to see these useless men and women sitting half dead, on top of black steel grates blowing warm, milky smoke out from somewhere below all across town, while a used, worn-out cup sat in front of them for handouts instead of working an honest job, frustrated the hell out of me.

Life isn't that hard to figure out. You are born into the families you are delivered into without a say, but what happens as you grow older and wiser, you have much to say about. More than people seem to realize, in fact. But they have to see it for themselves to truly understand that. They have to look at the opportunities around them, and they have two basic options from that point moving forward. They can find it within and use it to propel them into the right direction, or they can ignore it altogether. That is the difference between highly successful people and those that sit around complaining or begging from those same successful souls.

Jose was a man who seized an opportunity to better his life, although, in a way, that was not technically legal. He crossed over, and despite the fact he wanted to be a citizen of my great country, he was not legal. Again, I didn't bother to ask him why, because at least he was working hard and not begging from others, and anytime I needed a little extra cash, he knew how to find work for me. I pick my battles in life, and I decided having someone help me when I needed it would override my desire to complain about him sucking off from my tax dollars that I ultimately paid anyway.

At school, I studied business and finance. I figured that I would have a better chance getting ahead if I had the basic concepts down that other businessmen had learned. None of them had anything about them that was better than what I had, with maybe the exception of a better head start in life. I had a strong work ethic like those people, and I was intelligent enough to figure out patterns and systems for improving my chances at business, so if they could succeed, well, so could I.

As I entered into my mid-twenties, I experienced something totally out of my control, and it was crushing. The market crashed, and all the hard-earned money I had smartly invested over the past several years was wiped out almost entirely. I worked so many long hours for that money and educated myself about the laws of investing and saving and compound interest and buying the dips, that this made little sense to me.

What I learned the hard way was that it didn't need to make sense to me for it to be my reality. It was also the reality for millions of other people, but I had to focus on mine and what was happening in my center of the universe. not theirs.

I felt as if I was roughly starting all over again from rock bottom, and mentally I wasn't sure that I was prepared for this and what was to come. No one knew how long this horrid dry spell for the U.S. economy would last, but the truth was that I panicked. I was close to buying my first home, and the thought of not having to work two or even three jobs at a time was appealing to me as my investments grew.

At the same time, though, there were people far worse off. I had to at least see that reality to understand that it could be far worse for me. All across my city and across the states, people who had been living the high life for the past several years were spinning out of control and losing everything they had purchased during the height of the market. Literally all they made, was wiped away. Just vanished like that. Cars, houses, vacation homes, timeshares, all of it, just gone.

I heard stories that people were committing suicide over their losses, just as they had done in the great crash of '29. It literally destroyed families, and I wondered how the future would change for so many. How could people just give up like that? Did they not see that eventually things would turn back around for them if they just waited for the market to rebound and settle? As bad as things were at times for me, I always found a way to push through and never thought of ending my life.

I called my brother to check on him, but he knew it was me that was struggling. He knew me well enough to hear it in my tone, even though I think he always knew I had issues with my past. He could sense a different anguish and I had to give that to him. He read people and the situations they were in well. That's probably why he is so good at his work. He was most recently promoted to partner of his law firm just a year ago.

Was I happy for him? I mean, yea, I guess so. But the fact still remained, I took those extra senseless beatings so he didn't have to endure them anymore, and I wonder if that had something to do with his high level of success. Water under the bridge now, but still. I had to wonder where I would be if life was a little fairer, because I had the drive and the passion and the intelligence. I simply did not have the start that was needed, and it put me behind the eight ball. A level playing field would have made a massive impact on where I was now versus where I would have been.

For several more years, I was forced to work long hours, and was regulated to living mostly paycheck to paycheck, just to correct my financial situation from the turmoil of the crash. I had to get things in order, and that was going to take me years to work out, but eventually, things started to shift once again, and I made some smart moves while the market was low, and by the age of twenty-nine, I was mostly back on track.

It had been just about two decades ago that my dad passed, and my mother was still incarcerated, as she should be. But at the end of the day, I didn't need them to live my life. I had a built-in excuse for failing, but I was determined to do anything but fail. That was my issue with the homeless society. They had choices. They had options presented to them, and their past had nothing to do with their present. Just as mine did not. They chose to use it as an excuse instead as a catapult to a better way of living.

I remember being so angry one night, and it just so happened that this homeless bum was in the wrong place at the wrong time. He wasn't begging for money. Just sitting there under his piles of dirty mismatched blankets, sleeping away his life, and I don't know. Something pushed me into a fit of rage and frustration, and I unleashed a horrid, volley of words directed at this guy that woke him from his slumber, and a confused look began to cross his old face. He was just looking up at me, helpless, dazed, and probably hungover.

I said things I'm sure he has heard before, but I also said things he probably never heard in his entire life. It was bad, and after I was finished, I reached into my jean pocket, pulled out a twenty dollar bill, crumbled it up, and threw it at him, saying,

"Here. This is what you want, isn't it? Try working for it next time. At least do a magic trick, or dance, or sing or something to entertain me. Worthless gutter scum. That's what you all are. A drain on good, hard working people, because you would rather beg. Worthless gutter scum."

It wasn't exactly his fault, but like I said. Wrong place, wrong time. I also had a few drinks in me and a shot or two of tequila, maybe three, and it was just a bad night. I was seeing this girl, and we fought all week over stupid things, and then the friends I was supposed to meet up with bailed, and I ended up drinking alone, and...

Sometimes people don't get it. My past does come back to haunt me when I wish it would stay where I left it. I had no intentions of reliving those dreadful moments in my life, but every now and again, they crept back in like a bad stalker. I hated it, but most times I was strong enough to push it back and far enough away to forget it for the time being. Only, there were a few times I could not find that strength too. Those times were brutal for me, and usually caused me to rage, and when I added drinking into the mix, it was a bad night for anyone around, including me.

I never saw that guy again, but it wouldn't have mattered much anyway. What was I going to do? Apologize? Why? It wouldn't help him if I did. I probably did more for him by pushing him and making light of his situation, than any apology could ever do.

You have choices in life. All of us do. We go left, or we go right. We move faster, or we slow down. We work hard at whatever it is we do, or we don't. That's it. Those are the options we all have, and while our past can contribute to the number of options presented to us, they cannot make the ultimate decisions for us on the path we will take.

This guy, this man of gross dirt and utter filth with no purpose in life, had probably made a lot of bad turns and decisions throughout his own life. He most likely took a bad past, where maybe his parents abandoned him during his most needed times and allowed it to be his destiny going forward. Poor choices don't get you anywhere good in life, and although his current situation seems bleak, his life isn't over unless he's so far removed from wanting more than what he has.

That, no one can help him with. Not me, not society, no one. So did I feel bad? Sure. But not necessarily for what I said. I felt bad that he needed people like me to remind him he failed at life. That's it.

My brother called me not too long ago. That, I am sure,

contributed to my recent chain of mood swings as well. It seems my mother was up for parole once again, and he wanted me to attend the hearing. He felt she had spent the better part of her life paying for a bad afternoon, or perhaps a massive dose of many bad afternoons and nights of terrible decisions. My brother actually thought I may somehow care deep down, and that I would give a shit about her getting out and bonding with us again like some happy family that took a break for two decades.

My mother was a murderer. Plain and simple. It wasn't a gray area for me at all. It was as black and white as it could get. She purposely ran my father over with his own car, and the alcohol was just a vehicle in play. Her intentions were there, just as mine are when I am drunk and do stupid things. I know what I am doing is wrong, but the liquor just makes it easier to not give a damn. That is what my mother did those decades ago. She didn't give a damn that she was taking something from her kids, as little as it seemed to her. She only cared about what she wanted in that fateful moment and she got it.

So, no, I did not attend the hearing, and she was thankfully not paroled. I wanted nothing to do with that. Even when my brother tried desperately to tell me just how different she was after being locked away like a caged animal, and how she had found God and whatever else she wanted people to believe she had found. I had no desire to continue the conversations, so I told him I had to go, that I was glad he cared about something in his life, but that I had other things pressing that needed my immediate attention. For all I cared, she could and probably should die in that lonely prison cell, just like my dad did in the driveway underneath all that metal. An eye for an eye, and if she truly did find her faith? She would know that and accept that.

Chapter 3

* * *

Saturday was rapidly approaching, and I was beginning to wonder just how this whole Mudflaps community service thing was going to pan out. I didn't want to wake early and really didn't see the need. The homeless probably didn't wake early enough to need any real services at that hour, but what did I know? I was just going to do the required time and get this over with and return to normalcy.

I pulled out my old, weathered work boots with the soles worn down, found a pair of loosely fitted jeans I had been meaning to throw away because they were now torn in three places and I just had not found the chance, and a t-shirt I bought one of the times I was at a bar crawl downtown. That was a night to remember, or actually, one to forget. I learned exactly the number of beers it took me to pass out cold, like out like a light. I was cooked that night for sure and ended up waking up in a house I had never laid eyes on before. The guys that owned the house were cool about it though. They were probably out with our group at some point and maybe that's how I ended up in their dining room on the floor, but I never bothered to ask. I just wanted to grab my shit and get out. It was pretty embarrassing.

I called my girlfriend the night before starting the community service because she was traveling for work, and told her I didn't want to do this at all. I knew she didn't have the answer as to how I could avoid it, but I just wanted her to know I hated this and to hear some encouraging words.

"Babe, I get it. Think of it this way. You are always talking about how your past doesn't dictate who the person you are today, so maybe, I don't know. Maybe..."

Before she could get it out, I jumped in "What? Maybe I can be a better person and learn something from this sentence? Is that what you are implying?" I asked.

"No! I'm not saying that at all. I'm just saying, maybe you will find something in this all that will make you happier about your own life. I know you have a lot on your plate, but I fell for that smile of yours, and I just don't see it like I once did," she said.

When I met Hailey, she was this prep school looking type of girl, and I was just a grungy construction rat with an attitude. There was no way I could ever see us together, and for a few years, we weren't. We would talk here and there when we ran into each other, but she would date people more her type, and I would date women who just weren't mine apparently, but whatever. I was having fun.

It wasn't until earlier this year that we ended up getting together for the first time. It just happened one night out with friends, and everyone was pushing the two of us together, knowing we were both recently single, and things just ended up as so.

She's a good woman. I'm not sure what she sees in me, but she sees something apparently. I just need to be a little happier and more positive around her, but in this city, it's hard sometimes. Everyone is always rushing from place to place, and people don't seem to care where you are walking, because they are always bumping into each other, and no one ever apologizes, or rarely will. Plus, crime is high and it sucks wondering if you are going to get mugged or have to fight for your phone or your life if you end up in the wrong part of the city.

By the time we get off the phone, I feel like I am a complete mess. I can't possibly be good enough for this woman, and I just can't seem to find a positive vibe in my life for which to fall back on. Don't get me wrong. I like my life. My job is good and pays well, and my boys are always there whenever I need them. It's rare to find loyalty these days, and I have it with those friends. Now, I have this awesome woman who loves me for me, but she is missing something with me, and I'm afraid to lose her. I need to figure out my life a bit clearer, and as soon as this community service is up, I'm going to work on that next. I swear, it's the first project I will tackle when I am done with the bullshit.

That night, I didn't sleep well at all, and in fact, I would be surprised if I had a straight hour of rest. I tossed and turned throughout my attempted slumber, wondering what time it was over and over, and when my alarm was going to go off, but each time I glanced at my phone, it was still early in the morning.

Finally, I must have shut my eyes long enough that I went into a deep, sound sleep, only to hear my alarm go off in the most annoying way.

I'm pissed at myself for letting my anger get the better of me. I'm pissed at the guy who I punched in the mouth so he would shut the hell up, and the cops who arrested me for doing what guys do, I'm pissed off at them as well. I'm even pissed at the judge for forcing me to make a decision between this or jail. But jail would only remind me of where my mother is, and I am not my mother at all. I'm simply a product of her intoxicated desires and impulsive, somewhat uncontrollable actions one day.

I stretch my arms up high to the ceiling, yawning like an awakening lion as the sun hits his fur, and feel the dryness on the tip of my lips. I need coffee, and thankfully I remembered to set that before I tried to sleep last night. It's 6:00 am, and this all feels like bullshit to me. But this is only day one of eight Saturdays I will need to do so that I avoid the courts again, and more importantly, jail time. No doubt if I do not finish this exercise in humanity, that is exactly where I am heading.

On my nightstand sits the folded paper detailing where I

am to meet this Marcus guy that apparently no one wants to piss off, as if I really care, and the time I am to meet him. 7:15 am sharp written boldly. Who gives a time like that to meet? Why not 7:00 am, or even 7:30 am? Already, I feel like this is amateur night with this group.

After I pour my first cup of coffee, I text Hailey to let her know I miss her and that I will check in when I am finished up for the day. She's on the west coast at a conference, so she's still fast asleep I hope. At least she probably had a better rest than I did.

Then, I slip on the clothes I laid out the night before, lace up my old work boots, open the refrigerator to find the lunch I made for myself, and realize they never told me how long the day would be. Again, rookie move by this so-called community group who claim to be destined to help homeless people. Who starts a day at 7:15 and forgets to put an end time?

As I walk outside, the unusually cool, crisp early summer air greets me. It wakes me some, and I know it's only going to get warmer as the day drags on, at which point I hope to be back home and finished with day one.

The place I am to meet this Mr. Marcus is maybe seven or so blocks away from my house, and being that I live in the city, it's just easier to walk. I am always on alert most nights, but the mornings? Trouble sleeps in, so there are no worries about walking through the streets of Philadelphia early in the morning. Crime isn't even awake at this hour.

As I walk, I for some reason think back to that phone

call my brother made to me in reference to my mother's parole hearing. I had never followed up on her progress or the hearings she had over the years and wondered if she had had more since then. I have to admit I do not know how that all works, but it is what it is. She is in there where she should be, and I am out here where I should be. I know my brother wishes she would get released before she dies there, and I don't know if it's because he was too young to remember what she was like, or if he's just a better person than I am. I've never thought much of my mother after that trial and doubt I ever will again.

The thought of a different childhood comes to mind here and there, but I would be a different guy if that were the reality. Maybe I would be a prep school kid with a different set of parents, or maybe I would have been gay, or have two or three kids by now, or perhaps even be homeless. I don't want that, so to me, I am right where I was meant to be, and I accept that. Mostly, I do anyway.

The scattered thoughts shooting through my mind make my walk go by rapidly, and before I know it, I am two buildings away from where I am to meet. It's a simple, faded red brick front row home, with steps that have seen better days, and a railing that seems to be doing more harm than good. The front door has bars on it, and the sign above the door states, "Philadelphia Community Homeless Outreach".

Perfect. I must be right where I am supposed to be. Now, if I can just get this over with quickly and painlessly, I will be a happy person.

I knock on the door and wait. Inside, I can't hear anyone moving around, and so I look at my phone to double check the time. I'm a few minutes early, but someone should still be here. I would have to assume this was a group thing, with other men and women who decided to avoid jail time, helping out the homeless. Right?

"You Michael?" a deep, stern voice says behind me.

I casually turn around to see a man standing close to 6'4". He's walking by me now, unlocking the front door to this building with the keys he has dangling from his pants. My dad would always have his keys on his belt like this guy.

"Um, yea, I'm Michael. I assume you are Marcus?"

"You assumed correct. Follow me," he says.

I walk into the front doorway he opened just a moment ago and look around at the room in front of me. At first glance, I can't really see a lot, but then he hits a few lights, and I can see much clearer, that the room is full of brown cardboard boxes everywhere, loaded with cream colored files, and loose papers jammed inside each one.

Marcus isn't a man of many words. He walks around the boxes, grabs a few files from one that is opened on a desk, and places them in a bag he carries in with him.

"Take these files and meet me out front. I will be just a minute," he says.

I look around and realize that he and I are the only ones here. I begin to hope that when we arrive, there will be others to help out. I wanted to casually blend in instead of being a marked man. When there is a larger group,

I can blend in and do the minimum and no one would notice much, and that is what I was hoping for with this assignment.

Outside, I look around and don't see anyone else walking in the vicinity. Just a beat up brown Honda, with more files and papers inside thrown all about. You have got to be kidding me. This is my ride? Where the hell am I supposed to sit?

It's as if Marcus knows exactly what I am thinking, which is eerie.

"You just hang tight. I'll make room. We will find a place for you to sit," he says.

He has a strange way about him. He doesn't look at me when he talks and seems to know exactly where he needs to be, and what his next move is without pause. Like he is on a mission or something that only he knows about. Usually people look to see what my reaction is, but Marcus couldn't care about what I am feeling or wanting. He isn't interested in that, which leads me to wonder how he ended up wanting to help the homeless. I would assume one would need to have genuine care to help those that don't wish to even help themselves.

He tosses a few boxes to the back seat, and tells me to get in. As I do, I literally have my feet on top of boxes that are down below the dash, so that my knees are almost firmly into my chest.

But Marcus doesn't say anything else, so I guess this is how I am sitting until we arrive where we are heading.

I looked briefly the night before on my phone to where the river runs and tried to narrow down the areas this "Mudflaps" could be. There were a few areas that seemed like the only location for this, but I wasn't positive. I figured it didn't matter all that much because I was heading there regardless, and in a few months I would never have to see that place again, so why bother with any logistics. Just take me there and let's do this already.

The ride was dead quiet except for the loud muffler of his cheap-ass Honda. I figured he would start asking me about what I did that landed me here, or what my experience was helping homeless people, or about my background and family life, but he didn't ask a thing. He eventually turned the radio on, and we are now listening to sports talk, so I turned an ear towards the radio and listened as well.

I'm a die-hard Philly fan. Hockey, baseball, basketball, and football. All of it. I haven't been to many games recently, but I follow them as best I can when I have time. Philly is one of those cities where you either love the team, or hate the team, but you still love to hate all other teams. It's an unwritten rule here, and I follow it well. There are some morons who like other teams, but I swear they do that because they are looking for a fight. We are a fighting type of town so whatever. That city of brotherly love crap is just that in my opinion.

I have my eyes on the drive, trying to see if any of the locations I picked out were right for this hidden town. I am still shocked that growing up here and knowing all the people I do, that no one ever told me about the Mudflaps. It must be a really insignificant, unassuming type of place, because if it were anything else, I would know about it. I know my city. Trust me, I would know.

Eventually Marcus turns the old rusty Honda down a narrow road that doesn't seem like one you would find in a city such as Philadelphia. At the end of that road, he makes a left turn onto a winding gravel path and continues through thick vegetation that almost covers the ground below. As the trees and weeds start to disperse, I see an open area ahead, and then the river. It's not as wide in this part as it is in other parts, and looks more like a large creek, but it's still part of the Schuylkill river for sure.

We park the car, and Marcus motions for me to get out. I do as I am told and stretch from the car ride. My legs are aching from being up in the uncomfortable position they were, as I am not a short man either.

"Here, hold this," Marcus says as he hands me some files.

Without another word, he starts off down the trail and I follow, figuring if I stand where I am, nothing is going to happen. He lights a cigarette and walks calmly down the trail, almost as if he is at an office doing the same work over and over, knowing exactly what to expect.

Marcus is a dark skinned black male, probably in his late fifties or early sixties I would guess. He has a slight limp to his walk, almost as if he is carrying a weight on one ankle and not the other. He has no hair on the top of his head and isn't dressed for success. His voice is southern deep and commanding, and actually makes me a little uneasy at first. I can see what that woman was talking about when she said to not piss off this man. He just has an aura about him that he has seen a lot in his life and doesn't worry about what is coming any longer, because he knows he cannot change that fact, even if he knew.

At the end of the dirt path we walk down, I see it come into view. I see the makeshift cloth tents of different colors and materials, brown cardboard boxes scattered about in a somewhat strange but purposeful way, and a few small fires burning in the center of it all. There are several people sitting around having what appears to be coffee, while others appear to be just waking up, or maybe just heading to sleep. Trash piles up in areas for seemingly no reason, and there are overturned shopping carts tucked here and there, never to be returned again.

Marcus turns for the first time to look at me, and says, "Welcome to the Mudflaps."

Chapter 4

* * *

This place where I now stand, I somehow never knew existed. In fact, I am still unsure how it's even possible that a large community filled with wanderers and trash thrown all around, can be strangely hidden on a dirt riverbank, deep in the greens that surround it during the summer months, in a city as large as Philadelphia. I'm almost in utter disbelief, but standing in the midst of it all, I see that it's very real, right down to the people that are encamped here.

There are dozens of people tossed all around, dressed in various and somewhat curious styles. Most though seem to wear plain grays and beiges, or maybe that's just the film of the dirt covering their clothes. Some are dressed better than others, but no one here seems to care about any of that. They all seem to feel as if they are on the same level as one another, and it's an inexplicable sight to see from these eyes. How can they not care about how they look or smell? It's absolutely disgusting to me. This is where I say people need to have more pride in their appearance, but at the end of the day, it's not my business how they put their pants on. I am here for a short time, and this place? This place will be how it is, and I will be back home to a more civilized, better way of living while this place goes back into a suffering hidden realm.

Marcus walks on ahead and sits down with a few of the homeless, and I see him smile for the first time. He has the whitest teeth I think I've ever seen on a human. He's sitting upright on a long, moss-covered log situated around one of the fires, as a woman pours him a cup of whatever it is they are drinking, and he thanks her kindly as he nods her way. Who knew this large, deep-voiced and frightening, stern man could be so gentle? I half expected him to walk in and hand out expired bread and ladles of water from a metal bucket, and say nothing until it was time to go. Which, by the way, I still have no idea what time that is. He has yet to tell me just how long this is all going to be each Saturday.

I'm just standing there like an idiot, when Marcus pauses, stops his smile, and looks at me as if he is telling me to do something, but I haven't the faintest idea of what he expects from me. So I just walk over slowly towards where he is seated and place the files he handed me when we first met next to him and wait for his word on what to do with them.

The people seated to his right and left, with dirt smeared across their cheeks and hair sticking out through the wool hats they wear in the summer, just stare at me and then a few of them laugh obnoxiously. It's awkward being here with these people who suck the life out of a free society and expect others to fix all their mistakes, but I cannot worry about any of that. It'll just get me angry, and Lord knows, that's why I am here in the first place. My anger has to not be a factor here, or I will end up doing the time the judge allowed me to skip out on, which may or may not be a good thing.

As I think that, my mind goes back to my mother and the time she has served over the past few decades. It's crazy, that in all these years she's been incarcerated in a different part of the state, I have never once thought about the time she has done. I know she's been in prison, but to think about how she is actually doing that time has simply never crossed my mind. Was she frightened at first when her sober body was led into the metal and concrete cells with all those hardened inmates screaming? How did she sleep the first few weeks while away in a bed not familiar to her? Did she lose hope from the start, or is that something she has held faintly on to, knowing it was all she has left to escape from those walls?

It's funny how life can place thoughts in your mind without your approval, and you reflect on things you stashed far away in a place you never wish to visit ever again, only that isn't where they stay. I have learned that over my time here on earth. When I think I am over my miserable past and able to escape its clutches, it creeps in and reminds me that my past is always going to be there, no matter how hard I will it away. It's not for me to decide.

That same woman who poured the cup for Marcus walks over to the fire, pours the steaming liquid into an old mug that is cracked down the side, and walks it over to where I am.

"Here, freshly made and I used my favorite mug," she says with a smile that shows her mouth empty of almost all her teeth.

I don't do anything at first. My arms are down by my side, and I can't decide if I want to do the nice thing and take it, or do what my mind is saying, and politely decline, because I have no clue of what is in this mug, and where her favorite mug came from or how the hell they clean things around here, if they in fact do clean things around here.

But then, I notice Marcus staring hard at me from that damn log he is perched on, and without a word spoken, he's telling me to take the damn mug and not to piss him off this early in the day. For a man of few words, he says a lot without needing to say a lot. It's interesting how this man intimidates me. Most people don't possess that ability. I mean, I have been in street fights all my life. Through tight dark alleyways, behind rows of crumbling homes that probably once stood proud, and behind abandoned warehouses that almost seem out of a horror movie. I saw my own father killed by my mother in a fit of rage, and I have lived in places and areas of the city that most people would never be able to fall asleep in. Marcus is just built differently, and I notice that from the get-go. At first, I thought it was just intimidation setting in because that woman mentioned it when I first agreed to do this ridiculous service, but now I know it's more than that.

The hot mug is in my hands, seeping liquid from its crack that runs down the one side, and now everyone is staring at me. Damn, this really sucks something awful. I know what I have to do, but my body isn't responding to what my brain is relaying. My arms aren't moving from where they are, frozen at my side, and the few seconds that have passed by feel like many minutes. It's painfully uncomfortable and I am trying to remind myself that I have probably had drinks much worse than this in the past, so just suck it up..

The bar mat shot, or as we call it in Philly, "The Jersey Turnpike". At the end of the night, the bartender pours all the liquid that they spilled making dozens of different drinks throughout the evening onto the black bar mat, into a tall glass. It's never the same, because all of those people have been drinking all types of beer and wine and mixed drinks and shots throughout the night, and the excess spillage is collected on the mats. It's horrible, and disturbing what could be on that mat, but it's sort of a rite of passage when you are out with your boys. Everyone I know has done the Jersey Turnpike at least one time. I've done it more than once, I'm ashamed to admit.

I find myself finally placing the rim of the mug to my mouth, because the stares are not going away, and pretend to take a sip, even though I don't. I want to just tell them it's good and thank you, but I can't. I have no desire to talk with these people, and pretending to be thankful for all they don't do or contribute to society, is not going to happen easily. I loathe them to put it bluntly.

Marcus knows I didn't take a sip. I don't know how, but he shoots a stare at me, and turns away as if he's disappointed in me. Or maybe he just doesn't like me to begin with, but I have done nothing to this man. Once again, just get through this day and then you have six days in between that you don't need to worry about. One Saturday at a time, I remind myself. One at a time.

Everyone goes back to chatting away the morning and I see more and more people rising up from their sleep, stretching to the morning sun, and smiling as if something good is coming this day. For a place so unhealthy and unconventional, these people can't really believe there is good coming, can they?

I'm still unsure of my duties here, so I sit on a half-buried boulder that is coming out of the earth about ten or so feet from everyone else, and wait. Marcus doesn't direct me, so I figure he doesn't need me to do anything immediately. It's confusing, but without direction, I will simply wait and see what he tells me is coming next.

A half hour goes by, and still nothing. They are talking and laughing about who cares what, and Marcus seems to garner a lot of attention from everyone there. They respect this large man, but not because of fear. None of them show fear of him. They just have a mad respect for him.

I notice there are some men and women who sit alone, and either mumble to themselves, or make no sounds at all and just rock back and forth gently. I'm watching, waiting for something to happen where they are standing or seated, but nothing happens. It's as if they are all alone here in body and mind, and don't see what is going on around them just steps away. Weird, I think to myself. You would think they would at least want to have someone else to share in their grief and total lack of a quality life. You know, like misery liking company, but it's not that simple here. They seem trapped within their minds, unable to escape for any reason.

Marcus hasn't spoken a word to me, and hasn't directed me left or right, but I am sure he knows I am still here. Or does he? Did he forget that I was brought along here to help, delivered by the courts to his demands, or doesn't he feel as if I deserve any acknowledgement? Either way, it's making me extremely uncomfortable. I'm beginning to think this was a really bad decision on my part. Not worse than jail, but maybe removing graffiti from the sides of buildings wasn't a bad pick over this. At least with that, I would know what I was doing and the time would go by quickly. Here, it is standing perfectly still like a broken watch.

Then, about an hour into the visit, I see a humble man emerge from a makeshift tent, just off the edge of the river, and everyone trains their eyes on him. He greets the morning sun with a long deep breath of air that fills his lungs, and smiles at the sky. He points up, as if he is motioning to someone, or something, and right away, I think this man is plain nuts.

Marcus spots him, and immediately claps his hands together, smiling back at the man and speaks up.

"Good morning, Sir Von!" he says with a deep, loud belt.

This man, apparently named Von or Sir Von of royalty here, looks down from the heavens, and spots Marcus now standing up.

"Marcus, it's a glorious morning too, isn't it?" he says back.

They exchange a few more words, and this man walks on over to Marcus, and gives him a handshake at first, but then Marcus, with his large frame and massive hands, brings him in for a hug.

I'm still hanging back, and the man who emerged just a few minutes ago eventually spots me off to the right, and whispers something in the ear of Marcus, who turns my direction, and whispers back to Von. I have no clue as to what they are whispering back and forth, but I don't much care. Well, maybe a little I do, but I'm not giving that away to these men. They have yet to earn my full curiosity or any of my respect.

He walks over to me, and puts out his hand to greet me.

"Michael, is it? I am Von. It's a pleasure to make your acquaintance," he says.

Von is a thinner man, maybe six feet or just under, and his beard is showing his age more than his eyes do. He has lighter colored dirty brown hair that is in complete disarray, with just a hint of gray splashed in, and his posture is impeccable. He stands as if he once were a different type of man, and hasn't forgotten that.

I don't really want to shake his hand, because I feel as if that means I am accepting his life choices, which I am not, but I know if I don't, these next seven weeks are going to be hell for me. So, I reach out my hand, shake his quickly, and pull it back just as quickly.

"Michael, I get it. I understand you do not wish to be here, and that makes all the sense in the world to me. Trust me, though, Michael. We will treat you right here as you clearly deserve, and I hope that you end up learning a great deal during your time at the Philly Mudflaps. Mi casa es su casa," Von says.

This guy is out there if he thinks I am here to learn anything from him, these people, or this disgusting place they call home. If anything, I can teach them a thing or two. I can show them how they should be living, and how to work a normal job and not beg from good hard-working people, or how to let their past not dictate their present, but they, oh they are not going to teach me anything. That I can promise. They can't even bathe properly and their hygiene is probably senseless to worry about at this point.

Von tells me to come over and to sit with the others who are awake this morning. I'm hesitant, but it's either that or sit here alone for hours on end playing with my thumbs. It's not an easy decision, but I decide to go over to where a group of them are seated next to Marcus.

As I do, Marcus stands up, and simply walks away. He doesn't utter a word, and doesn't look at me at all. He just goes on over to another group of people and sits down, repeating the smiles and laughter that he had moments ago over here.

"Michael, is it? It's awesome to meet you, Michael. Come, sit. Sit," a woman mumbles to me as she shuffles over.

This one at least has few teeth, but her skin is loose and worn down. She has gray hair that is knotted almost entirely, and she smells bad. God-awful in fact, but the gentle breeze off of the river is pushing it away somewhat, thankfully.

I sit, and look down at the ground below me, wondering what I am supposed to say at this point.

The woman laughs slightly, and asks me if I am looking for something on the ground below me. She tells me that if I were, they would surely return whatever it was, as there are no thieves here today. I highly doubt that is true, but they were her words, not mine.

Von is looking me over carefully, but not saying much else right now. It's as if he is sizing me up, or maybe simply wondering what I did to end up here. They clearly know I was not born as one of them, but I am sure they are curious as to what I did that ended me here along the river's edge. I hate talking about it more than I need to, but I know it's a question I am going to have to answer at some point to these curious people who have nothing better to do with their time, and probably more than once.

Just then, Von breaks the ice with his words.

"Michael, what is it you see here? What is your heart telling you about this place?"

I look at him oddly, wondering if this man really wants me to tell him what it is I see with my eyes. He has to know I don't see any good here, but maybe I could lie and just make something up. The trouble is, I have an issue with that. I cannot lie about the feelings I have when I see bums begging for things they have never earned. I want them all to know how truly angry they make me, and how society can do so much better without them scraping from its bottom. I want them to know, they are worthless, blood-sucking leeches, and that a long bath would do wonders for all of them. I want to tell them that I despise what they are and represent.

I want to. But I don't.

Chapter 5

* * *

Most of the mid-morning is spent watching Marcus interact with literally every breathing human in the camp, and even those that appear as if they have no breath left. For such a seemingly hard-nosed man, he has an ability to make these people here smile as if they have everything they need right in front of them.

I stopped waiting for him to give me direction a while ago, as clearly he has no intention of doing his part. It's going to be a long, drawn-out day of standing around and watching these people do whatever it is they do all day long. I'm not even sure they have a proper plan in place for their own daily lives. Who wakes up in the morning and has no idea of what they are doing for the day in front of them, or where they are heading later in the afternoon? It's not even life, if you ask me. It's a waste of a gift of precious time to just wander aimlessly around in shapeless circles with no proper direction, as I am clearly doing here now myself.

Screw this. I'll just sit tight and watch the ever popular Marcus, and until he summons me over and gives me some sort of concrete task, it's not on me. He can't expect me to have any clear idea as to what these people need from me. I'm certain if they need something, they will ask. Or better yet, they will beg for it. It's what they are best at doing in life. In fact, it's the only thing they are good at doing.

Again, I am not trying to be an ass, even though it probably sounds as if I am. I've seen them all over the city holding up signs, begging for your money by claiming to be veterans, or stating that they somehow lost their job due to downsizing and have families they are desperate to feed. Liars. Every last one of them is a stone-cold liar.

Other than that twenty I tossed at that one homeless guy, I can't remember giving a dime to anyone who had to beg for it or clearly didn't deserve it. It teaches them to expect it from everyone else. Instead, they would be better served learning a skill or several different ones, and figuring out how to manage a formal job and a schedule that would allow them to prepare for the day. But nope. They are here, lounging lazily around a half-ass fire that will probably burn out before they realize it, living off of hard-working people who probably donate money less to help them and more to feel good about themselves. That's what I think, anyway. People seem to think that karma will somehow bless them if they are decent people and are seen doing something good for the less fortunate.

As the morning warms, and the bright sun sets higher

against the backdrop of the blue sky, people start to gather around a large rock, and as they do, they form a line that almost resembles a group effort. This is what I am talking about. They *can* be trained, but just on their own terms and when it serves them a purpose. I'm certain there is a purpose for this, and before I can guess what it is, I see it for myself.

A large white van pulls into this encampment through the same road we traveled by early on, and stops abruptly just a few feet from the rock. The side door slides open, and standing there are two middle-aged, what appear to be Middle Eastern people. One a younger man dressed in all white, and the other a woman who has this sensational, shy smile.

They begin to open a few boxes that are just inside on the floor, and the male steps out of the white van and smiles as he greets the line that has formed in front of him.

"Greetings my friends! I am so happy to see you all once again, and all so smiling this wonderful morning."

I'm not sure who he is, but quickly, he turns around and starts to grab what appear to be pre-packed brown paper bags from the shy woman who is pulling them from the cardboard boxes within the van. She gives him a bag or two at a time, and some sort of card along with it.

Each time someone grabs one of those brown bags and a card, there is genuine warmth in the man's eyes. He seems to be enjoying this very much. Not every homeless person seems to be saying thank you, but there are enough of them that do. Some simply grab the bag, turn around, and shuffle back out of sight into a tent, or behind a tree, or to the edge of the river that runs past this place. Others congregate around makeshift tables and wait for others to join them before opening the bags.

But I notice one common theme amongst them. Most of them are not eating from the bag just yet. They seem to be waiting for everyone to get something first before they take their first bite. For people that beg so much for food day and night, they sure have patience when they are not out in the public's eye.

Marcus heads to his beater Honda, and grabs a red mini cooler that was in the trunk. I walk over and unavoidably pass by him, without him saying a single word to me. I have no idea what I've done to him to make him hate me as he clearly seems to, but it doesn't matter in the grand scheme of my day. As I keep telling myself, in a few months I will no longer be here, but these people, including Marcus, will. They have no other options, but I have plenty. This is their reality, not mine.

I take my packed lunch out, and place it on the hood of the car. The last thing I want to do is eat next to these people that absolutely repulse me. It just makes me feel sick to my stomach watching people with so little teeth in their mouths chew and eat, all while talking and smiling as they do. There is no reason for that, but they do it anyway. It's just better if I stay by the car and out of that line-of-sight.

I receive a text from my girlfriend asking how my day

is going thus far. I could tell her the truth and bitch about all I have had to endure here, but I don't want to worry her while she is away.

"It's fine. Nothing to do but stand around a lot, but I'm fine. I miss you," I reply to her.

We message back and forth for ten or so minutes as I eat my packed lunch, and my attention starts to drift away from my phone.

It's that Von guy again. He's walking in my immediate direction, looking as if he may stop where I am seated and start conversing once again. I really don't want to be rude to him, but this man is starting to get on my nerves. How he doesn't understand that I am not here to make friends is beyond me. I am here to do as the judge has instructed, no more, and no less.

One thing about me is that when I am handed a direct task, I intend to complete that task as I am instructed, or in this case, ordered to without apparent instructions. It's part of my makeup. Nothing should ever be left undone in my thinking if you wish to get ahead in life. Nothing.

"Michael, may I?" Von starts.

Everything in me wants to say that I absolutely do mind. I mind and wish he would simply fade away into the crowd of other homeless people. I wish he would just vanish from my memory so that I can at least enjoy this moment of peace, but Marcus is looking over towards us, of course, I am sure he's watching me closely, ready to jump up and pounce on me if I step out of line from what he expects.

I am no fool, so I know he expects me to be polite to these people, and I will. Mostly I will. I'm actually a decent guy at the end of the day, but I expect a lot from myself, and others as well. People that don't reach their full potential are wasting talents bestowed upon them, and that may be the saddest thing in life. Not everyone is given the same set of talents, and there are those that would kill for some of what these people have been blessed with.

When I see Von, I immediately see that this man had strong potential given to him from the time of birth. He's not like the other people that are homeless, who are sleeping by rivers in made-up communities that the city continues to fight to shut down but somehow can't. Although, he does live here as best I can tell. He shows a spark of intelligence and drive, combined with a splash of passion and a unique understanding. Yet there is a sadness in those eyes that hide behind long thinning hair that he cannot completely hide.

For a second I am curious about what it is that brought him to such despair in his lifetime, but I quickly push those thoughts out of my head. It's not my business, and I cannot help this man who refuses to help himself, so it's a pointless conversation to me and my time is actually valuable, at least in my mind it is.

Before I can finish chewing the food I placed in my mouth right before he caught my attention, Von is standing directly over me, and is looking down at where I am seated.

He hasn't sat down yet. Instead he seems to be waiting for my permission. Odd, because I half expected this man to ask, and then just do as he pleased. I mean, I am in his domain. He doesn't really need permission to sit where he pleases, but I give a little respect to him for waiting. I will at least give him some credit.

I can feel Marcus' stare, although I am not looking in his direction at all. It's just a strong feeling I have in my bones.

Without much more hesitation, I nonchalantly nod at Von, and then to the place next to me on the old log I am seated on, and go back to taking another bite of my lunch that I wish I could enjoy in peace.

"Did you pack your lunch, or did a lady friend do that for you?" Von asks.

What the hell does he care, and what a strange question to ask someone you know nothing about. Who made my lunch? What is he going to ask next? Who dressed me for the morning?

I don't even bother to answer him, because it's a stupid question to begin a conversation with. I just continue to chew and pretend that I didn't even hear his ridiculous question.

"It's kind of crazy around here, and not what you are used to seeing, Michael. I get it. Give it time, though. This place grows on you once to gain an understanding of what your heart sees, and not of what your eyes tell you to see," Von says.

"Listen, Von, no offense? But I am here to do, well, whatever Marcus needs me to do with a few Saturdays of a few months, and then I am on my way. I have other things to tend to in my own life," I say back.

"Of course you do. Young guy like you? The world in front of him and a past left alone behind him, with all that potential at the tips of his fingers. Why wouldn't you have things to do?" Von replies.

I'm finished with my sandwich, and I take a long drink of my iced tea and screw back on the lid, placing the plastic bottle back in my bag. Lunch is done, because I feel I need to get back to standing around and passing the time doing nothing at all.

Von reaches for me before I can even stand and start back.

"Listen, we aren't bad people, despite what you may believe in your heart. I can promise you that with great certainty. There are better souls here next to this old Indian river, than out there where people feel safe in their comfortable homes and exciting, fast-paced lives. A soul is not shaped by the surroundings in which it is placed. It's shaped by the ability to give of oneself to better someone else, without expecting anything in return, despite one's surroundings. Sure, we can all become better ourselves, but to better someone else for the sake of just that is selfless and admirable. Remember that, Michael. You are helping others, even if you cannot see it," Von says.

"I'm not suggesting you or anyone else here is bad, but why? Why not work for more than this? Why not do something productive instead of begging from those that are actually productive? You said it yourself. You all should be helping others and not begging for yourselves. That's my issue, if I am being completely honest here. I came from a terrible background that would destroy most people and no one carried me when I needed it, yet I managed to do alright," I reply.

I can see Von smiling, as if he is wondering what then am I doing here, if I have done so great. As soon as the words came out of my mouth, I thought the same exact thing to myself. But this was a stumble in life. A bump in the road that shot me off course for a mile or so, and yet I have done so many other great things with my time that I get an exception, and Von doesn't need to approve of that for it to be so.

I'll give Von this, though. He is well spoken for a bum, and you can see that he once carried himself with a greater purpose than he seems to here. Maybe he held some importance at one time in his former life, but that must have been many years ago. He is only a shell of what he may have been, or could have been perhaps. I am unsure of which it is.

"Give it time, this place. Give it time. I have a peculiar feeling that this place, and the people of this wonderful group are going to grow on you. Learn something from each of the people here and their surroundings before you turn a blind eye, Michael. Trust me. You will see what you never could see, if you just open those eyes of yours a little more," Von says.

I just shake my head and smile at Von. He's trying to convince me of something that is never going to happen despite his poetic words of wisdom, but I give him an A for effort. He certainly is persistent and exudes a positive attitude for being in such a terrible place and owning nothing but his given name and the dirty clothes on his back.

This place is covered in old, worn-down gray rocks that the river has spit out onto its dusty banks over thousands of years. Those thousands of years that the Schuylkill waters have run over the once proud, larger rocks, has created gray trinket-sized ones that seem to serve little purpose. They are scattered about between patches of grass and weeds, that has created a fine dust from the days of no rain.

That dust covers everything in sight, including the people who call this place home. It's all they have, and I do feel a small bit of regret for these souls, but I remind myself that it was a choice they made, and not a sentence handed to them by someone in a higher position.

I am here because I was forced to choose a path, but they are here because they refused to choose a path, and I don't understand that at all. They must miss the outside real-world comforts. They must miss simple pleasures like cell phones, and hotels with warm, clean sheets and fluffy towels, that face the large skyscrapers of the city I call home. They have to be thinking about basic pleasures, like eating in the warmth of the sun at a restaurant's outside table overlooking the Ben Franklin Bridge, without being stared at for their appearance, or even about bathrooms that flush away the waste of the day in a place that is their own.

Here? None of that exists. There are no luxuries, and there is zero privacy that I can see. You are on display for everyone else here, and those that somehow accidentally stumble upon this useless piece of earth that would be better suited for a third world country.

"Michael, I believe lunch is over," shouts Marcus from inside the camp.

But that is all he says. Still not a word about what I am to do here now that lunch is indeed over, or when this day is going to end for me. I can't help but to think I may have picked the wrong community service, but at least I am getting closer to finishing day one.

Day one. This sucks so bad.

Chapter 6

* * *

For the rest of the day, I shuffled quietly around the grounds of the Mudflaps, casually looking at everyone who wandered in there, and I tried to image what their lives were like before they found themselves in this curious place. I imagine some of these people were, or are still, heavily addicted to drugs. I bet some were runaways when they were younger, who thought they owed their parents nothing including basic respect for having raised them, and decided they would be better off on their own somehow. Only they realized too late that they were dead wrong, or maybe their egos did not allow for them to rekindle that family environment they now miss dearly.

As I search the faces of these lost souls to determine where and when they lost their way, I begin to wonder about my own life as it has been. Was I living up to my own full potential, and was I heading in a direction that was clearly meant for me? I really hadn't given a lot of thought to that aspect of my life, but here, watching these people clean up from their free handout, or skipping rocks across the dark muddy brown river as they watch each bounce, I find myself wondering. Was I one wrong turn a degree left or right from ending up here as they did, or was I simply too strong minded for that to ever happen?

I had wanted to leave my foster parents' home since the first day I arrived, but I somehow stuck it out until the time I became an adult. What would have happened had I not had the patience to stay?

I thought back to that time when my father was run down in our driveway by my drunk of a mother and wonder, had I ran from that situation and never gave the state the chance to put me in the horrible system in the first place, would I have ended up in a place like this, or worse, dead?

Maybe I was blessed, or maybe I was a bit too smart for that to happen and somehow knew it would have happened if I made those decisions years ago, but whatever the case, I was not here. For that I am extremely pleased in myself. That one wrong left turn or one wrong right, never transpired for me.

But for these people, a wrong had occurred along the ride of life and they just rode it out all the way instead of getting off of it or going back and correcting what they could control. It's an excuse, although a bullshit one if you ask me. All they needed to do was backtrack a little here or there and make some minor adjustments, and life would eventually get back onto the right course, even if that meant suffering for a short time. It's all pretty simple in my mind.

I've also come to realize that prior to setting foot here in this appalling place, I pictured two different types of homeless people. In my mind there were the old, disheveled men with unkempt beards that had hairs shooting in all different directions and crazy eyes who always have a brown paper bag filled with some sort of alcohol. They stumble along the city streets looking for a place to rest, or someone to con or beg off of while being extremely incoherent. Then, there were the much younger ones who probably are hooked on their drug of choice and looking for their next score, by any means possible, and cannot or will not break that cycle.

The reality, as I look around the camp at this very moment , is that there are several different types of people who have lost everything over time which I could have never imagined. It's a larger demographic of people than I had previously believed it to be, and listening to them speak as they do, there are clearly many different nationalities and backgrounds, as well as ages to this group here. It's not as I had thought at all.

It makes me wonder, how did they all converge here upon the river bank? It's not as if I had ever heard of this place before, and I grew up within the city limits my entire life. There are no business cards that define the parameters of this plot of land, and nor is there a phone number to call that would direct you to here if you had no place to lay your head at night. I've searched on my phone to see if a website exists that invites those looking for shelter to come here, but again, it's nonexistent in my Google searches.

It's simply a place where these poor men and women have decided to at first rest for a short time, and then for others to live their lives out, or perhaps, to even die. Because I, for one, would not ever call this living in any sense of the word. I would see this as a spot to slowly waste a soul away until it was your time to move on to wherever we all end up when we die. For these people? It seems that is the only way out from here, to die.

When my mother went away, she had made a choice of her own doing. While I cannot remember all the details anymore, I don't know that she actually intended to kill my father. It was probably more out of a drunken rage on a day that started off like any other. She jumped in the car to leave, and more than likely never looked behind her before she put the car in reverse and hit the gas at the same time.

All these years later, I can't imagine she doesn't regret that decision each and every day she's incarcerated. How could she not? She's rotting her very life away behind bars that she created for herself, and there's nothing she can do to change that. It became her new way of life without her say. A different set of rules and a different view for decades, and who knows how that is going for her, except for her. Her life and mind are in a forever prison surrounded by very real walls, unless for some insane reason, they decide she has served enough time and free her back into the society she failed. Although my father will still reside where she put him, he doesn't get to be freed of her decisions or anyone else's decisions.

It frustrates me to no end, but I seldom think about it anymore. In fact, after it had occurred and I was removed from the only home I had ever known, I pushed all that pain away somewhere so deep, I am not even sure I would know where to search for it again. It was a defense mechanism that my body and mind forced on me so that I could survive. Had I not, I may have been forever depressed, or suicidal, or maybe a drug addict in the years to follow, and who would have blamed me. But I healed over time. Maybe not entirely, but enough that I focused on the one lesson my parents taught me. How *not* to live.

At the Mudflaps, these people have had chances to push through just as I had, because no one is forcing them to stay here. There are no bars or concrete barriers like my mother faces each morning she awakes, and the last thing she sees each night when she struggles to fall asleep. They can simply walk free at any time they choose and go wherever they would like.

It's more the fact that they have grown comfortable having very little to nothing in their lives, and for some strange reason, they accepted that. I think it's more a weakness they have learned to accept, but I don't get to be inside their minds, so who really knows for certain.

The city is full of places to suck off of, and I think that's a massive issue. The more you give to those people who refuse to earn it on their own, the more they will naturally take. It's teaching them to give up and never learn for themselves how to survive, just as a child does who decides to never leave the comfort of their parent's home. I have a good friend I grew up with, who still to this day lives at home. His excuse is that his mother is sickly, but I think it's much more than that. She provides everything for him including a security he desires, and he prefers that over trying to do so on his own.

Even baby birds are naturally pushed from their nest in order to learn how to survive on their own. They are taught the basic steps by their mothers, and then instinct takes over for them, or so they better hope. You don't see birds waiting around for others to take care of them all their lives. Well, okay so at the Jersey Shore you do. Those dirty, flying rats, otherwise known as seagulls, are bums. But people have created that by teaching them to beg and to rely on them over the generations. Just like the homeless have been taught since the beginning of time.

Finally, though, my day here comes to an end. Without notice, Marcus starts to say his goodbyes to the people who will remain here, and packs up his stuff in the duffel bag he has in his hands. He pulls Von aside, and whispers something into his ear, and they both have a laugh. I'm certain it was about me, but who cares. One day down. One day closer to being away from this depressing place for good.

As Marcus walks towards his car, he doesn't even bother to tell me. He just walks right by as if he's forgotten I came with him in the morning. I have to hurry over before he drives off without me and I am stuck to find my own way home. He's a son of a bitch for sure and I feel like telling him that, but he's a large man, in great shape for his age, and although I'm not afraid of much in this world, I know when to keep my mouth shut. I do have those street smarts about me.

"What did ya learn today?" he asks me.

"What did I learn? I learned that I have no idea of what the hell I am supposed to be doing there. You told me nothing, and so I spent all day standing around watching people roam back and forth aimlessly and accomplish zero. That's what I learned," I reply.

Marcus doesn't say a word. He just shakes his big ol' head as if I have missed some great lesson he tried to teach me. But he isn't telling me a thing, and so I am certain whatever lesson he meant for me to gain here, was lost in the wind, and that is entirely his fault.

"I still get credit for today, right? I showed up when and where I was told to, and was ready to work," I ask.

Again, Marcus just laughs under his breath, and nods slightly.

"Yea, you get credit. But if you are out here for credit, you are missing a whole lot, son," he replies back.

First of all, I am not his son. My dad is dead and buried in the cold ground. I have no father, but I don't expect this man to get it. He has no idea about my past, and probably doesn't care to. In fact, he's probably one of those men that calls everyone younger than him, son. As if he's some great philosopher, trying to teach grand lessons to others that they will carry on with them long after his time expires. Another ego thing.

We finally arrive back to where I first showed up, and I am beat. Not from the work, but from standing around all day in the blazing hot sun, doing absolutely nothing all day. I would have much rather worked my time off. At least then the time would have gone by faster and this day would not have seemed as wasted as it is.

Marcus gets out of the car and walks back into the building he came out of early in the day. He doesn't say a word to me, and I have no idea if I am supposed to follow him in, or just go home.

After a few minutes, I've had enough of the guessing game, and I decide to turn and walk back on home. If he has an issue with it, he can address that the next Saturday I am here because I have plans for the night and have no more tolerance for ignorant games. I've earned a drink or two tonight for sure.

The walk is actually nice. It's a warm Saturday, and I can hear music playing at the local spots where Hailey and I eat on occasion. I'll be excited when she returns so that we can celebrate day one in the books. Plus, I want to hear about her trip out west.

By the time I arrive home, I am ready to let loose. I quickly undress and jump in the shower to remove the stench I am positive I have, throw some food from the night before in the microwave, and text my boys. It's guy night tonight, and that usually means a late night is ahead.

I expect to be out well past midnight, but with tomorrow being Sunday, who cares. Monday is another day off.

I promised Hailey no heavy drinking, and no fist fights while she is gone. We can't go away for the next seven weekends because of both of those things, so I need to respect her wishes, and understand that if I break them, it could break her and I up. That is something I do not want.

By eight at night, I am finally ready to head out. A quick text to Hailey lets her know that I remember my promise to her, and I will touch base with her throughout the night to ensure her I am good to go.

I'll take a lot of ribbing from the guys, but that's to be expected. If they were in my shoes, I would give it to them all night as well, so they better rib me. It's part of being a male, really. We don't let each other forget things, but we do forgive things. It's an instinctual balance. It's almost a rite of passage for men.

Before I arrive at the spot, my phone goes off. It's my brother. I wasn't expected a call from him, but it's not unusual. Normally he'll just shoot me a text or something, but a call means something more needs to be said. I don't want to answer it just now, but after a few rings, I decide to just get it over with.

"Hey man, what's up," I answer.

"Hey brother, just wanted to check on your first day. Everything go well?" He says.

I love my brother. I have a great deal of respect for the guy he has become, and I also know my brother really well, despite having lost years of bonding that was ripped from us by our alcoholic mother. There is more to him calling than to ask how my day went. Even if he truly cares how it went, he could text that in four or five words. Not call me to ask, but he did call.

"It was fine. Nothing to do, really. Just glad it's done. I'm heading out for a few drinks. What's up, man?"

There's silence for a few seconds, and then my brother starts up once again.

"Michael, I know I've asked a lot about you talking with mom, and I'm sorry but I have to again. She's asked me to talk with you. She misses you, man. She's having a rough time more so than usual lately, and could use a little forgiveness," he says.

Forgiveness? She destroyed our only shot at a childhood, and while my dad was not a saint by any stretch of the imagination, at least he was my dad, and she took him from us. She changed the direction of our lives because she was selfish and pissed off one day. And now, she wants my forgiveness? Maybe she prefer I just forget everything and accept life as it is. Or that I go out to see her, and tell her how much I missed her all those years and wish she were on the outside so that I could hug her for the first time in decades without walls between us.

Man. I hate when he brings her up because it sets me off into a rage. I'm trying to forget this day and head out with my boys for a night of fun that I have earned, and he's bringing her back into my mind. I've asked him before, plenty of times, not to do that.

"Dude, listen. I really don't want..."

He abruptly cuts me off, which he also knows I hate.

"Yea, I get it. You don't want to talk about mom. I know, you've said it a million times. But Michael, she's getting older, and isn't feeling well. That place has taken so much from both her body and mind, even after she thought she lost all she had. She's not the same woman she was all those years back. She's a different person, Michael. She simply wants to tell you that she's sorry, loves you, and hopes that you will one day have forgiveness in your heart for all that happened. She needs that, man. She needs that," he says.

I know this conversation is going to go around in circles, and end up in an argument that I can ill afford tonight. I need to stay calm so that I don't find myself on the wrong end of trouble again. So, I need to relax, and just appease him for now.

"Yea, listen. I am heading out, but I'll think it over. I will give it some thought this week, and get back to you. Just give me some time, all right?" I respond.

When I hang up with my brother, I realize that his sense of urgency was odd. He's an attorney, so nothing is quick. They drag things on and on, arguing over sometimes important things, and sometimes just to brush up on their arguing skills, or to drain their clients of all the cash they have.

I have every intention of blocking this out of my mind, but I know he's just going to ask again and again until I either agree to meet with her, or find a stronger argument as to why I do not, or should not need to ever. Imagine that. Me arguing with an attorney and winning. That will be a reality check for my big-shot bro.

It's time to enjoy things for now, though. So out of my mind it goes, although the truth is, after hearing from my brother? It's on my mind more tonight than it's been ever, and I am struggling with the why. It's not as if I have forgotten I had a mother for all the years she's been away. I have replayed that day in my dreams and woken up in cold, drenching sweats over the years. But there is a conscience thinking going on, and I am not sure why I have decided to do that now, of all days.

But what I do know is that right now, I need a drink.

Chapter 7

* * *

With day one firmly behind me, I put it out of my mind as best I could, just as I have most of my childhood. It's time for me to enjoy myself after a long week of work rather than having wasted a gorgeous, sunny Saturday when I could've slept in.

My friends and I are tight. It's really five of us that have gravitated towards each other and have created this bond. Three of us are from the Philly area, and the other two are from out on the west coast. One is from the Seattle area where my brother resides, and the other from Mesa, Arizona.

The girlfriends call us, "The City Boys," but it's not meant to be an insult. We are clearly men for the most part, but tight as if we were raised as brothers. I know if I ever need anything, I can ask any of the four boys, and they will be there with no questions asked. That's kind of loyalty has been missing from this world, including a loyalty often missing from family born of the same bloodline.

Hailey messages me, and again I assure her that I am

going to be on my best behavior for the whole evening. I'm not sure if she believes me entirely or not, but no matter. Her best friend is dating my boy, Derrick, so I'm sure they have talked and Derrick is being put in a tough spot.

Honestly though, I feel as if I have learned a valuable lesson. Not from my time at the Mudflaps. There is nothing to be learned from that senseless, illegal encampment that houses the desperate. But rather from my time in a six-by-eight-foot jail cell overnight in the city, and from standing in front of that judge who was predisposed to hate everyone in the courtroom before getting to know the reasons they were there in the first place. While he did give me an option for avoiding prison time, he also reminded me that if I ended up back in front of him ever again, the choice he presented me with the first time would certainly not be there the next. I believed him and the wagging little finger he used.

The night starts out well enough. The boys are just messing around with throwing darts, and ordering pitcher after pitcher of beer from the cute waitress (who knows she's going to be tipped well tonight). Every now and again they order shots of tequila with no salt and no lime. I've told them well before I showed up that shots were absolutely out of the question for me tonight. They could tease me and offer them all they wanted, but it was not going to happen.

Derrick is a cool guy. He works in Center City not far from where I work, handling some type of software sales staff for a mid-sized company. He's a good talker, which is probably how he ended up in sales to begin with.

"Dude, tell me. What was it like at your community sentencing thing you did today? Did it smell like shit? It did, didn't it. You must have been gagging the entire time," he says.

For a second I actually need to think about it. I take a short sip from my glass and pause, looking around the room. It's packed tonight, and there is a band to the far end of the bar, jamming out. Life is good here in the bar, and I really forgot all about my morning until he just brought it up.

"Man, I don't know. It was...well, let's just say, I am glad I live here and not there. Tonight, while we are out having cold drinks, they are probably sitting around a makeshift fire, trying to figure out how to annoy anyone with a dollar in their pocket. Why would anyone want to live that way? Not me, brother. Not me," I reply.

But that question has brought to my mind other questions from this morning's adventure. What is Von doing? Is he one of those guys we see at night, panhandling along the side of the road, or holding up a sign claiming to be a veteran or out of work? I curiously find I have some respect for Von, but if I saw him out begging hard-working people for what they have rightfully earned, I would quickly lose it. I hate that. How can I have a weird respect for someone who goes against everything I stand for?

And the others? What are they doing? The ones with no will inside, or drive at all to do more than sleep and wake up and repeat. Those ones who saw the food truck come, and seemingly found a short will to get over to where it was, but then quickly retreated back to a state of helplessness, unable to stand or walk without complaining. Are they just sitting right where I last saw them? Did they have another delivery of food for dinner, or did they need to actually go and find that on their own, searching through trash bins outside of decent restaurants?

Why do I even care? I don't. I really honestly do not. This is MY night, and I did my service for today and that should be the end of it. Why are these people now invading my personal space and time in my thoughts? I did not give them permission to do so.

Hailey checks in.

"Hey babe, you good?"

"Yup. All good here. Just having one more and then going to grab a late bite, and then head back home. Miss you, baby," I reply back.

"She's a good person, Derrick. Far too good to be with me, but I'll take it," I joke.

Deep down inside though, I wonder. Am I really not good enough for her? She has a good background with her suburban upbringing, a strong work ethic she got from both of her parents who are very successful, and she's kind. Much kinder than I am. She seems to understand my upbringing was not a pleasant one, and she allows that to be an excuse for now. For now. But how long will she allow that to be an excuse I get to use?

When I was arrested for throwing that left hook, I was so worried that she was going to be finished with me. Who wants a thug who can't control his drinking at this age? Guys fight. Especially being born and raised in South Philly. We just fight. It's in our blood, and even though we are expected to grow out of that, we don't always.

But the drinking excessively, I knew I needed to stop. That was something that caused more issues in my life than I can count, and changed the entire course of my childhood.

My father, although a hard-working Irishman, was a lush. He drank on the days he would work, and more on the days he did not. It was as if he *needed* it. Like his body and mind were begging desperately for a taste of alcohol, and if they did not get it, he was not allowed to function like a normal human being.

He lived a drunk and he died a drunk. The only thing he did right in his time here was work and occasionally, take me and my brother fishing.

My mother, well, she's an entirely different story. She was not as functionally capable as my dad was when she drank, which was more often than not.

I remember this one time when I was a kid, she walked back from the bar three blocks away from our house, only to enter the wrong freaking house. She was an entire neighborhood over from where we lived and never realized it. The owners of that house, an elderly couple, were nice enough to help her to their car, give her a ride home, and never pressed charges. They thought they were doing her a favor, but maybe if they had pressed charges, she would have learned that she needed to slow down well before killing her husband.

That is what it took for me to learn a lesson. A short left hand to the jawbone of another human when you have a stomach full of liquor, can change your entire life. I'm still paying off the fines and doctor bills for that one and will for some time to come.

So I am working on slowing down, and so far, so good. If I lose Hailey, I'm afraid I'll fall right back into my heavy drinking, and I have no idea of what that will lead to next. But, I am truly working on not letting that happen because I don't wish to find out.

At the end of the night, I tell the boys I am off, while they continue to hang until the early morning hours. It's not that I am tired, or don't want to hang out with them any longer tonight. It's that I learned from an old neighbor of mine, who has lived much longer than I ever expect to, that nothing good happens after midnight. That, he would say, was the key to surviving the bar scenes.

"Get the hell out of them damn places before that dang clock strikes midnight, and you got half a chance to make it home without the cops tossing you behind bars, or some punk busting you up real good," he would say, usually while drinking a beer on the front stoop of his place.

DeRocco's Pizza is only a block and a half over, and they stay open late on weekends, probably expecting the drunk crowd to wander out of the city bars and go off searching for a snack before passing out for the night, or in the case of Philly boys, the early morning.

I grab two Sicilian slices, one with pepperoni and one plain. The slices are huge, so they take a little time to consume, which gives me time to unwind before I get back to my place.

As I am devouring my slices, I notice just twenty or so feet from me, a dark colored man with a colorful wool hat, that is, where the dirt hasn't covered them just yet. He's swimming in a heavy cotton jacket, much too large for his frame, and has pants that extend down past his feet, so you cannot see the shoes he is wearing, if he has any that is.

He's sitting there singing to himself, because no one else has asked him to sing, I'm sure. He has a half decent voice, but why the hell does he need to sing here and now, when people are trying to wind down? And why doesn't he just head over to the Mudflaps, where I am sure those people would enjoy his gift of voice, because what else do they have there to keep them occupied at just after midnight?

I go back to my eating, and ignore him as best I can. But there are a few younger kids who should be home by now, but for some reason aren't, and they spot him. I'm smart enough to know, he is now a target of theirs. I keep one eye on my food, and the other on what is going on over where he is still singing away.

At first, they are just acting as if they enjoy his singing. He's singing, but I don't know if he knows what is about to happen. Maybe I should go over so the kids see that someone is there, but I don't. I just want to mind my business and eat, and I can't afford more trouble anyway. Plus,

I've already done my community service for the homeless today and owe this man nothing more.

They are now getting louder and starting to mock him as they get closer to where he is seated on the ground. One has a pizza slice and is waving it in front of the old man in a mocking way, asking him if he wants some of it because it takes so good.

For his part, the man is staying pretty calm. He doesn't appeared bothered by these young idiots just yet. But that is about to change, and quickly. They are not just going to walk away, and I fear, he knows that.

Suddenly, the group starts to chant at the biggest of the kids, as if they are daring him, no, as if they are willing him to mess this guy up.

The man stops his singing, and starts to talk calmly to the group,

"Boys, now listen here. I don't want no trouble here tonight, you see? I'm just here to bring the gift of music to you all, and if you let me sing some more, well, I'm sure you'll all enjoy my gift to you. What do you say? Deal?"

"Gift? To us? Are you kidding me you old dirty bastard? Ain't no one want to hear your crusty ass sing nothing, okay? So here, take this pizza, eat it, and shut up," the biggest one says.

He extends his hands, as if he's going to give him the slice, and when the old man doesn't reach out, the kid slams the pizza on top of the man's head, knocking his hat from his hair, and the group breaks out in laughter. It's a sin, but if this guy would just somehow get moving in his life, he wouldn't be here now with these bullies. I'm not sticking up for the idiots in this group, but man, this is exactly the type of thing that happens all the time. These people need to learn from this and stay the hell out of the city at night.

"Why didn't you take the pizza? I know you are hungry. You's a hungry bum, right? It's me, isn't it," he mocks the homeless man.

"You don't like me, do you? I thought we were going to be friends, and here you are, acting like you are better than me," he continues.

Then, without warning, the big kid turns around away from this man, cocks his hand back as far as he can, makes a tight fist, and slams it into the side of the head of the guy. Bam. He freakin' nails him, and as hard as anything. The man is out cold, and the group is filming the entire incident with their phones, cheering on as they watch this kid hurt this man.

Bam. Another blow. Then another. He's pummeling this guy, and no one around is doing a thing about it. Then I realize something. Neither am I.

As much as I hate the homeless community and what they represent, I cannot stand by and watch these kids slam this guy, who is still lying motionless on the hard ground below him. They are giving him no chance to recover, and honestly, if they don't stop, they are going to kill this guy, if they haven't already.

I look around to see if anyone is worth recruiting to help

out, but my instincts tell me I am going to be on my own here. None of these people are worth a shit in a situation such as this. They are going to act as if it's not their issue because they are probably scared of what these kids will do to them for interfering.

Trust me, I have my concerns as well. Just because these kids are teens, doesn't mean they can't fight, and because they are in a group, they push each other and get stronger as they try to one up each other. So I know what I am up against, and it does put some fear in my blood stream.

But, I also know my father had no chance to fight back for his own life. He was run over and couldn't defend himself even if he had wanted to. He was forced to face what was coming because there was no one there to stop my mom, and my brother and I were too young to know how. So he died without anyone stepping in.

I look around for anything I can use to give me better odds, and see a branch from a tree nearby, about six feet in length, and about two and a half inches around in diameter. This is going to have to do. I take the branch, place it longways against the chair I was sitting on eating my food and minding my business, and with one swift motion, I stomp on the hard wood to break it in half. It's too big the way it is, and I can have better movement of it if it's a little smaller.

Before I even take one step in that direction, a guy sitting with his girl or wife or whatever she is to him, says to me,

"Dude, not your fight. Let it go before you get hurt."

This guy doesn't know me well. While I am not the largest person around, I have a good fight in me for sure. I'm Philly born and raised, and I know how to use my hands and my thick head enough to keep things interesting. This guy may not have balls, but I certainly do. Brass ones.

"Yea well, if I don't do something, he doesn't stand a chance. Watch this," I say as I head over.

Watch this. That's a line we have used many times as guys. It's usually associated with alcohol. We may use it when we are shit faced drunk and about to do something really stupid, like try to jump over a table in a bar after drinking all night. Or we may use it to signal that we are about to approach a girl way out of our league, but somehow, feel as if we have a shot with the amount of alcohol we have consumed. And sometimes, it simply means we are about to throw down, and we want our friends to know, we got this, even if we don't. You give your friend your beer, and say,

"Here, hold my beer. Watch this."

Most times, what you were planning to do doesn't go as planned. Your friends laugh their asses off while you come back either shot down by the chick, or holding your knee from slamming into the hard table you meant to hurdle but stood no chance of, or having a black eye from the dude that slammed you harder than you did him.

Here, I am aware I could come back in a bad spot, much different from the one I am leaving in, but screw it. This guy may be a bum, but he isn't bothering anyone tonight.

Besides, these kids need someone to show them they aren't as tough as they are feeling right now. It's a lesson I am going to give them, so I consider it a good deed of sorts.

Watch this.

Chapter 8

* * *

"Michael Kelley, you made bail. Let's go," the cop says.

I have been sitting in this dank holding cell for over a day now, wondering what the hell I should do. This was the one place I told Hailey I would never come back to just a night or so ago, and yet here I am. What a mess this is and now I literally have no idea who just bailed me out and why, as I haven't called a soul. I was hoping to get in front of a judge first to plead my innocence before Hailey got back or my job found out where I was.

Only, that's not what happened. I spent all of Sunday here and part of Monday morning, before someone decided to bail me out. Now I am heading out to see who decided I needed to be free.

As soon as I get to the front desk where they first brought me in and grab the things that I had on me that night, I turn around, and there standing just near the exit talking to a cop, is Marcus. I have no idea if he's there for me and the one that bailed me out, or there for someone else and just by some strange coincidence.

"You get your shit?" Marcus asks.

"Yea, I got my shit. Why did you bail me out?" I respond.

Marcus doesn't say anything else, as per his usual. He quickly turns, and starts to walk towards the front entrance of the police station, and puts his large hands on the door push-bar that leads out to the street where freedom lives. He doesn't turn around, but he senses I have not moved from my spot, as if I am wondering if I am supposed to follow him or not.

"Well, you gonna stand there all day, or what?" He asks.

Man, this Marcus dude is something else. First, I have no idea why he bailed me out and how the hell he knew I was even here. Second, something about him is incredibly intimidating, and that's hard to do to me. I don't get nervous about much, but he has this presence about him that commands respect and fear, and it works well for him without needing to try.

Ultimately, I would rather just head on out those doors to the street in front, and walk my dumbass home, but I know I owe this man at least a thank you. I just hope he doesn't feel like talking, because honestly, I just want to shower to get this smell off me and forget the entire thing happened. Plus, I am sore as hell and the entire left side of my face is aching and swollen.

"Yea, I'm coming," I finally manage to blurt out.

We walk down the steps to the road, and Marcus looks

straight up into the air, takes a deep breath in, and before he says a word, I already know what's coming.

"The smell of freedom, right?" I say before he can.

He smirks, which is the first ever emotion I've seen from this guy towards me outside of him being pissed off.

"Smartass," he says.

But he doesn't stop looking up.

"You know, freedom is interesting. Some people have it all their lives, yet don't realize that they do. Some people have never tasted a day of freedom, but feel as if they are free from everything, regardless. Freedom isn't always about what others give to you, Michael. Sometimes, it's about what you give to yourself," Marcus says.

Now the fact this large, intimidating mountain of a man just put together what managed to be a bit of poetic advice makes me curious, but I have no clue what he is trying to say. People have freedom when they aren't really free? What the hell is he talking about? He's a little delusional, I think.

"I know. You want to get home, back to your comforts and the exciting life that you think you live. I get it. But that all needs to wait some. Walk with me," he continues.

I knew it. I knew he wasn't going to just let me off the hook so that I could go home and figure out what to do next. Probably wants to have a hallmark moment with a cup of coffee and do some type of male bonding over an everything bagel, where he will tell me all about how what I did was wrong, and how I need to not let my anger control my actions, and blah, blah, blah. I seriously don't have the patience to sit through a Folgers moment, but he's kind of got me stuck. He did bail me out, so I owe him something I suppose.

He starts off down Girard Avenue, through the Fishtown part of Philly, and I realize we are back to where the Mudflaps are hidden away. I had been here of course just a few days ago, but never paid much attention to where it really was in relation to the city I know. I was simply driving with Marcus to do my time. Paying attention to the where, simply eluded me.

There's a cart selling fresh coffee and salt and pepper egg sandwiches, and Marcus stops by, gives the guy a ten, and collects two cups and two sandwiches. He doesn't ask me if I want anything or what I would want. Just orders, grabs the stuff from the guy, and heads over to a half-wall across from the cart.

"I'm sure you are hungry by now," Marcus says, handing me both a sandwich and hot white Styrofoam cup.

"Um, yea. I am a little. Thanks. Thanks, Marcus," I say back.

Marcus takes a few bites of his breakfast, and sips a black coffee that has steam rising from the brim.

"Freedom is an interesting thing, Michael. I know you don't get it yet. But one day you will," he says.

"I understand freedom. What I don't understand is why you bring it up. I'm out of jail. I get that. But that wasn't my fault. I was helping some dude who needed it. I was doing good, not bad," I say.

"Michael, freedom isn't about just being able to do what you like, when you like. Freedom is also the ability to not allow others your mental space. That place between your ears is not for others to occupy. It's yours. And ain't no man or woman able to occupy that space without your say-so. You hear me? You need to give folks that permission to occupy it. Just like your heart. You have a choice," Marcus tells me.

Man, he's getting deep. It's too early for deep, but listening to him spit out his knowledge is interesting to me. It makes sense, somehow. His words are hitting me hard, and I am actually feeling that in my bones.

"I get it, Marcus. But why, and how? Why did you bail me out, and how did you even know where I was?" I ask.

Marcus turns in my direction and faces me for the first time since I've been bailed out. He rarely looks directly my way, unless it was to show me he was watching my actions or lack of at the Mudflaps over the weekend. I remember his hard, stern stare, basically telling me to watch my step.

But here, he's genuinely looking my way as if he intends for me to understand his words clearer than I am able to hear them. I think he needs me to feel them more than anything.

"I didn't," he starts.

"It doesn't matter right now who bailed you out, because not everyone does things for recognition. Sometimes people have a bigger reason behind what they do. For starters, what you did Saturday night? It's not a good look on you at first sight, but the why of what you did, didn't go unnoticed."

So basically, he's telling me someone took their money to bail me out, and they don't want me to know. Got it. Also, apparently this "person," also wants me to know that while it was wrong of me to end up where I did, it was partially right of me because of why I did, what I did.

The funny thing is, I don't remember it all that well, myself. I remember going over and telling those stupid kids to knock it off. I think one of them told me to go f myself, and then another one or two hit me from behind when I wasn't able to defend myself, and all hell broke loose. That's where I blacked out. Not from the pain I was surely going to feel when the adrenaline left my body, but from my anger. I have this part of me that closes off my mind when I am at that point of extreme rage, I see red in front of my eyes, and my body reacts against everything my mind tells it to do.

"I don't recall exactly all the details, but I know I was trying to keep that man from getting his head bashed in. That much I remember," I say.

We are now finished our breakfast sandwiches and street corner coffee, and Marcus stands up and throws his out in a trash can not far off. He waves to the guy at the cart and thanks him again. Marcus has a thing for thanking all the people he encounters in his day. I've noticed that about him. All these people who are working thankless jobs for probably little money, seem to get his attention more than others do. It's interesting.

"Come with me," he says.

I don't hesitate this time, though. It's not the best area we are walking through, but being next to Marcus makes me feel a bit more protected. It would take a pretty brazen person to try and get over on him. Or someone extremely stupid. But the city is full of both at times, so you never really know what to expect.

As we casually walk along, I see we are turning this way, and that way, eventually finding a familiar path where I can see scenery that has crossed by my eyes before. We are back to where I first met Von and the others, and at first I want to remind him that this was my day off and I really didn't feel like putting in more work right now, but if that's what it takes to pay whomever back for bailing me out, whatever I guess.

Marcus stops short of going in, and instead, opts for a seat on an old log just on the outside of the 'Flaps. We are partially hidden by some overgrown butterfly bushes and senseless weeds that grab at your clothing as you walk by, and instead of talking more, Marcus just points over to where he wants me to focus my attention.

I train my eyes towards his outstretched finger and see a group of men and women who appear to be making some type of tent up, adding some flowers to the outside that they probably found growing along the edge of the river, and placing a sleeping bag just inside of it. They are making it up as if it's a home for someone, but it's a freaking tent, if you can ever call it that. I don't get it, but I continue to watch anyway, because I feel this is one of those moments Marcus needs me to get not what I am seeing, but what is really there.

"So, they are making a tent. I don't get it. There are dozens of makeshift tents thrown around here. Why is this one different?" I ask.

Marcus doesn't answer me. Instead, he just keeps his eyes fixed tightly, and eventually I turn my attention back to where he asked me to. The tent is just a plain tan canvas type with a band of dark green wrapped around, and a few loose blankets thrown over top for added coverage. It's nothing fancy, but they are treating it as if it's serving a better purpose than I can see.

Von is there. When I notice him, I almost instinctively sit up a little higher, either out of a strange respect for the man, or because I know whenever he is around, some great lesson is being served to anyone within earshot.

"Are we going to sit here, or are we going to go over and talk to them?" I ask.

"Sometimes you hear more from simply watching folks do, than you do from hearing what folks actually say," Marcus replies.

Here he goes again with his fancy poetic talks. I roll my eyes up, thinking he's trying to explain something to me that he doesn't even understand. He's throwing words together that clearly make zero sense, at least to me. Who the hell hears more by *not* hearing people talk? I mean, is this guy really certified by the city or state to help these people? Have they vetted him or any of the helpers well enough or at all? Because he seems a little mentally off when he speaks sometimes, but whatever. I really don't care all that much for any of this as my last night was not a comfortable one.

"Listen, Marcus. I don't mean to be rude, or act as if I am not grateful for whomever bailed me out, but I have to call my job. They probably have no clue where I am and I need this job. I have a lot of explaining to do, so do me a favor? Can you just thank whoever bailed me out this morning, and let them know I will repay them whenever I get the chance?"

Marcus looks at me, shakes his head as if I am still not understanding some great message he somehow hoped I would, and laughs to himself quietly.

"Your job? No need. That's already been handled. They are aware you needed a personal day today," he starts.

"You see, there are things in your life that you don't need to understand, to truly appreciate. Sometimes, it's just that way, and you accept it or you don't," he says.

I look at Marcus as if I am questioning his thought patterns. I'm looking him up and down for a sign that he's bullshitting me, but I see none. He doesn't change his demeanor, and doesn't adjust the expression on his face at all as he looks ahead. Either he's telling me the truth, or he believes what he is selling, even if it's totally untrue. Either way, I need to check in with my work, because I need to find out for myself.

As I pull my phone from my pocket to dial, I see a message already there from my boss.

"Michael, you are covered for today. Take your time. We got this handled buddy."

Strange. What are they talking about, and who called them, and more importantly, *what* did they tell them? I am thoroughly confused. Nothing is making any sense here but I feel a sense of nervousness through my body, wondering if they know I spent the night in jail.

"Michael? Michael, is that you? Come. I was hoping to see you today," a voice says from the distance.

It's Von. He somehow now knows I am here and is motioning for me to join them.

So I do as he asks.

Chapter 9

* * *

Since I am relaxed, not feeling the shackles of the court system tightly around my hands and feet, forcing me here to whittle away my day like last Saturday, I can see this place a bit more clearly, and I have the opportunity to look around and observe in detail. All simply because Von spotted Marcus and I sitting here off the outskirts of the Mudflaps and invited us over.

A few short weeks ago, I was unaware of this tiny part of the city hidden away from the bright lights, nor did I know of Marcus and Von. They were outside of my circle of friends and my comfort zone, so they simply did not exist to me, but they existed, nonetheless.

It has me wondering what else I may be unaware of, both here in their shanties and further around the city of Philadelphia as well as beyond. Although I have spent my entire life roaming these mostly unforgiving streets and understanding the blessed good and unforgivable bad of the different sections of town, I imagine there is an entire world right beneath my feet that I have failed to see, and therefore, failed to understand or accept its existence.

Von is busily working away, navigating those who seem to need him greatly for his leadership skills. He's like a fined-tuned crossing guard, directing breakneck traffic on the busiest of streets with a skill beyond any others. As a kid, I remember seeing them out on JFK Boulevard looking so focused on the task at hand, rushing cars past with a perfect grace, and stopping them just as quickly so that the pedestrians could cross safely without fear of harm. I looked to them as authority figures who commanded respect because of how well they managed to do their work. But as an adult? They were simply people who were there to collect a check the easiest way they could, or perhaps the only way they could.

Funny, as a child, you see things done for various reasons, and most of those appear truly admirable, if not hero-like. But as you mature and life's responsibilities take priority, bills need to be paid, so that when you head home from work, drained entirely of all the energy you gave away to that day, it becomes about the paycheck. I haven't looked at anyone doing a job as more than that in many years.

But as far as I can tell, Von isn't getting a paycheck for helping those that cannot or will not do for themselves. No one is paying him to orchestrate the many different personalities who need direction at every step and every imaginable level. He doesn't seem to be in a clocking in and out mindset here, wondering when his day is officially going to end so he can pack up, and head home to his family for a nice dinner. Instead, he's focused on the task and smiling through it as if he begs for more to hit his plate.

I'm curious as hell as to how he ended up here in purgatory. What did this unusual man do prior to finding himself in a tiny one-person tent hardly fit for a human of any kind, along the edge of the Schuylkill River? Was he an alcoholic at one time like my parents were, unable to function in that environment without causing pain to himself and those around him, which eventually ended up costing him his once flourishing career? Maybe he ran out of luck while aggressively investing in the stock market at a time when people lost their fortunes, losing his investments because he forgot that pigs eat and hogs get slaughtered.

Whatever it was, he is here now and maybe it doesn't matter that I know the how and the why. It's really not my business at all, and the less I know, probably the easier the next seven weeks are going to pass so that I can get back to my life.

"Michael, can you give me a hand over here? We have three more of these tents to set up, and it's a little warm out with this sun dancing across the sky. It is being a little less forgiving than I had hoped today, as it sometimes does. We could sure use your strength some," Von says.

Marcus walks right past me and grabs a stack of what appears to be hand-cut wooden tent pegs, and one of the tents that is laying in a makeshift pile on the ground. He walks over to an area that has been freshly cleared of jagged rocks, and begins to lay out the next tent in line. His large hands grasp one pointed peg at a time, and with a swift, easy swing of a mallet, Marcus is securing the base down tightly.

Von didn't need to ask Marcus for his assistance. He instinctively knew what to do, so I assume he has helped them more than just Saturdays over the years.

I make my way over to where Von is working under the rays of the blistering hot sun, and shrug my shoulders, as if to say, "what is it exactly that you want me to do?"

Von smiles gently as he uses an old torn shirt to wipe away the sweat from the top of his forehead, and hands me a small, worn-out mallet. As I turn around, there are two other homeless people laying out what appears to be another tent and unfolding the contents of a gray duffel bag. These two look almost lost and helpless, more so than the others. Now I see why Von called us over. He needs the help with people like this wasting time because of the ignorance for such simple-minded task as they have in front of them.

"Here, let me," I say, motioning for them to get out of the way. I don't want to be here longer than I need to be in this damn heat, so they just need to let those that understand the basics of camping to do what they are doing so we can complete this quickly.

These two are a woman and a man, and as hard as it is to tell their ages accurately with all the grime and filth they have on them, if I was forced to, I would guess maybe late fifties. They just appear to have that aged, weathered look where your body starts to wrinkle a bit more despite your wish, and your posture begins to slump ever so slightly, almost mocking you, letting you know it's just going to get worse from here.

"I'm Mae, and this here is Wallace B," the older woman says to me.

She's just a short being, with thick, graying hair down past her shoulders, and she appears to have more clothes on than someone should for this heat wave we are in, but I've seen that before many times over the seasons.

The homeless have so little that what they do possess, they hold on to for dear life. It's as if they are afraid to lose in the warm summer months what they will surely require in those harsh, cold, winter ones ahead. So, they dress in multiple layers, despite the climbing temperatures. It's making me hot just sitting here, and to be honest, it's not helping that the stench coming off of her is almost enough to make me gag.

The male seems to know her well, as they have very similar mannerisms that seem almost earned together over many years. He's a bit taller than she, with most of his hair gone from the top of his head, and hands that show signs of a rough, cruel life.

"Yea, I'm Michael," I reply, trying to keep the small talk to a minimum.

"Yes, Michael, we are aware of who you are. It's our pleasure to make your acquaintance," Mae says.

I think maybe they have me confused with someone else, because I literally came here two days ago, stood around like a jackass the entire time, said maybe a half dozen words all day, and then just arrived here again less than an hour ago. There is no way they know me, but hey, let them feel as if they do. If it makes their day brighter, so be it.

I'm working fast and furious, because I want to show Marcus I have a use beyond what he thinks he knows about me, and then I want to find a way to make my exit without much attention. I know my job seems to be okay with me off today, but tomorrow is a different story. I need to get back home and figure out what I am going to do with the next hearing I now have to have. That judge is going to be super pissed off that I am back in his presence so soon.

I've learned in life that you cannot go back in time and make changes to your past, so worrying about what you have to face because of prior decisions makes little to no sense. It doesn't mean that I am not worried about what lies ahead, but I am not going to stress over that just now. There will be plenty of time to deal with those emotions as we get closer to the hearing.

If I have to go to jail because of this, it's going to be pretty ironic. I will join my mother as a hardened criminal, and I'll be embarrassed to be compared to someone like her. I guess it's best to call my brother when I get home and see what he suggests. Maybe he can point me to a local attorney he trusts that isn't going to take all my money while convincing me he is working hard for my case. My brother is going to judge me for my choices. I can feel it already.

Without much more exertion, the tent is up in place, and I drop the almost useless mallet and stand back to take a quick glance. At first, I feel a small sense of pride come over me. A sense of accomplishment darts inside, and I feel good about what I have just done. But just as quickly, I shut that down. It's a tent, in a homeless community with a strange name that makes absolutely no sense, no less. What is there to be proud about? No one who matters is going to see this and give me props for doing such a magnificent job.

"Michael? Nice work. I do believe you may have a future here after all," Von says.

This guy is entirely delusional. A future here? What kind of idiot would give up a well-paying job to come here and help people that cannot even help themselves? I am no Mother Theresa, that much I am aware of.

Marcus glances over at me and drops his mallet down to the ground as well. He's cracking a slight grin, and I am unsure if it's because he thinks I am this cocky punk who is being brought down to a harsh reality, or maybe, just maybe, this small deed has impressed this hard man enough that he believes I am something more than a criminal.

Before I can look around to see if there is an opportunity for a quick exit, I see Mae and Wallace B walking back to where we are with flowers in their hands. Wallace bends down and uses a small handheld shovel to dig a few holes into the hard, dry clay. As he does so, Mae walks down towards the river with a small plastic bucket in her left hand. I assume she's heading to fill it with water from the river for the flowers. Her pace is snail-slow, as is that of Wallace's, but they are at least steady at what they are doing.

Mae fills the pail with foul smelling river water and turns to walk it back to where her partner is. She sets it down a few times after every four or five steps, bending over and catching her breath, and no one seems to be paying her any mind. It's literally going to take her an hour to get back here to water these plants, so I just hurry myself down. As she attempts to pick the bucket up, I place my hand on the handle to the bucket, and tell her that I will take it from here.

"Well Michael, thank you kindly. This is one of the nicest things someone has done for me all day," Mae says with a laugh.

What type of life do these people expect, if someone carrying a stupid small pail filled with dirty river water a few yards is the best thing they have experienced all day? I mean, I can name a dozen things that happen in my normal day that would trump this. Maybe not today because it's been a rough start, but a normal day for sure. One where I do not need to be bailed out of a cell for fighting underage kids early in the morning.

That brings me back to my original curiosity. Who the hell bailed me out? Marcus never told me much, expect that it was not his doing. I don't know whether to believe him or not, but to this point, he's giving me no reason to think he would lie about such a thing. He's a proud man, and I think he would have no care about letting me know if he did. But someone did, and he's not allowing that name to part through his lips. Marcus, while proud, is also stone loyal apparently.

When I return to where Wallace B has dug the small holes, I can see he's already planted some of the wildflowers that traveled along the banks of the river through wind and seed. Carefully, he's managed to move them away from the dirty banks, to where they will be planted.

"Ah, thank you Michael. Thank you very much. This water is so important for these wildflowers to thrive. They have the soil, and they have a new place to call their own, but without the water, life for them doesn't exist. Their voyage here is empty without the gift you bring to it, Michael," Wallace B says.

I'm starting to feel as if everyone around here is pulling my leg. Like they all decided to pretend to be homeless and dirt poor, just to get a rise out of someone, because they all seem to have this strange knowledge of life that no one I ever met has. Maybe they are doing improv from a local theater group, but homeless bums? I don't know.

Or maybe it's because they have nothing else to do with their time. Perhaps they have a past with a background in education or literacy, but let that slip through their filthy fingers because they got lazy at some point in time. Imagine, having a gift to understand life, but no will to actually *live* life.

I pass along the water to Wallace B, and look around

at the remainder of the camp. Looking down towards the old river, I can see there are many more tents and people than I first remember. It's like an entire small town here, and dozens of people are walking around, tending to small tasks that would seem mundane to most, but to these people, they seem as if they are creating a legacy. It's strange.

"It's something, isn't it?" says Von.

"Huh? Oh, yea. It's something. Only, I'm not sure what exactly," I respond.

Von laughs. He laughs and smiles an awful lot for someone down in the dumps. I can feel a lecture coming on.

"I know you think this place is dirty, and full of useless people who don't care about life, but that is the furthest thing from reality, Michael. It's not what you see here that matters. It's what you feel here. You see, your eyes can deceive you long enough to make you feel as if you are blind, but your heart will always allow you to see beyond that."

Rather than try and figure out what he is preaching to me, I am trying to understand how so many people can live here without the city doing something about it. It's a slice of river that could be used for so many other projects like a park, and I cannot imagine the city doesn't want to use it for something more important than this. I mean, how does this place even exist today with how important land is in a city like ours?

I turn to ask Von what brought him here, but as I do, I see he is gone from the spot I saw him last, and now is over talking with Marcus. They are looking my way and nodding, but I haven't a clue as to what they are talking about. Nor do I care. Well, a little I do. I care somewhat. It's more of a curiosity.

Then I see Marcus wave me over. He turns around and starts to walk from the 'Flaps just as he walked in hours ago. I look over to Von, and he offers me a gentle smile and a wave, as if he's telling me it's time for me to leave and follow Marcus.

I hurry myself along to catch up to Marcus, who is walking his normal, slow, cocky pace, but he carries himself with a confidence I've never seen before. I have friends that walk "tough", especially at night when they need to carry themselves with a little "extra", but Marcus walks with a peculiar pride. He walks as if no one around him can ruin his day despite their best efforts, and no one around him should dare challenge him either.

I want that exact confident walk at some point in my life. I'm finding myself jealous of another man's stride. That is interesting to me and yet, somehow concerning.

Chapter 10

* * *

Over the next few days, I have slowly gotten myself back into my regular daily routine. My hands, while still bruised a deep shade of blue from throwing lefts and rights, are no longer swollen open. Hailey is back in town, and we've had a chance to catch up some. And although for now I feel we are okay, I am still concerned that once my court date hits, that all will change for our relationship. I don't want that night to be the deciding factor in our union dissolving.

My brother has been extremely busy out west, but promised that he would call me with some help as soon as he could break free. He asked that I get a copy of the initial police report and send it to him, which I now have. He must think I am such a screwup, but I am not. I just happened to be in the wrong place at the wrong time with a slight amount of adrenaline. Nothing else. I wasn't looking forward to a fight like that night in the bar. That evening, I was most probably looking for trouble and feeling unquenched until I found it, which I obviously did.

This was a case of some idiot teens trying to impose their strength in numbers on a helpless human, and while he was a bum laying around where he should not have been at that time of night, he didn't ask for it. He simply didn't use his head well enough in the city and that caused him all those troubles. He sang to garner attention, and he got the attention he was seeking, even if not the way he was after.

As my father once said before he died, probably while he was drunk no doubt,

"Be careful trying to get someone's attention. You sometimes get it."

He was a drunk bastard most times, but a tough son of a bitch. I once saw him reel back his hand and hit a guy who was at least six inches taller than he was, and my dad knocked that guy clean out. Back then, though, the cops rarely were called for fights that involved using only your hands. It was a much different time where men settled beefs like men. You hit and were hit back, until one of you had enough, and called it off. And then that was the end. Period.

Usually that ended in the busted up men shaking banged up hands afterwards, but on rare occasions, the beef wasn't totally squashed, but respect was surely gained. That was something my father instilled in me. Always gain the respect of those around you, even if it means having to throw a few lefts to get their attention.

I miss my dad. I don't remember a lot about the man he was outside of his drinking, but there are a few things that have stayed with me over the short years I had a dad. I find myself fondly remembering those things in the times when I feel most perplexed about life. It's as if he's still teaching me things at the worse moments, even though he is no longer around. I appreciate that. Only he never told me he was teaching me, but instead said he was learning me a few things. I never knew if he was kidding or just out of his mind.

My mom, it's just a shame that she couldn't amount to anything more than a convict in the eyes of the State. Had she never touched a drop of alcohol or at the very least learned to control the amount she consumed, I wonder what type of person she would have turned out to be. Maybe she would have been a better mother to my brother and I, and taught us to love ourselves more, or to build solid dreams on strong foundations and to chase them with all our intentions. Maybe, just maybe, she would have been there for me today with words of encouragement and advice that would have pulled me through, just when I needed her most. But she's not, and because of her, neither is my father.

My week goes by quickly for some reason, and I find that it's Friday night again without it feeling like it. This means that tomorrow is day two at the 'Flaps, although technically it's day three, but no one is counting that day on my behalf.

Hailey wants to stay in for a change, and we agree to cook together just something quick and easy. I have a feeling she's worried about me going out with her in public, and someone pushing my buttons again. Really who could blame her? She's probably concerned that if I end up in another scuffle before I even have my second court date, that they will lock me up and throw away the key without the need for a hearing.

She's a bit over-dramatic most times, but I can understand her genuine concerns. I'm feeling the same way. Tonight it's better to stay indoors and ensure there is no trouble on the streets with me in the middle. I cannot afford it again.

" I know you don't want to talk about it much, but tell me about this community service thing you are doing. What's it like there? What are the people like, Michael?" Hailey asks.

I take a bite of the Italian bread she picked up for us and swallow hard, knowing she was going to ask at some point. I get it. She's curious, but to be honest, I am confused by that place. It's only been a week and I have a feeling that this isn't going to go as I had planned. I expected a quick couple of months' worth of Saturdays to come and go without me remembering much at all about my time there, but after only a week, I have come to realize I am learning a lot more about the homeless community than I ever cared to know.

Somehow, something within that community of theirs is playing stories through mind. I am growing ever the more curious about the people who call it home, and about the startup of a place like that. How did this place even exist, and for how long has it? I mean, was it just sitting there unused and a group of bums decided to just camp out, and one thing lead to another, and boom, instant tent city? You know, like squatters' rights?

I've read stories online about situations where a vacant house is inhabited by someone who refuses to leave and it's hell trying to remove them. Some loophole in the law books that allows people to basically take over a place they want as theirs, and they do just that without ever having to pay a dime. Maybe this is one of those cases, but instead of just one person squatting, it's an entire congregation of people, making it nearly impossible to remove them all.

I bet if I ask my brother, he would be able to look into it some and get me some information. It's funny really. I couldn't have cared less a few weeks ago about everything having to do with this entire assignment, and here I am, wondering why this place exists in my city as if I should care. It's not that I have an issue with it being where it is, but more the fact so few people seem to even know its whereabouts.

Hailey seems to be pretty interested in my time there. There's a difference between that and when someone asks how your day was, really just preferring to hear a "good," or a "not too bad," because they are not really looking for an answer. But she wants more than a canned phrase and isn't willing to settle for less. She wants to know what is was like for me the morning when I woke, how I arrived there and what the building I met Marcus in was like. She wants to hear me talk about the ride over in his shitty car where I was initially nervous around this guy, and how my first interactions with the homeless I came into contact with was like. She begs of me to tell her about the people who live there, and what their individual personalities are like. The what makes them who they are.

It's crazy to me that she wishes to know so many intricate details of a day that was to come and go without much of anything, but she does. And the day didn't come and go as it was supposed to go. It shaped the next several weekends for me before they have even arrived.

"So, are you excited about tomorrow? What are you planning on doing tomorrow when you first get there? Are you meeting that Marcus guy first, or heading straight there?" she asks.

"Whoa. Slow down, Hailey. Slow down. Excited? No. Why on earth would I have excitement for a community service I am being forced to perform, early on a Saturday morning that I should be sleeping in? I literally have no clue as to what I will be doing when I get there. Marcus doesn't seem to give me any direction, so I guess I will figure that all out when I get there. I guess I will meet Marcus like I did last week and ride over with him. Seems to be the way this is going to go," I respond.

We continue to pick at our food, even when it starts to cool down to room temperature. I don't want to have our night end, but I know it's getting late. Still, I feel like I need to walk a fine line here with Hailey and give her all I can before it's too late.

"So, these people. They live there, full time, right? Do you get to talk with them, or is it more like you are handing out things as they line up, like in a soup kitchen?" she asks.

"No, it's not like that at all. They are basically living there and fending for themselves most of the time. I met this one guy there, Von, and he seems to be in charge of the others. He doesn't tell me he is in charge, nor does he seem to want that title bestowed upon him, but clearly the others all look to him for help, and he gives it without question. He's, I don't know, there's something compelling about him. It's hard to explain. It's almost as if he doesn't belong there, but somehow, at the same time, he does," I say.

I can see Hailey is growing more interested by the minute as I tell the story, but I am feeling the need to stop for now. This place has taken up way too much of my time already, and I want to focus on other things. Afterall, it was Marcus who told me no one can occupy my head space without my say-so, and that includes places as well.

"Listen, can we not talk about this right now? I'm exhausted from this week and that God-forsaken place. I just want to forget about it for a little tonight. I'll go there tomorrow, and when I am done, I will come home and if you want to talk more about it then, we can. Deal?"

The morning comes much too quickly, and to my surprise, Hailey is up before I am and she has breakfast made and laid out, and a lunch packed for me in a brown paper bag. She's dressed in her workout outfit, her hair is up in a tight bun, and she has no makeup on at all. She looks absolutely adorable, but I'm not going to tell her that. She would get pissed at me for calling her anything but pretty.

"What are you doing up?" I ask confused.

She's not a morning person at all. In fact, she's the exact opposite of a morning person. But here she is, chipper and bright-eyed, sitting at the counter where there is space for only two high top chairs, waiting to have breakfast with her screw-up of a boyfriend.

"Well, I wanted to show you that I support you. If you need to get up early Saturday, then I will get up early Saturday with you to make it easier," she says.

Man. Let me tell you this and this is for certain. I do not deserve this girl at all! She is far way too good for someone the likes of me, but I am not going to tell her that. If she has not figured that out for herself, well, that's on her. But I know just how lucky I am that she sticks with me through all this shit I cause with my temper.

We sit and eat, but I am still half asleep, so I am not so talkative. It doesn't matter though, because we are together, and although I have to leave in roughly ten minutes, for those ten minutes left, I am blessed. That is what I am focused on. Not where I need to be soon, but where I am now. I learned that also from my parents. When things were good, which they rarely were, I tried to live longer in those moments with them. I knew things were going to turn bad at any moment and without notice, but those moments could wait. I wanted to enjoy the good for as long as possible.

I guess I have learned that my life is all about the balance of any situation. I understand that both good and bad will come with time, and if I forgive the fact that both move at a pace I don't desire, I seem to grasp the balance more and accept most situations.

I'm learning that about the 'Flaps. It's an act of balance for me there. I want that time to move quickly, and in fact, I try to will it to, but then there are moments where that place captures my undivided attention, and I stand and watch in utter amazement the different variables it provides.

I think Von is a huge part of that for me. He could be miserable and complain incessantly about all the things he doesn't have in his life, but he chooses not to. He seems to appreciate the little that he does have, although most people could never get that. I've only met him on two occasions but so far, he's proven to be the type of person people gravitate towards, with a strong purpose and truly admire. All the people there that I have met absolutely adore that guy, from what I can tell, anyway.

I kiss my girlfriend on the lips goodbye, grab the lunch she has packed for me, slip on my old Timberlands, and I am out the door. The walk is peaceful this morning, and I am once again focused on getting another day of this bull-shit behind me. Plus, it's a bit easier today knowing what to expect from Marcus and what not to expect from him. He's going to have a harder time intimidating me, because I expect so little from him to begin with.

It's another warm summer morning, and it's only going

to get hotter as the day stretches on from what I heard, but today there is a chance of rain, which we desperately need around here. The plants are all dying, and the little grass within the city limits is sapped of color and drained of energy.

I haven't thought much about what these people do in the rain, and for that fact, what they do come winter when the ground is frozen solid, and the snow packs along the roads and ice covers everything in sight. How do they exist in those conditions? It has to be brutal to live outdoors when the temperatures drop below thirty degrees, or far less even.

Those are the times you see the homeless huddled together against warm grates as the welcomed heat rises from somewhere below, with four layers of clothes covering them and black and white newspapers spread across their bodies, hoping to keep in just a little bit of warmth.

It reminds me of flowers. You know, the perennial kind that come back each year after the cold weather has all but killed them off. The flowers drop their petals, and then their stems die off to below ground level, exposing nothing of what once was something magnificent. But underneath? Underneath in the ground, something magical happens that we don't get to see with our eyes. Those plants hibernate, and when the ground begins to warm to just the right temperature, they emerge once more, just as magnificent as they did the year before, as if nothing ever changed. It's fascinating how nature just knows when it's time to emerge and grow once again. That it knows how to go to the very brink of death, and not die off entirely because it has more to give.

I wonder, is that what happens to these people? They hibernate somewhere that people cannot see or refuse to see, and find a way to skate through the coldest of months, barely alive by the end, but with a strong will that is pure enough to get them through to the next season, then and only then they become what they once were?

It's strange, but it's crossing my mind where-as before, it never had. I never gave a second thought to them as they laid sideways on those smoky, metal grates, half alive or half dead. I just preferred to ignore them and move on, wishing they would simply vanish from my city forever.

But, alas, I am back where Marcus is waiting for me, sitting on the stoop of his office and reading a newspaper he probably found lying nearby. I can't remember the last time I read one, or saw someone else reading one. Today, we get our news from social media, and have little use for the black and white papers anymore. But it reminds me of a time long gone where as a young kid, I watched the neighbors walk out in red robes and white slippers with their hair a freaking mess, in the warmest of days and the coldest of mornings, to get their news. It's a pretty cool memory, but I had let it sleep awhile until this moment when Marcus has woken it up..

"Anything good in the world of news today, Marcus?"

He doesn't answer me. I swear, either this guy hates me

like no one else, or he's deaf. There is no other answer. I don't get him, but I remind myself that one more Saturday will be checked off the list today, and I will be one day closer to never having to see Marcus ever again. Thank God for that.

"You ready for today?" he asks.

Ready? I'm here, but ready? I don't even know what we are doing today, so how can I answer his stupid question.

I decide to play it cool like he does, and not answer him. Although it clearly doesn't have the same effect as it does on me, because he simply doesn't care that I don't answer. It's like he has this something over me, and only he can dictate how I will feel on these mornings. Damn this guy is annoying as hell, but I am not going to let him change my life if that is what he is after. He may not appreciate his, but I do value mine.

So, as he gets into his beater of a car, I open the passenger side door and again move things out of the way so I can sit. Only as we start out, we don't head in the same direction as we did last week. Instead, he heads into the center of the city, and I begin to wonder, just where are we going now? I agreed to help the people of the Mudflaps, and nothing else. This crazy man is messing with me, and I am not happy at all about it. He's lucky I don't call that lady back at the center where I signed up for this job, because he would most likely be out of a job, or at least reminded that I am not to do anything but what was on that paper I signed.

He pulls into a large parking garage where I can see the

Hospital of the University of Pennsylvania in letters across the top. What the hell are we doing here? He doesn't look sick to me, and I am certainly not sick.

Chapter 11

* * *

As we pull into one of the empty spots, I ask Marcus what we are doing here and if he's feeling okay. He nods. Then I ask him if we are visiting someone here before heading off to the tents, but he doesn't answer me. Instead, we are back at a food cart on the street corner across from the hospital, and he's once again ordering two egg sandwiches with cheese on them this time, and salt and pepper, with another two black coffees. I literally just ate, but I am not about to tell him that. He's at least decent enough to buy me something, so I'll eat it. Besides, I never turn down a hot cup of coffee in the morning.

We sit on a wooden bench adjacent to the hospital, and I watch as people are heading in to work their shifts, relieving others who are coming out the same doors from a long night. It's a busy morning, but I guess sickness and injuries don't really have a peak day of the week in the city. Maybe they do and this is it. What do I know?

'We going in, or just hanging out here for a while?" I ask.

"Visiting hours don't start until eight, so we are hanging out here for a while," he responds.

His voice doesn't shift tone at all, and his demeanor is stoic. Nothing seems to rattle this man. He's eating his food from the foil packaging it is wrapped in, and sipping that hot coffee from the white Styrofoam cup, and he couldn't care less that I am asking what we are doing here. It's as if he doesn't think I have a right to know, but I do. I don't like hospitals to begin with, but not knowing what we are doing here is a little troubling to me.

I sit after I finish my food and just continue to people watch. There is a homeless man walking around as if he is lost in his own mind. I wonder if Marcus spots him, but I don't have to wonder for long. Marcus walks over to the food cart again, places another order, and then proceeds to walk it over to this guy. The man doesn't seem to know Marcus, but then again, I am not even sure he knows who he is himself. He's definitely confused about things.

As Marcus hands the man the food and drink he purchased just moments ago, he touches the guy on his shoulder, says a few words that I cannot hear, and smiles at him. The man looks anxiously around, but for a split second, he seems to acknowledge what Marcus has done. It's super brief and I would bet that most people would have missed it, but it's noticeable enough to me.

Then, just as quickly and as nonchalantly as Marcus walked over, he walks back to where I am, sits down, and waits.

I may never understand this man, but maybe that's the way he prefers it. Mystical, strong and brave, but kind as anything when the time comes. He's unique, and although I want to hate him for many reasons, I cannot find one. He's growing on me, but I am not about to tell him that.

At five minutes to eight, he stands up and starts to walk to the front entrance of the hospital. I know not to wait for an official invitation, so I just follow him to the street where we need to cross. The guard knows Marcus by name, and does one of those head ups, where he says, "what's up," without actually saying anything. Marcus nods in his direction in return, and I do the same, but the guy has looked away before I even finish my "what's up".

Once we reach the doors, we walk in to the front reception area where things are busy as can be. Marcus waits his turn patiently, and then when the woman behind the desk asks him what she can help him with, he responds,

"Here to see Mr. Terrance Carver, ma'am".

She looks at the computer screen in front of her, finds the man's name on it, and tells us that he's in room 307.

Marcus walks casually to the elevator and pushes the button for the third floor without any more hesitation. I have no clue who Terrance Carver is, and why we are here to visit with him, but I assume he's a friend of Marcus' and we are just paying a quick courtesy visit before we head to the 'Flaps. Not a big deal, I guess. He's human and has a right to visit with a friend if he so chooses. I'll just wait in the waiting room for him to do whatever it is he needs to do. Afterall, it's killing time that I don't need to be outside in the early morning sun, and that is totally fine by me.

As we exit the elevator, Marcus first looks left and then right, looking for the right direction to head into for room 307. It's right, so he pushes on that way while I stop where the waiting room is. Without turning around, Marcus somehow knows that I have stopped, and asks me what I am doing.

"I'm going to wait here for you to visit with your friend, or whatever. Marcus, I don't want to visit with someone I don't know," I say.

He stares at me, and gives me a look as if to say, you aren't waiting in no damn waiting room.

I roll my eyes, and proceed to follow him. Marcus turns around and continues to room 307.

As he stands just to the outside of the room, waiting for a nurse to finish whatever she is doing in there, he motions to me to stand over beside him. I reluctantly walk over, and stand uncomfortably besides him, and wonder why the hell I have such a hard time telling this man no. But the fact is, I do have a hard time.

The nurse walks by Marcus and I and smiles quickly. Marcus starts to walk in to room 307 and sits beside this man who is laying out, placing his hand on his old swollen hands, and smiles at him.

"Terrance, my friend. How are you feeling? I know it's been a rough week for you, but I'm here and I've brought a guest to visit with you. His name is Michael," Marcus says.

What is this guy doing to me? Now I need to talk with

this guy, who is semi-conscious and laid out on a hospital bed in clear pain, and I have no idea who he is and what I am supposed to say to him. Marcus is losing his mind here, and I am really uncomfortable with this all. I even think of just leaving and heading back home, because this is not part of my job description and no one can hold this against me, including that judge. I want to desperately, but instead I decide to live by my rule of balance. Just get through this moment, because something better is going to come along in the next one and this will be gone from my mind.

I have no idea of what I am supposed to be saying, and all I can get out of my mouth is,

"Hey, what's up?"

That's it. Marcus cracks one of those smiles that you do when you are trying to act pissed, but can't because you find it too damn funny. I wasn't trying to be funny, but I don't know this man from Adam, and really, what am I even doing here in the first place? I'm a little uneasy at the moment, so maybe he can cut me some slack.

"You don't recognize Terrance, do you Michael?" Marcus asks.

I lean in for the first time to see why he is asking me this question. Do I know him? I have no idea, but now I have a strong urge to see if in fact I do. He's asked me for a specific reason, so I'm sure this is one of those rhetorical questions, but how would Marcus know anyone that I have crossed paths with in my life?

"I don't think...," I begin, but then as I focus on his face and those eyes, now slightly swollen but still open partially, I realize I do know him.

"Wait, oh this is the guy from Saturday night! The dude, I mean the guy who was singing near the pizza place, when those idiots came over. Right? It's him, isn't it?" I ask.

Terrance can't seem to speak at the moment, but he reaches a damaged hand out in my direction, and shakes it back and forth, telling me that he wants to grab mine without using his words.

I'm terribly reluctant at first, but then for whatever reason, I reach mine out to meet his. He touches my hand and pats it gently, before placing his on top of mine while holding it down against the bed. It's weird to me, but not grossly uncomfortable as I may have thought at another time in my life. He's cleaned up, and they have cut his shameful hair back, bathed him thankfully, and trimmed his facial hair neat and tight, to allow his features to shine despite the swelling. I can still tell it's the same man, but he almost looks normal, sans the bruises and swollen eyes that have transformed his face just a bit.

"Hey Terrance, um, hey, glad you are here. Well, I'm not glad you are here, but what I mean is, you are safe here. That's good," I say.

I'm clearly confused on how to talk to this man. First, I don't think he can talk back to me, which I clearly accept. He's pretty banged up, probably on a major dose of hard prescription drugs, and has clear plastic tubes up his nose and in his arms. I don't know that even if he could talk, he would feel much like doing so just now.

Marcus is watching this man, and I can see two things on his face. One, is sheer angrer. Angry that this man, who apparently is a friend or acquaintance of his, is lying here in this bed, roughed up for the crime of lending his voice late at night. And two? I can see Marcus is treating me with just a slight bit more respect than he usually does. He isn't high-fiving me or anything like that, but he's clearly throwing a shade of respect my way, and I appreciate that gesture probably more than he understands.

"Michael, sometimes doing the wrong thing, is the right thing to do. And sometimes the right thing, well, not everyone is going to understand or accept why we do what we do in tough spots. Either way, Terrance is here healing because you stepped up. That is the only reason you were bailed out. You stepped up, and that did not go unnoticed," Marcus says.

If this is a thank you, he's not entirely convincing. But for the little I know about this man, Marcus, it's probably as thankful as he's ever going to be. So I'll take it gladly. But I'm not telling him that. He's not making me drop my guard just yet.

We stay there another twenty minutes or so, just sitting quietly and every once in a while, saying a few words to Terrance, but mostly just sitting. There's really not much more for us to do, but I sense that Marcus feels Terrance could use the company this morning, and I feel Marcus needs this almost as much as Terrance. He seems to thrive off of giving his time and energy to others who need it much more than he does. It's an impressive thing to witness, but I wonder. What is his ultimate goal here?

Then Marcus stands up tall and tells Terrance he will be back in a day or so, but needs to head over to the Mudflaps to give them a hand for the day. Which makes me wonder, why was Terrance not sleeping there that night? If he knows Marcus, and he's homeless, he surely must know all about that tent city by the river. It would make sense to know about it if so many other homeless people do. They must talk amongst themselves because really, what else do they have to do all day and night?

Marcus does his usual get up and walk by me without so much as a "you ready?"

It makes me drop my head, shaking it back and forth, but this time, with a proud smile. He has to be doing this on purpose now. Like it's his calling card to me. As if to tell me he comes and goes as he pleases, but I am not afforded that same luxury. That, I have yet to earn that.

Down the hall I catch up to him before we hit the elevator, and I ask him,

"Marcus, why was that man, Terrance, why was he not at the 'Flaps? Doesn't he know about that place? I mean, it seems like it's a bit more secure with sheer numbers and all, and people there seem to call it home. Why wasn't he there that night?"

I was waiting for Marcus to ignore me again as he does most times when I ask a question of any importance, but this time it's different. He shakes his head and mutters,

"The 'Flaps? You come up with that nickname on your own?"

I guess somewhere along the line I had. I've heard it called Tent City, The Mudflaps, the community down by the river, even the shithole where people go to die, but the 'Flaps must just be the slang term I used when talking about it to others. Maybe laziness kept me from saying the entire name, or maybe it just sounded cooler. I don't really know, but is that his response? He's not going to tell me the answer to the question I just laid in front of him?

"Not all folks feel as if they belong places, and not all folks want help. Some want more in life, and at times that first step is right hard, but it also grants a strong feeling of independence. Terrance is one of those folks. He wanted to prove he could be on his own. That's all," Marcus says.

Well, it's more for sure. And I guess it makes some sense, although there are a dozen follow up questions I have, but this is just not the time. We are out of the elevator and heading right back to the parking garage, towards where he parked his car.

The day has started somewhere else, but it's still the community outreach for the Mudflaps we are working on. And my day is that much closer to being over, but for now, we are heading over to the river, and we shall see what they have in store for me there, if they decide to tell me.

Chapter 12

* * *

It's just after 9:20 am, and the day is still new and mild thus far. The sky has a slight overcast, and a hint of rain can be felt in the air, but the people here cannot be concerned with that. They have things to do, and apparently, so do I.

"Michael, here. Grab one end of this, will ya?" Von asks.

It's a large, wooden table that has seen a few seasons of weathering for sure. It's one of those you would find at a campsite, or along a park where large families barbecue for the afternoon, while throwing back a few beers and playing a little cornhole, as music plays in the near distance. Those days have the best types of afternoons. I don't get to do that much because, well my family isn't close by for various reasons, but I have been invited to events with my friends as their families do this over the summer.

"Where did you get a picnic table from, Von?" I ask.

Von is shifting it left a little, then right, trying to plant in on the ground so that it sits stable, as the earth below is nowhere near level with its rocks and roots protruding through the top coat of dirt . He seems like a perfectionist for someone that has nothing to his name outside of this place, and I wonder why he can't implement that into a successful career of some type and get the hell out of here.

"Well, it fell off a truck," he answers.

I look at him, trying to figure out if he's lying, or telling me the truth.

"I'm messing with you, Michael. It was generously donated. There are a few groups throughout the city that, from time to time, find ways to give the people here a little bit of their warm side of the sidewalk. Everyone deserves to experience happiness on different levels, and while this may be a small thing for most, it's not for those here," he says.

I smile, which is funny for me. I don't want to be here, but when I am, I somehow find a strange bit of wonder cross my mind and I feel as if I am learning a great deal about something I apparently knew so little about. It's hard to explain, because I don't really understand it yet myself.

After we set the table in place as flat as the unforgiving ground will allow, I see there are a few others lined up at one end of the area these people inhabit. They look as if they were dropped off purposefully and neatly in a row, and are ready to be transported to where their new function will be. I can see a few of the people who live here are trying to pick them up in groups of four or five, and that at least feels good to witness, seeing them attempt something of use finally to help themselves.

"Here, let me. I got it," I say.

Von grabs one end and I grab the other as we work side by side, shuffling the tables under a bit of shade, trying to find a level piece of earth for these people to sit and eat without them rocking too much. I know when I go out to eat with Hailey, and we sit at a table that can't stop tilting from left to right, it drives me crazy. And those are on mostly level floors to begin with, so that makes it even more frustrating, but this spot is anything but flat and level, so we do our very best with what we have to work with.

Marcus is showing his sheer, brute strength, because when I turn to head back and grab another, he's on his way to where we just placed the last one, and carrying the damn thing himself. I would say he's showing off, but I don't think he does it for that reason, honestly. He just enjoys doing things for others as efficiently as possible, and the fact he is insanely powerful is just something that is natural to him. I feel as if I want to tease him a little about him being like the Hulk, but wonder if he will take it well or not. Screw it.

"What's wrong, two at a time a little too much for you big man?" I tease.

Marcus places the large, wooden table down where it needs to be, and turns to look at me. He's not smiling. He's just looking hard at me and I feel a sense of nervousness shoot down my spine. I may have said something I should not have, and he's letting me know that he did not appreciate it.

But then, he cracks a smile, and relief flows through my veins, where just a moment ago, I felt a sharp fire ride through them.

"I didn't want to make you feel too bad about yourself by doing twice as much as you need help with, little fella," he shoots back.

Von starts laughing hysterically, and then the others of the 'Flaps join in. I doubt that many of them heard what he said, or if they did, even understand what it is he meant, but it doesn't matter. These people are laughing and enjoying a moment that most of us take for granted on the outside. They get to laugh together as a whole, and that seems to change the entire mood of the mysterious city they have created.

My face is probably a bright shade of fire engine red, because to be fair, his response was quick-witted and perfectly executed and timed, and I did not expect that from this simple man. But I'm not mad. In fact, I feel a bit human here for the first time. I've felt like I was here physically but not mentally, and now I feel a little of both. It makes me feel a tad relaxed and able to let my guard down just enough.

This place is growing on me a little, but it's still a merciless, sad environment. I mean, these people need baths something fierce. There's a river right there just yards away from where they walk, and I wonder why they don't feel the desire to jump in and wipe the weeks of grime, dirt and filth off of their bodies. There are a few that seem to take better care of themselves than others for certain, but those are far and few between. Most of them just seem to have accepted their forlorn fates here, and no longer care what those outside of this place think of them or their humble existence.

Von confuses me. His intelligence is beyond that of others here and honestly far beyond most people I know elsewhere, and although he does hold himself well for having lived in filth for years, he's not one of the cleanest and I don't get it. I even think about asking him if he needs to shower at my place, but then I decide it's better not to. I don't know this man well enough and the last thing I want is for him to think I'm strange or gay. I am neither. Plus, if I let him shower at my place, it may send the wrong message to others that they too can share in that cleansing, and that would create a massive problem for my girlfriend and me.

The sky closes off any remaining rays of sun that were moments ago peeking through and gracing the ground around us with bright beauty. Now where there was sun, there are clouds, and those clouds are dropping tiny bits of salty water onto the tops of our heads. It feels good actually, because it's still warm enough out to make a man sweat without doing much manual work.

"Ah, the heavens are opening up and cleansing our village I see," Von says to me.

I look around and see that the people here are coming out from their humble tents to enjoy the coolness of the droplets of rain, just as I am. Each of them could be anywhere but here in their minds, the way they are acting. I would be miserable if this was the highlight of my day, but the simple mid-morning shower is a genuine gift to them. It's positively real and something they can be a part of, without anyone's say and without money to buy it.

It's almost like a party has started, but there are no colorful balloons or streamers, and no rectangular tables covered in finger food of all varieties for guest to consume. There are no large canopies to sit and eat under while the rain waits on the outside, just out of reach. There are just a few old, splintered picnic tables, and the hard, clay ground all around. But these people seem happiest when they have less. I may never truly understand that.

Even Marcus is smiling with others around him, and slapping a few gently on their backs. He looks as if he understands this moment more than I would expect, but he gets it. Oh, he gets it.

"Marcus, now what do we do?" I ask as the warm rain gets heavier and drops harder from the heavens.

"Do? You worry too much about what you need to do. You are doing now," he replies over the pounding drops of rain.

I'm doing? All I am doing is getting wet. And cold. Wet and cold doesn't seem like a part of the job description either.

But looking around in all directions, people *are* doing. Marcus was most likely trying to tell me that I worry too much about what is coming, and that I try to control the situation more than I need to. But that is just how I am as a result of my upbringing and life experience. If there is a task placed in front of me, I want to complete that task as quickly and efficiently as humanly possible. For me, that is the easiest and most direct path to success, but for all these homeless people here, they aren't worried about success in the sense that I am. Their success comes from their happiness they find, and the moments that give them pause long enough to enjoy the change that came from somewhere other than here.

This reminds me of a day of fishing my brother and I had together after my parents left our lives, while he was back visiting the old stomping grounds. It was just him and I, fishing an early morning along the banks of the Schuylkill, but a spot further up from where I am now.

There could have been others out fishing that same day and time as us, but I don't recall right now. That morning, it was just us brothers, and our old fishing poles, plus a six pack of beer. I generally do not drink before noon as a rule, but this was an exception. He was leaving again shortly, and we would not get an opportunity to do this again for some time. I never knew when the last time we would fish together would be, and I hated to even think that this could be that time.

I remember we sat mostly in silence, with the occasional," was that a bite?"

It wasn't about the conversation we were sharing that morning. It was more about the time spent between two young brothers, heading on two very different journeys in a life that didn't always seem fair and balanced. He was heading for much bigger things, and I, well, I was staying in the same city that taught me how to fight back, and how to push on when I felt the urge to give up.

I don't regret staying here, although I would like to get out to visit with my brother for sure. I've never been out west past Pittsburgh and could use a change in scenery. Maybe next year. That's what I have told myself for the past several years. Maybe next year. Only, something always comes up, and I get sidetracked and forget to plan it out for later.

I know my brother feels as if I don't really want to visit him, but that's not the case. I really ought to one of these days just show up and surprise him.

But today, watching people dance crazy in the rain and laugh and smile, reminds me of family and how it should be. A good, strong family finds happiness in the smallest of moments, and creates memories out of them that travel a lifetime and are handed down from generation to generation. Like that morning with my brother. It's one of my favorite memories, and I carry it with me all the time and will share that story and plan those types of trips with my own children someday.

I wonder if any of these people will carry this one with them and for how long, or if this is just another day to get through to the next for each of them? It seems like so much more, but it can be hard to tell. They seem to be pretty damn happy for having zero to their names but a rainstorm, a tent, and their given names. I mean, if food stopped coming in, most of them would starve to death.

If the winter is harsher than the one before and the tents fail, and no one cares, they will freeze to death. They don't have a say in much of anything over their lives, and that would scare the shit out of me. I need absolute control of my destiny. I don't trust others enough to let that go.

But for now, they don't worry about what is out of their control, but instead, they relish in the fact that they have rain on a hot summer's morning, when rain was needed desperately. It's as if they prayed for the rain, and that prayer was granted to them.

But there is still work to be done, and as much as I have remarkably enjoyed this small moment of theirs, I have other things to get back to in my own life, and I would like to get through week two of this. There are only six more to go, and I remind myself that I can breeze through the remaining six weeks if I just continue to do whatever it is I need to, and if I have a little enlightening along the way, well, then so be it.

"Hey Marcus, I'm going to head on over and clean that brushy area up over there, because if we get any more of these picnic tables, we can use the flat land better than here," I say.

Marcus just throws a hand my way, waving me off, probably wondering why I cannot enjoy the simple things like the rain he and the others are thoroughly enjoying. But he needs to understand something. I have seen a lot of rain in my time, and it's never changed much about how I feel. I look at my life like the weather. Sometimes it's warm and sunny, and the air is calm, allowing me to live in the moment and enjoy what the day brings. Other days, the harshness of the day, like an ice-cold Philly winter evening, with its second straight day of snow, ruins my mood. There is nothing good to see on those days, especially on the second day of snow.

Those types of days I know they are coming, but I still get frustrated when they do arrive. The first day that the pure white snow touches the tops of the pavement, it's peaceful. During the heavy storms we see sometimes once a year, no one leaves the comforts of their homes. The blanketing snow covers the tiny side streets of Philly, and there is simply no where to place the snow, even for those brave enough to shovel their cars out when they have no choice but to head to work. It's almost perfectly enjoyable. But that second day? The one where the heavy salt trucks and plows come through the streets they are able to, pushing piles high into the air, and turning the once perfect white snow into a gray and black slush? Well, that second day sucks. It ruins what was once so nice, in just one day.

The rain, though, comes and goes. It doesn't change much in my day. It does not leave a trail of ugly gray slush behind for days on end, and when the sun makes an appearance again, it dries up the ground quickly, changing my mood very little.

I ask Von if he happens to have any shovels or rakes around somewhere, then I almost feel stupid for asking. Why would they? It's not as if they have a shed handy for tools like that just sitting there waiting for someone to store things. They have what they can carry, and not much else.

"Well Michael, the shovels and rakes are all being used by the gardeners right now, so I'll let them know when they are finished with them that you would like to use those as well," he says.

Okay, funny. Make fun of the guy who is here to help and actually has ideas, because he's not used to what others don't have. I get it. It was stupid of me to ask. But seriously, how the hell am I going to clear that area of the brush now?

"Let's see if we can't find something around here of use to you, shall we?" Von says with a wink.

He walks away from where I am standing, and through the rain drops, stops by to talk with the others. As each one shakes their heads back and forth, he smiles and moves on to the next. He continues until a woman disappears into her tent for a moment, and comes back out, handing Von an olive-green duffel bag. She looks at him, and says a few words, as she reaches back for the bag she just handed him. Von smiles and touches her hand, in the most calming gesture. She seems reluctant at first, but he continues with some more words, points over to where I am waiting, and then starts to walk my way, with her right beside him, holding her hand the entire way.

"Michael, this is Emma. Emma, Michael. Emma was kind enough to provide some small gardening tools for us to use. She's looking forward to giving you a hand. Is that okay with you?" Von asks.

Honestly, I work so much better alone. She's old, out of shape, and her helping is going to be more work for me, but what am I going to do? Tell Von no? Marcus would not appreciate that, and I seem to be on his better side for today, so I want to keep it that way if I can. It'll make my time here go by much easier. So I will let her help, but hopefully she stays out of my way and allows me to just get this done as quickly and easily as possible.

"Yea, sure, whatever she wants," I respond without any enthusiasm in my words.

I grab the bag, and can see Emma is nervous about that. I need to remind myself that this is her life in that bag. It's part of all she owns, and when I grab for it, it's as if I am grabbing a part of her directly, and acting as if it's insignificant. To me, it is. To her, it's everything. It is hard for me to be so different here than from where I came from, but I am trying my best.

"Emma, do you want to carry it over there and help me? Would that be okay?" I ask.

She smiles, and nods quickly. I look at her face, and for a split second, for some unknown reason, I see my own mother in her eyes. She has some eerily similar features, although she's about ten years older than my mother is. But wow. Something inside me hurts when I see Emma up close. Normally, I see them as basically all the same. Homeless, dirty, and a drain on society. But in this moment, I feel for this woman, Emma. I feel sad for her situation, and wonder where she comes from, and if she has any family that should be helping her instead of allowing her to be in this situation.

We walk slowly over to the area where we are going to work on removing the scattered brush, and as we do, the rain ceases. It's nice because it has softened the ground up just enough to make the work a little easier on us.

"Emma, what sort of things do you have in the bag to help us?" I ask her, hoping it will be of use.

Von is somewhere else doing whatever he is doing, so it's just the two of us here now. Emma reaches in and pulls out a pair of old, soft blue looking work gloves, a small wood handled garden rake, two small garden shovels that have a slight bend to them, and a book on gardening probably from the late 70's. We won't be needing that, but it's nice to see she can read, or maybe she simply enjoys the pictures.

These tools aren't exactly what I was hoping for, but rather than make Emma feel bad, I decide to show her my appreciation by doing what I can with them.

"Perfect, Emma. These are going to be just the tools we need for this. You ready to get started?" I ask her.

Emma looks at me curiously, as if she's trying to read something deep in my soul, and then she gets to work without a word spoken. She goes down to her knees, and starts to dig at the annoying brush in front of her, pulling it from the ground a little at a time. I watch for a moment, imagining working side-by-side with my mother in a small vegetable garden back home in the city, as it should have been in my life.

But it's not. That part sucks. Because that garden and that moment never happened.

Chapter 13

* * *

Week two is officially in the books. I have a full week of not worrying about the 'Flaps, and I can get back to my other life problems and goals.

Hailey and I have not discussed my past all that much, mainly because when she brings it up, I give her short, nonchalant answers and change the subject quickly. It's hard to talk about a past you would soon rather forget, but I understand it's a part of me, and the past has shaped me into the man I am before her.

I trust her most days, and value her opinion and advice when she offers it up. Even when I don't necessarily agree with it. She has my best interest at heart, and I think she really just wants to peek into the window of my past so she can learn more about what makes me, me. My exterior can be a bit rough and hard to see past most days, but she knows that I have put up a wall to protect myself.

I am my own worst enemy in this world. When things are

problematic, I often resort to remembering a past I wish to forget, even though I don't seem to try quite hard enough. It's something that creeps into my space at the most grueling of times, and it reminds me of what Marcus told me a week ago. I am allowing my past to occupy my personal space, but I do not know how to stop that from happening. I'm sure if I went to therapy of some kind, they would tell me all about how I need to deal with my past better, and how I need to forgive and accept, and on and on and bullshit and yea. Well, I don't forgive my past because no one has apologized for how everything went down.

But lately, with this new "job" of mine on my normally free Saturdays, Hailey is beginning to ask more questions, and before, where I wanted to skip right past answering them, I feel as if it's not the most terrible thing to give her at least some of the answers. For one, she's my girlfriend and she's just genuinely curious. For two, I have someone to bounce things off of, and with all that I am experiencing there at the camp, I do have things that I am eager to discuss.

"Hailey, you should see this place. I mean, people live there as their only residence. It's dirty, full of people that smell horribly from ten feet away, and they have literally nothing but a small number of personal possessions, and their names. That's all they own. But, they seem mostly happy. I don't get it," I say to her.

Hailey thinks it over before responding. She likes to find the right words before she speaks, and isn't one to waste a good chance to enlighten someone.

"Well, maybe they are mostly happy because they don't really want more than they have. You know how people want a new car, or a second home down at the shore, or something just out of reach and they spend so much time fighting with themselves over how to get it? Maybe they are mostly happy because they don't have that need or desire to fight with themselves," she responds.

"Hailey, how can they not want more than they have? They have to. A place with a shower with running hot water and soap to scrub off the filth they have been laying in for weeks at a time. A reliable car that allows them to travel wherever and whenever they want, so they can see things they never have. A home to call their own, where they can decorate anyway they please, and invite friends over to have a few drinks and a charcuterie board. How can they not want at least those things?"

"Michael, those are things you enjoy and want. They aren't you. Just like you are not them. They have their reasons for living the life they have, and whether they decided to live like that or not, they seem to have accepted it as fate. I guess you can wish that they would want more, but maybe they are genuinely happy, where we seem to frustrate ourselves chasing more than we have," Hailey says.

I still don't get it, and I'm not sure I believe her, but who am I to say that someone else *has* to want more out of life. It's not my life, so I really shouldn't concern myself with it, but I am. I want them to want more.

"Babe, I was there helping to clear out this part of the

camp, and this old woman, Emma, she just reminded me so much of how my mother would look today, minus the layers of dirt and years of loss in her skin, if my mother would not have done what she did. I don't really know why, but she brought up a lot of lost moments for me that I should have had."

Hailey takes my hand, and rubs it gently. She's smiling at me, as if some great breakthrough has occurred, but it hasn't. I'm simply giving her a glimpse into my week, and this was one of the moments that stood out for me. It makes me want to stop opening up, but I feel safe with Hailey. I feel as if she's not going to judge me, or give me a lecture about how I need to forgive my mother and give her a second chance at a life she desires. She knows how I feel about that kind of talk.

Surprisingly she doesn't pry much more. She just sits there, probably hoping that I continue to release some of what is buried inside of me. And that is what I start to do.

"You know, my brother called me a little while back. My mom apparently had another parole hearing and it was denied once again as it should be every single time she has one. But he continues to feel as if her time is coming and she will gain her eventual freedom. He seems to have this reasoning that she deserves to spend her days out here, even though my father doesn't get to. I don't know how he can be so forgiving," I say.

"Maybe it's his way of healing from his own past. You are two entirely different individuals even though you come from the same set of parents, and so naturally you are going to look at things from vastly different angles. One isn't right, and the other wrong, though. It's all in how you choose to see it Michael."

It reminds me that I need to get back to my brother. We haven't spoken much lately, and as I grow older and find myself taking on more and more in my life, I realize that I am allowing time to pass by without my permission, and it's going by fast. Much faster than it seemed to just a few years back.

He, too, has been tied up with work and the successful career he has built for himself. Sometimes, though, I feel as if I am the one that should have had the greater career path and all the awards and recognition. But perhaps being the older child also hurt me. I remember more than he does, and I can see that night clearer than he could ever have.

He would ask me about that afternoon and if I could remember any of the details, such as who started arguing that day, and what it was over. He would ask me if my mom had rage in her eyes before she grabbed the keys and left the house, or if I believe she unintentionally ran the car back over him, and was it really her intent to hurt or kill him, or was it a stupid accident that ultimately changed the course of all our lives?

Maybe anger clouds my perception of the events that day, so it makes it hard to know for certain. I generally answer with something about how her drinking was more important than her living, or the lives of those around her, and how she was entirely selfish, but who knows what she intended for our father that day. I never wanted him to believe she intentionally killed that man, because deep down, I know he loves her still as a son should. He remembers moments of joy, and to take that from him would be both selfish and cruel of me.

But truth be told, I can't remember all that much about it anymore. My mind has locked a good deal of my memories far away in a dark pit, to a place that probably will never allow light to visit them again. And that's a good thing as far as I am concerned.

Trying to figure out what the truth is would serve me no good purpose now, and people waste entirely too much of their precious time focusing on the things they have no control over. I prefer to focus on what I can change, because that is where my energy needs to be placed to get the results I desire.

It's like the 'Flaps. I cannot change anyone there. There is little I can say to those people there that is going to change how they live from one day to the next. No words are going to magically come from my mouth to their souls, enticing them to abruptly change their outlook on the world around them, so why even waste my breath?

As far as Hailey is concerned, I love her and want her to know as much as she wishes, but that doesn't make it easier for me to open up freely.

And it's only been two weeks. I am bound to have mixed emotions over helping out people who have thrown their own lives away and giving up when they had a shot at something normal. This time seems destined to remind me of a past lost before it began, and yet somehow I was able to find some success along the way, regardless.

"But are you enjoying it there? I know you resent that way of life, but what are you *feeling*?" Hailey asks.

It's a fair question. I do resent their way of doing things and that plot of land along the river is a waste of a resource, just as they seem to be. But to be fair, some of them show small signs of life.

Take Von, for instance. I know I have a perplexing respect for what he *could* be, but what turned him to a life of begging in the first place? He had to have had a chance at greater things in the past. Did his parents do something that altered his natural course towards success and take it from his hands? Or did he maybe get sidetracked by an addiction that completely took over his world, and forced it to crumble right before his eyes?

The same goes for Marcus. I know he doesn't seem as if he's the most educated human around, but he has spots of true inspiration that come through when you least expect it. He, too, seems to have lost his way, but at least he is gainfully employed. His job, while not the highest paying, is legitimate enough and seems to put a smile on that old rough man's face. He genuinely loves what he does.

Those two men interest me. They are extremely different and from opposite worlds, and if you placed them both in front of me, and you changed their voices and I had to listen without seeing their faces, I would tell you the roles were reversed. Von would be the one helping from behind the comfort of a steady paycheck, and Marcus would be the one living in the tents, laying on the hard ground, just accepting his fate day in and day out.

"Babe, I don't know that enjoying it is the right word. The first weekend was pretty pathetic. I hated that I had made the decision to sign up for that community service and thought it would only get worse. Then the second week came, and I don't know. Things just went differently than how I expected. I saw that in two days, I had somehow made a small impact on their lives there. That part feels kind of decent, but I just wish I could talk more sense into some of them. They aren't all able to do more, but most of them, given the right chance, and if you laid it out for them so they could easily understand it, could," I say.

It's a constant struggle for me in my life. Watching people fail and give up when they have so much more potential to give. People fail and quit way before they ever should. It's as if at the very first sign of a struggle comes up, they panic and give in to desperation. A fear of missing out causes them to miss out. How is that so difficult to understand for them?

I wonder if I will ever get to know more about Von and Marcus, and some of the other people there. My curiosity about their past is not part of the job description, but it's absolutely part of the job.

The job. I am not even getting paid for this, and yet I still call it a job as if I am. That is puzzling for me. I've always been someone who hustles to gain an edge in life. That person that when it snowed as a young boy, was the first one running from door to door, asking the neighbors if they needed their sidewalks cleared for a few dollars. No one works like that anymore, but I know it made a difference in my life. Whenever times were financially rough, I found a way through them by doing whatever I needed to do.

These people probably know what that feels like on occasion. I see some reaching into trash bins, pulling out the empty aluminum cans of a day's drinking for someone who worked that much harder. There are times I judge them for such a foul existence, but then I am reminded of the days when I too, did whatever needed to be done to survive.

Long ago, before my mother ended two lives in one thoughtless moment, my father was injured at work and was forced to rest. He fought that at first, but eventually relented to the notion that he was better healed than he was forcing the issue.

We were starving, and so my mother, before her hey-days of consuming liquor by the quart, picked up my infant brother, and grabbed my hand, leading us down a few blocks to where the railroad tracks were. She walked us along the iron tracks, as I held a small magnet in my left hand. I remember skipping along the tracks, pretending to jump from one cross beam to the next, as if I was running from a street gang, back to my hideaway.

My mother would stop me and point out something in the brush and ask me to go look closer. We were searching for simple, metal cans that others had discarded over the years.

Each can needed to be touched with the magnet. If it stuck to the can? We put it back where it had rested for probably longer than I was alive. If it did not stick to the magnet, I handed it off to my mom, who placed it in a large black trash bag she had tucked under her arm.

We spent the day covering the tracks back and forth, in search of the "treasure," as she called it. When a train would pound slowly down towards us, we stepped back into the brush and waited. I would wave to the engineer and sometimes he would wave back, while others would shake their heads as if we were doing something very wrong.

But they did not know. What they did not realize was that we were surviving.

I didn't ask my mother that day about the game we played, but a few years later when I saw her place a can in the trash, it reminded me to ask about that day.

She told me that with dad not working, things were tight, and we needed to eat. The only way she could think of to make extra money in a pinch, legally, was to take her kids out along the train tracks, and to gather cans so that we could take them a few blocks to where the recycling yard would pay us for them. She was given a small amount of money for the cans, and apparently it was just enough to get us a meal or two that day.

Funny, that recycling yard is still there today. I drive by it and each time I do, I am reminded of that game of survival. I had no idea that we really weren't playing a game at all, but truly trying to find a way to enjoy a basic necessity in life that is so often taken for granted.

I almost laugh as I remember that now, and even hesitate when I go to toss a can in the bins we use for recycling, probably trying to figure out what it's worth and if I should keep it just in case or if I should let it go. I always let it go now, but there is that tiny moment where I wonder, and it's hard to let go.

Just then, my phone goes off.

"Hello, this is Michael," I answer.

The man on the other line is Marcus. He has some bad news, and it actually hits me harder than I would have thought.

"Babe, you alright? Michael?" Hailey asks.

Chapter 14

* * *

The direction of one's life can change over the course of a millisecond. With a simple thought, or a spoken word that reaches an intended target, or even the simple gift of a beautiful song that is sung for others to appreciate even if they do not, life simply comes and life goes.

I've always said that if my parents had had one less drop of alcohol that day, or if my foster parents had treated me as one of their own with the basic respect everyone deserves, my life would have been vastly different. But those things did not happen, and here I am.

But for some, those decisions and turns and those heartfelt songs given away for free, at times take a great deal more from those that give. This is one of those times, unfortunately.

"Michael, what? What is it?" Hailey asks again.

I place my phone down next to me and take a moment's pause. It was just a short while ago that Marcus and I ran into each other when I was bailed out by someone, and just a short time ago that we walked into the hospital doors to see the man who was beaten over who knows what exactly. But now? His voice is no longer going to give to others whatever he felt like singing about.

"That guy that I went over to help out that night, you know, when those kids were messing around with him?" I begin.

Hailey could see disappointment take over in my expression. She knew before I told her.

Marcus wanted me to know as soon as he found out. He knew I would eventually hear about it because the charges filed against those boys were now going to be upgraded to murder. Who knows what that all meant for me? I knew my charges included assault, but I had no clue if somehow they were going to think I caused that situation to escalate and charge me with more counts as well. I have a hate/hate relationship when it comes to the court system and feel as if justice is simply a play on words to make others who never find themselves defending an action, feel warm and fuzzy and safe at night. There is little justice in a city where crime happens at an unimaginable, breakneck pace.

"Man, I just saw him. He was in rough shape for certain, but he didn't seem like…how did this happen?" I ask.

The reality is that Terrance was not well. He had not been to the doctors since maybe he was a young boy, and his life was covered in years of bad decisions and heartache, which caused him to forget how to love himself for most of his time here.

When I went over to help him out of that jam he somehow managed to get himself into, I felt as if he put his life in that position by expecting others to ignore his faults in life, but really, why should he expect others to ignore him? He had a gift, and he was sharing that, although a little late at night, but who cares. He wasn't hurting anyone by singing on a corner where no one else was standing. He wasn't screaming obscenities at people passing by because he was angry with the world, and he certainly didn't ask to be treated any differently than another human should expect to be treated for simply living.

My mind races to those boys who made such a horrible, stupid, and now tragic decision that night. Where were their parents? Did they know, or did they even care, that their kids were roaming the dangerous streets late at night with other high-energy kids? What did they think would happen, really? Kids do not go out in the city late at night in tough neighborhoods to play stick ball. They go out to cause trouble, and to push each other with dares that sometimes are minor, and other times turn deadly, without a second thought for consequences. Like this time.

Marcus was hurting. I could hear it in his voice that had a different tone for the first time. He said so few words as per his usual, but he needed only those few to convey his thoughts. He's not the type of man to show emotions to others and certainly not the type that cries in front of people, or even while alone. He's what people probably consider a man's man. One that never shares his inner-most feelings more than is needed or expected, and one that when there is something to do, or something that needs fixing, does it and expects nothing in return.

He's the type of human who if there was a riot going on around you, you would want that man standing in front of you. And the rioters, well, they would think more than once about heading in his direction, even in large groups. But I feel for Marcus. I could hear the pain in his voice that dropped off as he finished his sentence, and know he just wants to let it out, but still holds back.

I wish I had asked more questions, but Marcus was quick on the phone. He had a mission to tell me what was going on, and he completed that part of his day. That was that.

"Do you think they will have a funeral or anything for him?" I ask Hailey.

I know she has as much of an idea about that as I do, but it's just talking out loud for me. I don't really care what her answer is because she doesn't know. It's all just a guess at this point for both of us, but I am truthfully curious.

He was homeless, and probably hadn't spoken with his blood family in years, if he even has any left. How would anyone know he died today? Honestly, how would anyone know that he lived? That sucks, wondering how a person can depart from this place, disappear without a trace and that all their breathing, words and motions are not even a memory. As if they had never existed in the first place and had left no imprint of their time here.

But it's a part of that lifestyle they chose that they either accept fully on their own or are forced to accept. Their entire world is wrapped up in a single old canvas bag, or a water-stained cardboard box they sleep in to gain just a small piece of privacy. Or in a small, donated tent, laying mostly flat along the banks of an old river, side by side with others who are living the same damn nightmare.

"Are you going to go and find out?" Hailey asks me.

Truthfully, I had not even thought about that. Where would I go to find out? I don't want to bother Marcus about it right now. I literally just got off the phone with the man, and he needs some time to come to terms with this still.

I could ask at the hospital and see if they have any details on his next of kin, or where they took his body, and then ask the funeral home if they could give me that information once they were told.

But the best place for me to find out? The place that probably can answer my questions more than anywhere else? The Mudflaps. Von, if anyone, would know. He's the guy who knows more than a man in his position should. He seems to have an answer for just about everything and anything, and I would bet that Terrance crossed paths with Von at one point or another, as everyone in tent city seems to know everyone in their position.

Do I really even want to go if there is one? I met this guy twice. Once when he was being pounded mercilessly as I tried to intervene, and the other when he could not speak at all, and could hardly see me through eyes tightly swollen almost shut. That's the extent of my interaction with Terrance.

Still, I feel a strange urge to learn more, and a desire to be there for a simple reason: respect. I feel the need to learn more about his lost past, and to possibly try and reach out to his family. If there is anyone left, they may not care anyway, but so what? What if one of them cares enough to know? That is the one I am worried about. The one that might actually care to know.

"Yea, I think after work I am going to swing by and see what I can find out, if that's okay with you, babe," I respond to Hailey.

Work is busy lately, so the days go by pretty fast, but not today. I am watching my phone to check the time constantly and waiting to see if Marcus sends me an updated message or calls while I am working. He does not. I don't really think I expected him to, but occasionally it's those times you most likely get the calls.

When my last meeting for the day is completed and I only have a few more files to go through, I decide to skip out ahead of the rush hour. There is always time tomorrow to get those done, and besides, I feel like I am ahead of my workload, so thirty or so minutes early isn't going to change much.

On the way out, I slide into my boss's office and tell her that I need to jet just a little early.

"Michael, is everything going alright? You seem a little distracted lately. Everything okay?" She asks me.

"Huh? Yea. Oh yea, everything is good. Just, I've just been tied down with some things at home, but nothing big. It's almost all sorted out, no worries," I reply.

I wonder how much she knows. Does she know that I have a court date approaching for beating on some underaged kids? Or that I am doing community service, helping the homeless people that most of us would rather pretend don't exist? And who called who when I was arrested this last time, to let them know I would not be in work while I needed to be bailed out by someone I didn't even know?

I head to the bank of elevators, and push the down key so that it illuminates, wondering why I even care about this turn of events. Some of the guys I work with see me heading down early and give me a look that asks me if everything is cool. I just give them a thumbs up and enter the elevator without much further ado. I don't need more people feeling as if I have a problem when I don't. It's bad enough that I am struggling with why this is on my mind so much. Talking about it to half a dozen people isn't going to bring me the answers I am seeking.

The distance between my work and the trail leading to the entrance to the 'Flaps is long enough that I decide to take the bus that will eventually drop me off within a quarter a mile or so, which isn't bad at all.

I board the city bus and realize I haven't been on one for some time. I usually take the train everywhere I go, but the train won't get me as close as the bus will, and I want to get there and back home before it gets too late.

The ride is about twenty minutes or so with all the stops, and so I sit back and look out the tinted window as we go from stop to stop around the center of the city. Philly is a fairly large city, and there are a lot of things to see along the way if you take the time to look. Sculptures line city parks, and men and women dressed in smart suits walk by busy on their phones, ignoring everyone around them as if they simply don't exist. I, too, probably have done this without realizing it, but here on the bus, I begin to notice more about the city where I was born and raised.

When we pass the arts area, and head deeper into the smaller sections of the city where the homes are joined together and the streets are small enough that only one car at a time can get through, I realize the great difference from what I had just seen three minutes ago.

The sculptures are replaced with graffitied walls that are crumbling, and the tall, glass enclosed skyscrapers, while still in view to the rear of me, are shadowing broken homes with boarded up doors and windows that hold nothing but maybe some of the elements out. You would never know these places were here if you only came to the center of the city to work or visit and went back down 76 to the suburbs. Your idea of city life would be only a miny portion of what it truly entails. That is exactly what the city wants from you.

I've been through these neighborhoods more than once but seeing them while sitting on a large city bus, knowing that each homeless person I am seeing on the corners is alive, reminds me that I live in a closed-off universe by design. One where I only see what I choose to see, and although things exist without my permission or without my input, they only matter if I let them matter. As Marcus would say, "Ain't no man or woman able to occupy that space without your say-so".

Well, he's right. I don't think about the sorrowful people I don't care for. Maybe I don't care for them because I am inherently selfish, or maybe because my way of living is, in my mind at least, far more superior to their way of traveling through time.

There is an old phrase I have heard several times in my life that will always stick with me; Don't be the smartest person in the room.

What they mean is that in order to better yourself and what you understand, you need to be around better people that know things you do not. Iron sharpens iron. Smart people teach things to those that are not on their level, because they simply know more or have had the experiences you have yet to have.

But I now question that theory. What if that is mostly true, but not entirely? I am learning from my time helping the homeless community, and as far as I can see, none of them has more knowledge than I do. Few of them seem to be as educated, or as traveled as I am, which still isn't a lot. But they still somehow show me things that I could not find on my own. That's a powerful gift to possess, and they have it for some strange reason.

Stop after stop, I see dozens of people who appear to be homeless, but it's hard to tell if they all are. These neighborhoods are poor. Dirt poor. But many still have a place to call home, so they would not qualify as "homeless". Interesting that all of a sudden, I am distinguishing between the different levels of poor, when it's something I never gave a second thought to. You were one of three things in my mind. Poor, middle class, or lucky.

Eventually I see a bus stop that is probably going to be closest to where I intend to go and I get off the bus.

As I walk down the road with my head lowered but my eyes pointed up, I wonder why it is that I have never been down this way. As a kid, we ran from neighborhood to neighborhood, and even while living in foster care, I would do mostly what I pleased, because I just wanted to be free.

After just about a half mile trek, I come to the clearing that has become a little more familiar to me. It makes me feel both a sense of calmness, and a feeling of acceptance, for this place has accepted me as they have everyone else who comes through. They may judge me, but they never show me that they do. It's a warm feeling to walk in and know that people are going to smile at me and appreciate me being there, even if only for the short time I stay.

This is the fourth time I have been to the 'Flaps in just two weeks, but it feels as if I have been here many more times than that. It's becoming extremely familiar, and I am enjoying that as one would anything good and familiar for them.

When I approach the area where I typically see Von mulling around, I notice he is not there. The place seems virtually empty, with the exception of a few souls that probably have little ability to move, even if they wished to.

Strange. I expected this place to be just as it had the last few times here, but something is off. Something is very different indeed.

Chapter 15

* * *

"Hey babe, I'm going to be a while. Don't wait for me to eat. There's only a handful of people here, but Von and Marcus are nowhere to be found. I'm going to hang out awhile and see if they show up," I say as I call Hailey.

I can tell she's slightly concerned, but I do my best to assure here I am perfectly fine. There's nothing to worry about, but it is strange that they are not here. I've only been here a handful of times, but it's not the type of place that sits virtually empty for any period of time. You may have a few that wander off in search of who knows what, and then you have those that come into camp, disgusted with themselves for feeling all alone, and this place gives them a pickup they desperately seek.

That is something I will say about this strange confusing place. It gives of itself to everyone that enters onto its grounds. The weak feel a moment of relief, and the frustrated feel a sense of much needed calmness. For someone like me who came here with preconceived notions of wanting to vomit the entire time I would be here, it's taught me that those things I do not fully understand, are not necessarily bad. I just needed to see better, and through a different lens than I have been looking through.

Two weeks. That short time has changed a lot of my understanding of the homeless community. I still feel they should be able to give more of themselves and that they could fight through this stalled position of helplessness, but I'm learning it's not as easy as wanting to. Sometimes, there are more extenuating circumstances at play, even if I don't recognize them.

"Excuse me, sir, but are you Michael?" a voice calls from just a few feet from where I am standing.

"Me, yea, I'm Michael. Do I know you?" I respond back.

Standing there is a tall, lanky young man, who can't be more than twenty-five, if that. His front teeth are worn down so that they no longer touch together in his mouth, and his hair is cut close to his head, like a military style buzz cut from years ago. He has varied style tattoos along the sides of his neck, and up and down both arms, but none of them appear as if they were done by professionals. He's looking around anxiously as he stands before me, as if he's nervous that someone is looking for him.

"Me, sir? No, you don't know me. You know Von?" and he pauses, again looking around, which is starting to freak me out. I'm watching his hands in case he's going to reach for a weapon or something.

"Yea, I know Von. Is everything okay? What's going on?" I ask sternly.

This man, almost a kid really, is strung out on something. I've seen a lot of people sucked in by the lure of drugs and the rush it gives off, who get hooked hardcore, and it ruins lives. Families get ripped apart, and relationships fade quicker than they began. It's sad to see, but these people had a choice, and they chose wrong for whatever reasons.

I'm not a fool. I know quitting isn't as easy as just wanting to. I know that having an addictive personality can drain nearly all the hope out of someone and make it nearly impossible in their minds to even attempt to quit. In fact, it reminds me of sugar. Basic, and simple enough when you look at it, but try to stop using it in your everyday eating habits. Oh, you may not add it to your food directly, but look on the back at the ingredient list of the foods you eat, and go down to where it says, "added sugars," and there you will be shocked. Some companies hide it even better in the form of fancy words. But it's there in most of what we consume that isn't pulled directly from the earth, or that wanders on the earth.

I stopped ingesting it at one point to get in a little better shape before I went on a trip to Florida a few years back. I wanted to look lean without my shirt on, and so I began working out some and changed my eating habits overnight. It was fine the first day, but then each day that came after? Brutal. My body craved sugar constantly, and it was going through a terrible withdrawal from depriving myself of it.

I would never had thought that sugar acts just as a drug does. I had headaches for days with it out of my blood, and it almost made me give in.

So, I know it's not easy to just stop something because you want to or need to, especially when it's hard to see a better future in front of you. When you work a job in a large company, you may be able to see clearly ahead to a management spot, or a position as a vice president of a department, or something along those lines. You have something in front of you that is real and obtainable with the right amount of well-placed effort.

But let's say you never attended school after the twelfth grade, and you've only worked jobs that were positions fillable by anyone with two decent hands and a beating heart. What are you looking forward to from there?

Now imagine that, and then imagine you are giving a taste of a drug that makes your body feel a sensation it never has before. You feel alive with an odd sense of power, and any pain that your mind made you believe you had, is now far gone in the past. You enjoy the satisfying feeling, but as soon as the drug wears off, your body begins to beg for more. It cries out loudly and grips you with fear and desire that it needs you to just give it one more, just one more and it will all be fine. Just another small taste.

Over time, you forget how many hits you had, or white lines you've snorted, or multi-colored pills you've popped into your mouth in any given night. You want to forget, because knowing the truth will serve you no good, you tell yourself. As long as you don't think about the amount of times you have given in, it doesn't change anything for you. It's just one more, after all.

Except that it does. Your body is built to withstand a lot and to adapt to a beating for sure, but you must take care of it as well for most of the time. It relies on you to keep it strong, balanced, and free of toxins as best you are able. When you fail at that, your body begins to rebel against itself, and you come to a battle that may or may not destroy what you were asked to protect.

That's how I see this kid, this young guy in front of me. He's losing a battle he may not even be aware he is fighting. I don't understand it, but he's here and needs to tell me something it would seem.

"Von, he told me, that if Michael comes here, you are Michael, right? The Michael?" he asks again.

"Yea, man, I told you I'm Michael. What did Von say?" I snap back.

"Oh, yea, sorry. Just being cautious, you know. Never can tell. I'm always being careful, you know? Anyway, Michael, listen. Von, he said he would be back by Saturday. He had somewhere to go and would touch base with you when he saw you Saturday. Wait, yea, I think he said Saturday," he says.

This guy is all over the place wacked out of his mind, but I get the gist of what he is trying to say. Von isn't here, and for some reason he's leaving his home and heading who knows where, but that doesn't explain the lack of other people here. Where are they? There is no way they all went with Von, wherever he went, right? It would be noticeable big time. Imagine an entire entourage of filthy homeless people walking around the city like a Mummers parade. The police would be all over that trying to herd them back to the safety of hidden grounds away from the eye of the general public. Not for their sake, but more for the city's image I imagine.

"Saturday? Hey, did he say anything about a funeral for a man named Terrance? Did he mention anything about that?" I ask curiously.

"Oh, um, Terrance. He's being cremated. Von said so. When, I don't really know. Hey, you have a cigarette by chance? I can't seem to find mine, but I promise I'll get you one back when I do," he asks.

I don't even know this dude's name. Not to mention, I don't smoke. I never have. Weed, sure a few times, but I've never smoked a cigarette in my life.

"Nah, man. Sorry I don't smoke. What's your name, anyway?" I respond.

I feel bad. He's shaking nervously, and I imagine a cigarette would calm his nerves some, but I just don't have any. If I did, I would give him one for sure. Just to stop him from tweaking all over the place like a fool. He's making me want to smoke.

"I'm Aaron, but people call me Jitters."

Jitters, that figures. If anyone earned a nickname bequeathed to them, it's this guy right here. He bounces around like he has the jitters for sure. Jitters. I want to laugh, but I won't. Not now anyway. Later I may just to get it out of the way.

"Well, Jitters, listen man. Thanks. I really appreciate it. Are you staying here awhile?"

"Oh yea, for sure. Von is going to help me get on track. He tried before, but you see, I had a small setback come up that was totally out of my control, but Von? He told me if I ever needed to come back, he would be here to welcome me this time for certain. So, here I am," he laughs, and the fact he doesn't have a full set of teeth at all suddenly isn't funny.

I can see this guy needs major help, but I can also see he wants something more for himself. He at least attempted to leave this place behind, and when he stumbled, or crashed, whatever the case may be, he knew he needed to come back to where he first asked for help. I admire that, truthfully. Not everyone can come back to a place like this and admit they failed.

"Why didn't you go with the others, wherever they went? Why did you stay back behind?" I ask.

"Well, someone needed to stay to keep an eye on the others here that couldn't go. I know I may not look like the best choice, but I wanted to prove to Von that I can be trusted. I owe him, man. I own Von a lot," he says back.

It actually makes some sense, what he is telling me. Jitters seems like outside of drugs, he would be a cool guy to hang out with. He seems like he just lost his way and desperately wants a push in the right direction again. He understands that he is probably going to fail, again and again, but he also understands that failing only matters when you refuse to try again. He's trying again.

"You mind if I stick around awhile and hang? I just got here and honestly, I already told my girlfriend to eat without me. I don't really have much else to do," I say.

"Yea! For sure, man. Stick around. I could use the company. Hey. I have some water over here that Von left. You want one?"

Without me having a chance to answer, Jitters walks off briskly in the direction of one of the newer tents we put up the last time I was here. He disappears for a second, and emerges with two bottles of water, one in each hand.

"Here, Michael. Here, have a water. They are still a little cold. Hey, you want to fish some? I have a few poles I brought with me. You like to fish?" Jitters asks.

This guy is trying his hardest to be friendly, and that's cool to see. He's struggling and still all over the place, but he's still desperately trying to put on his best face, and pretend as if he's just a normal guy, home from work, ready to fish a little, in order to forget the problems of the day. Maybe, in a sense, he is.

"You know what? Sure, Jitters. I haven't fished this river in a little while. The last time I fished here, I was with my brother. It's been a while," I say.

"You have a brother? That's cool. Does he live here? What does he do? Is he cool, man?" Jitters asks.

We talk. We fish. We talk some more. For the next few

hours, Jitters and I fish the narrow end of the Schuylkill River, as we talk about our past, and all that we have seen. He realizes that I have a similar story in many ways to his. He listens and then he has a mountain of questions for me, and he peppers them off one right after the other. But I don't mind. He's from a city too, but the city seems to be far different from here. He tells me his favorite spots to eat when he's home, and I tell him mine.

If I had met Jitters a few years back, and he hadn't ever picked up the habit he has, he would be the type of guy I would fish with more often. He knows how to cast, and he knows how to find the bait we use to catch the bass and catfish the river provides. The river is full of crawfish that the bass and catfish live off of. He walks out where it is shallowest, rolls a rock over, grabs the crayfish behind the head, and places a hook through its body. It's fishing 101 here on the river.

We catch some sunnies, or sunfish as they are more commonly known as, and toss them back. Even the carp Jitter catches is thrown back in the river. We are not here for food, but for the sport. Two guys from different neighborhoods and cities, just casting and talking about bullshit.

I miss my brother right now. He would love this. We haven't been next to each other in some time, and it's getting to be time. I need to plan that trip west and put the excuses away. I'm always going to have excuses, but I am not always going to have a chance to fish alongside of my brother. Time makes sure of that.

"Hey Michael, what makes you come here and help? Von only told me that you volunteer here and will be for a few more months. Is this some missionary work of some sort? You don't seem like the religious type," Jitters asks.

Von seems to be one of those guys that tells your story just enough, to let you fill in the blanks. I respect that. He doesn't know if I am okay with everyone knowing why I am here, so he allowed me to tell that side on my terms. I don't mind, really. This guy, Jitters, he gets it. He will understand that sometimes in life, shit just happens. Sometimes we must fight our way through the day, and most of the time, no one cares. It's what boys do. But every now and again you get caught and have to pay the price. No biggie. I'm paying my debt to society for cracking some guy for bumping into me too hard. It's not a big story and made no headlines.

Before I know it, the sun has gone down, and I'm sitting there still casting away. It's growing dark, and I have lost all track of time. My phone is next to me, but I haven't paid attention to it at all. I've been too wrapped up in letting go for a while and must have realized the distraction that my phone going off causes.

"Man, what time is it?" I eventually ask.

I forget that Jitters is homeless, probably has no phone, nor a need to know the time of day.

"Don't know, homey. Check your phone," he responds.

Homey. My friends and I call each other homey now and again. Not as much as we once did, but yea, it's a slang term we have used for years. It's funny that he just called me that.

It's almost nine at night, and Hailey has texted me a dozen times, worried out of her mind. I don't blame her, as I would be worried too if she was in a strange place and not responding to my messages.

I decide it's best to call her instead of texting her that I am all right. She probably needs to hear that I am and not just read it.

"Babe, my God, I am so sorry. I completely lost track of the time," I start before she cuts me off.

"What the hell are you doing? You said you were going to look for Von, and that was hours ago. Then you don't reply to any of my texts, and I have no idea if you are alive or dead. Don't do that to me again, you hear me?" she screams.

"I won't. Trust me. I'm sorry, babe. But honestly, I'm good. You won't believe my night," I say.

"Well, when are you coming home? It's late. I don't have my car to come and get you, remember? It's being inspected. And your car is stick, and you know I can't drive stick. I have no idea how to get you home," Hailey says.

The conversation is loud enough that Jitters hears it and offers a plan of his own,

"Dude stay here tonight. No one will mind. There are tons of places to sleep, and the tent next to me hasn't had anyone in it yet. You can stay there. Honestly, I could use the company," he says.

"Who is that? Where are you, Michael? I thought you were at the Mudflaps."

"I am. I'm here. That's just Jitters, I mean Aaron," I say, trying to not panic her anymore with some crazy nickname that still fits him so well.

For a second I am actually thinking about it. I mean, I haven't been camping in a while, and no one is really around. I could crash here, take the bus tomorrow morning back to the center of the city, shower, change, and get to work just a little late. I would still get all of my work done, and if I remember right, I am ahead of my workload anyway.

Hailey thinks I am insane for wanting to even consider this idea, but she's also aware that I am kind of stuck. I could call my friends, but they are probably out getting hammered. I could call for an Uber, but really, I'm learning so much from this place, and staying here might allow me to dig deeper into my curiosity.

My phone is about to die and there is no place to charge it. So basically, I need to make a decision fast and let Hailey know.

"Babe, if it's alright with you, I am going to crash here tonight and head back first thing in the morning. I can catch an early bus, okay?"

And that is that. My phone has died, so I hope she got that last part, because I never heard her answer, if she even responded back with one.

Chapter 16

* * *

Mornings come fast and hard when you aren't in the comfort of a familiar place. The air feels a little less familiar, and the sounds are different from the noises I hear at my own home. I don't have the usual noise of my phone to wake me and the smell? It's not home by any means.

Jitters promised me that he would get me up, and on top of that, I have an internal alarm that seems to get me up the moment before my phone wakes me. So, I wasn't overly worried about rising to the sun, or just prior to the sun's rise.

"Hey, you up, man?" Jitters asks.

I'm up, but I just was laying there hoping it was not morning just yet. I had a horrible night's sleep, with the rough ground below me, no central air to cool me off as I slept under that makeshift tent, and the noises all night… hard to explain really. There were screams, and loud bangs from who knows where, and on top of that, the entire night it seemed as if people were coming in, either drunk from a full night of drinking, or perhaps just looking for a place to lay their heads for a night. Others could have been heading out to God-knows-where.

It was surreal, laying here all night under the blanket of the dark sky, as the city lights shine just a few miles away, as if you could almost touch them. The constant sounds of the nearby roadways and the noise from neighboring places could be heard from everywhere in the camp, serving as a reminder that there is an entire world far different from here, just steps away. I seriously took for granted how quiet my condo is, despite the loud radio or two in the night driving by.

Jitters has a plastic bag a third of the way full of partially smoked cigarettes in his one hand, and a bottle of water in the other. He's just as jumpy in the morning as he was the night before, and I wonder if he's even had a moment of sleep. It's hard to tell as he looks no different.

I remember we were talking about my brother and his family for a part of the night, but then I told him I had to crash or I was going to be late for work, and I can't afford to do that right now.

"Yea, I'm up. What are you doing with a baggie of used cigarettes, Jitters?" I ask him curiously.

"Ah man, people throw away so much stuff, dude. Some of these are hardly used up at all. I can get several drags out of each, man. They just throw this on the ground, and I pick them up," he responds with a smile of accomplishment.

"Wait, you pick up used cigarette butts that others discarded because they were finished with them?" I ask.

"Yea, I mean why not? Smokes are so expensive now, and I ain't got a job or nothing like that, so you do what you need to do in order to survive my brother," Jitter says, lighting one of the half-smoked butts up.

I'm sitting there, still wiping the crust from the corners of my eyes, and wondering where I can get some decent coffee, and this guy is walking around with trash that others didn't want anymore. Not just trash, but disgusting trash. It's bad enough that they are cigarettes, but they were in the mouths of complete strangers that who knows what they may be carrying, or when they discarded them. Does he not even care?

Apparently, he does not. He's proud of his haul. He told me he was up at four in the morning, and said he walked along the outside of the grounds to the park, careful not to get himself noticed by anyone, and then picked up any he could find lying around on the ground. To him, he's done good this morning, and is on his way to a better day.

I think about that while I stretch and pull myself out of the small tent that was my bed last night. I managed to climb out, which I do each morning I leave my own bed, while Jitters managed to achieve a goal for his own day far before I even opened an eye, although it's not a super healthy one.

"I won. I own the day," he says.

"What on earth are you talking about, Jitters?"

He smiles.

"Von taught me that. He told me anytime I do something useful for myself, or for others, and I find a small bit of happiness in it, I own that day. So, I own the day already," he says as he smiles proudly.

I mean, he's not entirely wrong. If he had woken up, and had a craving for a smoke and had none, the morning would own him because he would be craving one bad, but instead, when he is craving a long drag from a cigarette, he just places one of his hands in the bag he has with him, pulls a choice one out, and smokes it until there is nothing left of it to inhale.

I own nothing this morning, yet. That actually bothers me in a peculiar way, or maybe it's because my muscles are moaning and screaming at me from the awkward positions I managed to place them in all night. They are not going to be good to me today. That I can tell already.

Jitters is in a peculiar place in life. As I talked with him last evening through the odd sounds around us, I felt his struggles and his losses. I felt how much he experiences doubt in his thoughts, and how the days can mostly feel like a complete waste of time. Then, here and now, I watch him smile proudly over something no one I know would ever find themselves doing. Or so I thought.

Was this on the same level as my mother walking along the steel tracks collecting aluminum cans as we avoided oncoming trains? My smile was probably just as proud and as bright that day as Jitters' is now, and I bet if people knew that story, they may look at me in a different light. Not many know that part of my life, because I was proud then, but I am not proud of it now.

"Man, I have to get going. I have a long day ahead, and if I don't get started, I'm going to fall way behind. Thanks Jitters. If you see Von, tell him I stopped by, and that I will see him Saturday I suppose, unless he needs anything before. He knows how to find me."

With that, I put my shoes on and lace them up, push my hair back so it's not sticking up all over the place, and I head towards the trail leading out of the park.

"Hey, Michael? Appreciate you hanging last night, man. I needed that brother more than you realize. Thank you," he tells me.

I smile as I turn away, because I know I did some good. As odd as my night was, I feel as if I accomplished something after all. I helped someone by simply hanging out with them and shooting the shit. That took less from me than jumping in the middle of those kids did. And it hurt a lot less too.

I'm almost to the top of the road, and I hear from a distance, Jitters singing something to himself, but he stops and screams my way,

"Michael. Own the day! Own the day brother."

He's a wild kid but has a huge heart. And when I stop to think about it, he probably helped me just as much as I did him last night.

I'm heading to wash myself of the night before, get

dressed in a nice button-down shirt with a tie, and long, creased pants with a pair of clean socks, boxers, and shiny shoes, and Jitters is going to stay in the 'Flaps, with no access to an easy shower or running water, and no clean clothes washed after a single use and laid out neatly in a folded pile. He won't have a full, healthy breakfast where he can simply order whatever it is he wishes, and he won't have people telling him good morning as he walks into an elevator downtown. He won't have any of those simple comforts that I have day in, and day out.

And I hate that for him.

As I first arrive home after a trip along the roads in a bus and on foot, I see that Hailey is up with breakfast laid out, and fresh coffee in a pot. She has music playing in the background, and she's dressed herself, ready to head out the door to start her morning.

"I figured you would come home first to clean up, so I made you this. I need to head out though," she says.

I can see she is certainly frustrated, and I am a little confused. She wanted me to learn something, anything from this place, and to appreciate people on a different level than I have my entire adult life, and here I am doing my part. But she's not happy about something, and I cannot figure it out.

"What's wrong, babe? Are you mad at me?" I ask her.

She puts on her shoes and throws her head back in my direction.

"I was worried about you. No call, no text. Nothing. I

almost called the police, but realized I had no idea of what I would say. It's not as if I could tell them my boyfriend preferred to crash in a homeless community in a tent over staying here with me, and oh, by the way, he's not on drugs or anything like that. He was just bored," she responds.

I'm partially confused, but I also see her point a little bit.

"Listen. I get it. My phone honestly died, and I had nowhere to charge it. They don't have electricity there, and I had no way to reach anyone. My last call was to you, and then my phone died. Period. I knew you were worried, and I appreciate that. I don't know, but it just felt like I needed to stay there last night. I can't really explain it because I don't fully understand it myself."

"Fine. But next time you decide to sleep out in a park with no electricity? Charge your phone before you go, okay?" she says to me.

She's a good-hearted person, but I know this community service I am doing is not easy on her either. I am trying to just get through the eight weeks I must do, and that's it. I am done after that, because as much as I am learning and helping others, I have a life of my own to get back to and invest in.

People like Von and Jitters and the others I am learning about are going to come and go and in their place, there will always be others who need attention, until they move on somehow and then more will continue the pattern. It's a cycle that will never cease, and so I can only do so much and then my good deeds will be lost in time and meaningless.

Like Terrance. He had a gift with his voice, but because he has no one to carry on his legacy, and no one to record his soulful tone, what does it matter that he gave of himself? It doesn't. He died and so did his gift. He cannot pass that on to anyone and no one will be gifted that in a will. All he had, died with him in the hospital and that is that.

I feel bad, but I know in a few short weeks no one is going to be talking about him. His family probably has no idea where he had been for the past however many years he spent on the streets, and so how would they know where to find him in death?

People like Marcus can make a difference because they leave something. He leaves his advice, which is passed around from one homeless person to another. They listen to his words, almost as if they are gospel. He's a tough dude, but he has a way with his words. Maybe his parents were teachers and they passed that on down to him. He had to have learned it from somewhere.

Anyway, I need to quickly shower and get ready. It's getting late and I don't have a lot of time to sit and drink coffee and eat. But it was nice she did this for me, even though she was pissed off. But if she returns from work before I do, and this is all out just as she left it? Yea, she's not going to think I appreciated all she did.

So, I shower in record time, and dress myself in whatever clothes are clean enough and to the front of the closet. As I run down to put on my shoes, I throw an over-easy egg in my mouth, drink the pulp free orange juice she poured for me, and grab the coffee to go. The dishes are just going to have to wait, but at least I'll get them into the sink. Effort is important in my mind, even if I don't finish the cleaning until long after I should.

As I am out the door and rounding the corner, I remember that I haven't charged my phone. That's going to suck, but I can charge it at the office. I'll be too busy to mess around with it anyway, and Hailey already is aware that it was dead, so I am sure she knows it won't be charged right away.

Maybe not having a phone for a little is a good thing. I know I have become so reliant on it that I forget to "smell the roses," as my mother would say. My mother. She's lost a generation of years and will never gain those back. Such a waste, and honestly, I feel bad for her for the first time in forever.

But the bus is here, and I have to focus on the now.

Then, I think, I need to talk with my brother today. Maybe it's time to finish that conversation we started.

Chapter 17

* * *

"Erik? Hey man, it's Michael. I want to ask you something," I say to my brother.

It's been many years of hiding my deep-seated emotions and my torrid hatred with my past. I've come to realize that running from the things that have hurt me the most, the things that have damaged my soul and my belief that everyone can do some good in the world, is never going to allow me to get far from it.

I have also come to the realization that life is not meant to be easy, no matter how much I will it to be, and forgiveness is even harder than anything else I've ever had to do. I want to be able to grant forgiveness and forget all the damage that others have inflicted on my journey, but I simply cannot yet. Why? Well, I still need to figure that part out.

For some reason, Erik has a heart that allowed him to love, when he should have been only hurting. A heart that allowed him to forgive when it should have made him filled with regret and hatred. We come from the same blood, the very same line of people, yet we stand in completely different spots, no matter where we are in the world.

He loves my mother unconditionally, and for the life of me, I cannot figure out why. I want to have love for her. I want to walk into the jail she calls home, and I want to hug her as tightly as I can, and tell her I miss her and forgive her for everything. Then I want to push those metal bars aside, and tell everyone in my way that no, they will not be keeping my mother there for any more of her days. That no set of steel or iron bars, and no count of guards on hand will prevent me from breaking her out and bringing her back home so that we can rebuild what was torn down.

Yet, I cannot even stomach the notion that it's even a possibility. To my understanding, she may never get out and she may end up dying behind those thick gray concrete walls. They may end up burying her in a simple common lot, where other aged prisoners rest next to her, as their sentence is completed by only death. And would that bother me? To be fair, I don't know. I don't really know. But I believe I am going to need to explore that idea at some point before I no longer have the ability to.

"Michael, are you okay? What's going on?" he asks.

My brother knows me probably better than I know him. Over the years that we have talked, he has asked questions about my life and my hopes and dreams. He's tried to figure out my path, and wondered about what makes me who I am. He's offered to listen whenever I needed to vent, or whenever I was in trouble and needed someone's advice. He knows when I am feeling conflicted about something important, and me? I barely know his birthday. In fact, I am sure he had one recently, and again, it passed by like a quick summer sun shower, and I paid it no attention.

I forget to check on him, and here he is, once again, ready to step up and do whatever he can to help me. I love him. I just wish I knew how to tell him better.

"I'm, yea, I'm alright. This community service I am doing? It's not at all what I expected," I respond.

"Tell me about that. What it's like for you, being around others who are different from you in so many ways? Is it showing you a different side to others?" Erik asks.

"Man, on one hand, these people are as different from you and I are as a pear is to the color seven. I mean, there is no comparison to how they live their life and I live mine. But then, when I look just a little deeper, and I ask a little more about who they truly are or who they once were, I learn that maybe they aren't entirely as different from who I was, or even who I am. It's hard to explain, really," I say.

He laughs. Not a laugh as if he is trying to tell me I've lost my mind, but a laugh as if to tell me that he gets it. That a lesson I am possibly learning from all of this is one he learned long ago about himself.

"I get it. Michael, they are people like you and me. I see it all the time. A past that no one asked for can change a person's direction without their say, and it can be hell gaining the traction to get back on course. It's not as simple as, well, thinking everyone should act and push through things just as you or I have done. It's not that simple at all," Erik tells me.

He's right, but still, I just get so frustrated because if I could give them a direction to start out on, would they all take it? No. They would not all take it. Some would just shake their heads to appease me, and then go right back to whatever simple task they were doing right before I blessed them with that knowledge and a real hope they should all desire. It would go in one ear and directly out the other without stopping for a moment to give them pause.

Why? Why is it so damn hard for them to understand that there is a way out of this cruel lifestyle, and there is a better future than the one they are currently about to create? That all they need to do is find someone who has pushed past a difficulty, and learned to use it as an advantage instead of a crutch, and follow in their footsteps.

"There's this guy Von, and man, you would really appreciate Von. He's so well-spoken, and doesn't seem to let anything alter his happiness, including his surroundings. It's as if he is right where he was meant to be, and to be anywhere else would be a sad way to live for him. This guy? He has the brains and the ability to easily turn this around for himself, yet..." I stop for a moment.

What if there is more to everything I see? What if Von has a purpose here and if he decided to improve his position in the world, it would impact the positions of so many others near him? Could he be that selfless?

"Brother listen to me. You need to stop worrying so much about where people are heading on their journey. Michael, it's their journey, not yours," Erik says back.

In all my life, I have always looked at my direction, my journey in this world as a source of pride. I came from hell, no denying that, and found a place for myself where I can thrive and be mostly happy. But then I look at others and wonder why they are not where I am, and truthfully, I have never really noticed that I do that.

"Yea. I know. I know. Maybe when this thing I am doing is done and over with, you and I can meet up. I can come out there this time, or if you have anything back here you want to do, you can come back. I've got a few months of Saturdays left in this, and then it's over with." I say.

My brother would fly out here if that was really what I wanted him to do, but I don't know if that is what I am asking. Maybe I just need to get out of Philly for a week and clear my head some. It might do me some good and I can bring Hailey with me. It would be like a nice getaway that we both could really use.

"Sure. We will figure it out. Let me check my case-load and see when I am going to be free for a few days. It would be good catching up. Is there anything else you wanted to ask me?" he asks.

There is. I just am unsure of how to ask. So instead of making it my usual beat-around-the-bush type of thing, I decide to just let the words form as they need to without letting them dance around.

"Yea. Mom. I've been doing a lot of thinking about her lately, and I don't get why. I'd put those feelings of anger and hatred behind me I thought, and now they are creeping back, but not so much hatred for how she left us. It's more hatred for how she is living now. Does that even make any sense to you?" I ask.

Erik sighs on the other end of the line. It takes a moment to put the words together in his mind before laying them out for me. He seems to be a bit caught off guard by this, and for an attorney who can turn off his emotions for the grisliest of moments, he can be truly emotional with me.

"It makes more sense to me than it does for you, Michael. We really need to figure that one out but listen. I still have all those letters mom wrote you over the years. Maybe I can put them together and send those out to you if you want?" Erik asks.

As much as I am trying to understand these emotions and the sudden concern for the wellbeing of my mother, I am not ready for that dump of emotions just yet. I honestly don't know if I will ever be ready for those letters. Twenty years of I'm sorrys and I wish things were different and how are you doing being raised by people I never picked for you? I can't even imagine the amount of trauma reading all those letters at one time would do to me.

"One thing at a time brother. I am not there yet. Listen, get back to whatever it is you are doing. It was great catching up and let's figure out our schedules and get something on the calendar. For real this time," I manage to say back.

Most times I talk with Erik, it's me wanting to hurry the conversation up, but this time I found myself wanting to explore more of our past, and to understand how he has this insane ability to just forgive his. I cannot even imagine seeing myself as he is, forgiving and forgetting so much that others have done to hurt me. I feel a massive sense of loss for all those changes in my life due to a bad decision. Perhaps it was more than a bad decision. Maybe it was a trail of them that lead to the inevitable because there was nowhere left to go for them.

I wonder what would have happened if the car didn't start that day. Would my father have been able to wrestle the keys from her hands, and then what? With his Irish temper, would he have trounced on her until she stopped breathing, just as he had, and ended up in his own jail?

I know I give my father credit for things he probably never deserved credit for, but it's my hatred of what my mother did that makes me offer that to him. He probably deserves at least some of the blame for that day. Had he been sober, like he should have been with two young boys at home watching him, then he would have had the reactive capability to move left, or to move right and to avoid her rage.

I say this all the time. A simple move in a different direction can alter the course of an entire life. That was one of those times where had he moved just a little, he would have continued on with his life, and we would have still been one family. Not happy, but you know what? Families aren't always happy. Just like being raised by some kooky Sunday church-going people didn't make me happy. It made me rebel.

I hope to talk some more to Von Saturday. For some reason, when he talks, I seem to gain a different perspective. One that I was unable to gain on my own.

Plus, I really want to learn more about Terrance and what happened to his ashes, his family, and his belongings. I have so many unanswered questions, and hopefully he will provide me those answers. I know he loves to talk, but will he be open to talking about something so tragic? I really don't know.

The week goes on and Saturday cannot get here fast enough for me. What once was a miserable weekend morning to have in front of me has become an almost necessity for me now. I find myself trying to control my emotions and practically excitement about heading to the 'Flaps early in the morning.

I have not heard from Marcus all week, which in and of itself isn't strange, but what is strange is that when my phone lets me know that a message has arrived, I almost hope it is Marcus giving me an update on anything.

Saturday comes and I am out the door. The summer is that time of year when it can be blazing hot still first thing in the morning, or starting to cool off for a few hours, especially early on. I love this time of year when the morning temperatures are not always in the 80's, and instead wake you with a calming cool breeze.

When I arrive at the office, Marcus is already in the car with the engine turned on. I am a few minutes early, so I assume he wasn't waiting around long for me.

"Hey, good morning, Marcus," I say.

He nods, which I guess is the same as saying good morning back for a man of few words.

Not much has changed since the last ride we had together. The talking on the way is nonexistent, and that is okay with me this time. It's almost a mutual respect we have going into this ride, and I appreciate that for a change. He isn't being rude or harsh. He's just being Marcus, and me? I am learning that sometimes words aren't necessary to convey a feeling or thought. I don't always have to see or hear to understand.

This is week three for me, and I have five left to go after this one is finished with. But week three seems almost the most important week yet, because I am more aware of what my duties are without the need for someone to direct me, and because this will be the first time we are there after the passing of Terrance.

Will anyone bring him up, or will that be taboo from here on out?

Whatever happens, I am going to just do what I can today to help, observe, and most importantly, learn from this experience.

Chapter 18

***

Thinking back on past times can be both a curse and a blessing. At times, I look back on a memory like opening a pack of Topps baseball cards at the store a block away from my home, and I am reminded of innocence. A time when nothing mattered but that moment, and when the excitement of finding a particular card caused a wonderful happiness throughout my body.

But I also remember times when my mother worked late into the early morning hours, and my dad was passed out in the living room, and my brother and I were starving. I would go into our kitchen and just start opening cans and heating the contents in a pot on the stove, rather than try and wake my father. I hated to wake him because I never knew which one I was getting. The father who understood and was thankfully hungry as well, or the one who was pissed off at the world and for me waking him to remind him that this world was his reality.

Those memories, while powerful lessons that I could

never see at the time, still sucked the happiness I had on many a days. So, although I try to block them out from my memory, on occasion I have used them as a tool to remind myself I can overcome anything life wishes to throw at me. If I can make peas and potatoes mixed with green relish into a meal we appreciated, I can do just about anything.

I'm looking around today at all the people carrying on with their lives, and I can't help but wonder how many of them knew Terrance and how many of them have a fear as a result of what happened a few weeks back. I know being on the streets isn't easy for anyone, but after witnessing what I did, I would even be leery of traveling out late at night alone if I were in their shoes.

The tasks are pretty much the same. People are cleaning up around their tents, and people are helping the volunteers who are delivering food that morning by distributing it to those that cannot or will not go over. At first, you would think to yourself,

"How dare they expect someone to wait on them and not only bring them food to eat but serve them as well".

But then if you think harder and look deeper, you understand that not everything is as it appears. Some of them are either physically or mentally sick, or a combination of both, and have enough trouble waking up, let alone walking over to where others are waiting in line. There is also the strong possibility that there are those with some pride left in their spirits, who have lost their way more recently and are ashamed to show their face here, or anywhere.

Today is also the first time that I see children here. I had thought of this place as a hideaway for adults who wanted to sponge off of others, but seeing children here is breaking my heart. What child deserves to be in a place like this? No child should ever start out life homeless. None. So why are they here and where the hell are their parents and what are they doing about this?

"Michael, over here," Marcus calls me.

He noticed that I spotted the kids and he can clearly see I am raging and want answers.

"Not only adults need us here. Homelessness doesn't discriminate. It could care less if you are black, white, or brown. It does not care if you were once rich, poor, or middle class. It does not bother to check your information to see if you are of legal age or not. It does not have a need or a care for those sort of things," he says.

"So where are their parents?" I ask in a manner that shows I am concerned but pissed off and ready to judge.

"Either here, or out looking for work, or maybe dead. Some of these youngins have guardians who swore to take care of them, and somehow that changed along the course of time. Some of the kids couldn't handle their home life and decided enough was enough. There isn't one answer here that fits them all, Michael".

That is the most I have ever heard this man speak. In the weeks leading up to today, he maybe managed half of those words combined, but clearly, he's a much smarter man than he looks. He is reading me well enough to tell that I need to be calmed down. I am trying to stay calm, but this sucks something awful.

"See that boy over there, running a small stick through the ground, making a game out of barely anything? His father told him he would be back once he found some work. That was four days ago," Marcus says.

I try to read his expression to see if he gives a hint of sadness, anger, or indifference, but he doesn't change his countenance much at all, so I am left to wonder about that myself, unless he decides to share that with me.

I begin to focus on the little boy playing in the dirt, who cannot be more than seven or eight at the most. He must be scared and confused out of his mind. And what about his dad? You are telling me that after four days you cannot even return to take care of your kid? Who does that? In what world is this a normal thing?

My Irish blood is boiling over, but I need to focus on what it is I am here to do. To help, and not to judge. And certainly not to beat the shit out of a man who leaves his young child here with strangers and decides not to return until he is good and ready, if ever.

Just before I try and decide what to do first, I feel Marcus' large hand reach over and grab my shoulder. He squeezes just enough to let me know he understands. He understands my anger, and my sadness about this. He seems to know that there are deep wounds tied up within my soul that are unleashing a flood of memories I wish I could keep tied away but can't. He knows.

"It's all right, Michael. Go ahead over and see if you can make that boy's time here a little easier," Marcus instructs.

What the hell do I say that is going to first not scare this kid into a crying fit, and then help him feel at ease about his parents not being here for him when he most needs them? Do I ask where his mom is or is that off limits? Can I ask him about his father and where he went to search for work? Maybe I could try to locate him and reunite them, or perhaps a reuniting is the wrong thing for this kid. Maybe he needs a better family to guide him away from living a life like this. He is far too young to understand that this type of place even exists.

I wander over in his direction casually, and he doesn't look up at me at all. Either he is so focused on what it is he is playing in the dirt and rocks, or he doesn't want to draw attention to himself and hopes that I will simply back off and let him be. I can't, though. What would that say about me?

I have done some bad things in my life and placed myself in situations I knew had a better chance for bad to happen than good, and for that, karma has caught me and repaid me for almost every single time. I am not about to walk away from this one empty handed when there is a real chance I can help someone other than me and know I made a real difference. I've learned at least that much. Not all of these people are here because they want to be here. Some are here because in their minds they have nowhere left to go, and this is a last resort that offers a little bit of protection from the harsh reality of the outside world. And possibly even a little hope.

Sad to think of it as that, but it's the truth.

"Hey buddy, what's that you are making?" I begin.

He starts to place his stick down, and then slips back into one of the many tents lined up in almost a perfect circle. I follow, but slowly so as not to alarm him.

I can imagine at his age, that if a strange older man approached me and I was here all alone without the protection of my parents, I would scream my head off "stranger danger," and that is something I am not after here today, or any day. I have enough trauma going on in my head that I do not need to add to that.

I look over to where Marcus was last standing, and he is speaking with others but has one eye on the situation I am in. I want to make this guy proud for some reason. Like I really want Marcus to understand I am not a terrible human, and that despite my preconceptions about the people staying here, and the ones out on the streets that are literally covered in trash, my mind is shifting somewhat. I am learning that just because I see something in a way that fits my ego, doesn't mean I am seeing it correctly.

"Hey, bud, I'm not here to harm you. I'm just chatting with you some. Hey, want some gum?" I ask.

Great, now I am feeling as if I am the old man in the white van that has "Free Candy," painted on the sides in red spray paint. I am not that guy, but I just offered a young boy gum, which is basically the same as offering him a piece of candy.

He shakes his head no, while hanging it low to the ground. I don't know if it's because he is afraid to take it, or just doesn't want it.

"Okay, not a problem. Listen, I am going to walk over there where the picnic table is. You see that over there?" I ask.

He looks up just a small amount, and sees the table to where I am pointing. He nods ever so slightly that he sees it, and I feel as if I have made the tiniest of breakthroughs.

"Good. Listen, I know things are tough for you right now, but I am here to help you. I am here to help all of the people here, and if I can do that for you today, you will make my day. So listen. Anything you need, you just come on over and ask me. My name is Michael. Listen buddy, I am not here to hurt you. See that large man over there talking to those people? He would make sure no one here harmed you. Trust me. You are safe here with us."

But is he really safe here? Marcus doesn't live here. I certainly do not. We leave at the end of the shift, and this boy cannot leave. He has no clock to punch out when he's had enough here. He cannot simply walk to the bus stop and catch a ride home to where his family is waiting for him with open arms. No. He has to stay right here for as long as time holds him here. If he left, where would he go? His father, although I use that term loosely, told him to stay put and wait for his return. If this boy leaves and his father does come back, what then? How would we even find him?

What a mess this kid is in, but man, I do not want him

to end up like I did. With a family that only cared for the appearance of nurturing an inner-city kid with nothing to his name. I don't want him to have years of regret and nightmares that come out of nowhere at the most inopportune times. I want this kid to have a real shot at life, where he makes the calls and he works for what it is he truly wants for his journey. Every kid deserves at least the opportunity at that. What they do with that opportunity is entirely up to them, but he and every child at least deserves that chance.

I pat him gently on the head, wondering if this is even allowed here, and leave a pack of gum right next to him. Then I stroll over to the table I pointed at and begin to strike up a conversation with others who are just hanging around, looking for something, anything to happen.

Marcus joins me after a few minutes and sits down to rest his legs.

"I know you don't think I am a decent guy, but I promise you Marcus, it's not that I don't want to be. I am not a bad guy. It's just..."

He quickly cuts me off, and begins to speak directly to me.

"Bad? I don't think you are bad, Michael. I think you are harboring demons from a time you cannot live in anymore. You have a past, just like everyone here has a past, but you have much more than that. You have an ability to live outside of that past, and to create something good for you, and good for your heart. But that starts with letting go, Michael. Sometimes we have to let go," Marcus says.

"Let go? It's hard to let go. You don't understand my past, and you don't understand all that I witnessed. If you did know, you would understand why letting go is not an option for me. It just isn't," I respond.

Marcus draws in a deep breath and nods his head firmly up and down.

"I understand more than you realize, Michael. I know your past enough, and I know what happened to your mother and father, and what that lead to for you and your brother," he begins.

How does this man know that? I haven't said a word to anyone here, or anyone really in a long, long time. Is he stalking my life? What is he doing?

Marcus knows I am wondering exactly what it is I am wondering. As I said before, to look at this man, you would never see what he is capable of. He's smart and has a great sense for reading people who cannot even read themselves. He can see deeper into a person's soul than even they knew existed.

"I have your records in my folders. Every man and woman that comes to this place and offers to help, be it on their own or by the hand of a judge, I look into. I need to know not only who is coming to help, but what they need to gain from helping. People can gain from anything they see and do, and it's not just my role to supervise you all here. It's also my role to help you figure that out. What can you gain, Michael. What is it you need to gain?" He asks.

I'm speechless. For three weeks, I saw this guy as someone

here because it was his job and dealing with me here was just part of his job description. I figured he wanted the eight weeks' time to go just as fast as I was begging it to. But now, here with him sitting next to me like two old friends catching up over a long absence, I feel something different. I feel he, too, is gaining from this place, the people here, and from helping me find whatever it is I need to.

"I see. I had no idea you had access to that. What do the records say about me? What do they think of me?" I ask.

"The records say nothing about you. They are pieces of paper that include the opinions of those who had to write them to justify their jobs. They tell me nothing of the man you are here today. They are useless except for the fact they give me a glimpse into your troubles. I don't rely on paper to tell me who you are. I let you do that by your actions, and you are doing just that," Marcus says.

We spend a half hour or so just sitting there, looking out to all the people of the 'Flaps talking here and there. No more deep thoughts, and no tales of a sad past that should be forever forgotten but can't. We are just two guys from different generations, backgrounds, and situations, shooting the shit.

It's nice to have Marcus understand me without me feeling the need to explain myself. I feel I am seldom understood, and that makes moving on from a past shadowed in what should have beens almost acceptable. Almost, anyway.

Eventually, that little boy whom I shared a few moments with and a full pack of gum, comes over to where we are.

He sits down on the opposite side of Marcus and I, and listens. He nods as we talk about the weather, or where we need to do some cleaning the next Saturday we are here. He's gaining from us right at this very moment. He wants to feel a part of something other than what his existence has given him thus far and hanging with two guys who are talking about nothing important is granting him that.

I am making a difference here today. I feel that.

Chapter 19

* * *

I have yet to see Von all day, and wonder if he ever came back from where it was he took off to last week. Usually, I hear him with a pleasant, "Hello Michael, how are you today?"

Not today though, at least not yet.

After lunch, I start to walk around the grounds and try to study the people living here in a different light. I look at their hands to see swollen bones hidden underneath thin skin, and I look to their faces and find sadness masked behind acceptance. Where I once saw pride, I see a sense of guilt that was not easily seen before.

Most of these people appeared happy and excited the first few weeks, but now when I take a closer look and I turn off the preconceived notions about why each is here, I learn that I am far off from what I once believed.

I want to get to know their stories, their backgrounds more, and just exactly where they made that left instead of that right. I want to know who they were before, and who they are now. Those people seem generations apart, but in reality, they are not all that different. They just gave up some, or had things removed from their lives that gave them stability and purpose.

Purpose. God, I never really thought much about that here. These people just need a sense of purpose, and something to give them a hope for a better tomorrow than they can see now. They need something to look forward to, other than just surviving. That life is not suited for them, even though most seem to have accepted their fate as just that. I am not as accepting as they are.

I see years lost that will never return, but I wonder, what if these people could be reunited with family that loved them, or perhaps still does? There has to be someone out there for each of these people. An uncle, a second cousin, maybe someone from a church they once knew. Anyone.

Marcus is over with that young kid, and I realize I never got his name. He has a name. Sometimes that is all they have, but no one is taking that from them. I want to know what to call him, other than buddy.

He's picking up some tree limbs Marcus has cut that were in the way of some of the picnic tables. God, he's so small and frail, but here he is, lifting a few at a time in the hopes Marcus can see what a big helper he is.

It does not go unnoticed. Marcus doesn't miss a thing around here. He understands that this kid is looking for some basic acceptance, and he is just the man to grant that to him.

"Whoa little guy. You are going to make me look bad with all that work you are doing," he says to the boy.

You can see this kid light up, and he goes back for even more branches the second time.

Marcus has done what few other people have been able to do in this child's life. He's made this boy feel a part of something simple and allows him to feel a genuine worth that he's been missing. Just as he has made me feel here. After three short weeks, I feel a sense of worth here. Like what I am doing matters to more than just me, and more than to the courts. I feel I am making a difference in the lives of a few souls, and never knew just how powerful that feeling is.

"Michael, you better watch out. He's going to outwork you next," Marcus says to me.

I want that gift. The gift to be able to read anyone at any time, and to know just what to say and how to deliver it. But that gift is reserved for Marcus, and not me. It's his, and although I am a little jealous of his gift, I am happy that I know this man. He was tough on me when he needed to be, and he is kind to me when I need that instead. It's a truly remarkable balance he exhibits.

I'm laughing, not because of what Marcus said just a moment ago, but more because of how he taught me such great lessons, when I thought he was simply trying to get me out of his hair, of which he has none. I want to tell him thank you, but I know I don't need to. He already knows.

I walk back over to where Marcus and the boy are, and

on the way, I make sure I smile and acknowledge each person along the path. Not all respond, and in fact, most do not. But that's okay. It's not about what they can give to me today. It's about what I can give of myself to them. And if it's just a simple smile or good afternoon, then so be it.

"Hey, buddy, you sure are strong. You work out a lot?" I ask the kid jokingly.

He smiles bashfully and continues on with his new found purpose.

I whisper to Marcus,

"Anything on his pops? Is he coming back Marcus?"

Marcus looks over to the boy and points purposefully to where the other branches should be placed. As he does, he speaks without taking his eyes off of him.

"Don't know. Truth is he dropped off this kid and left before I even arrived. I never saw him."

I can't understand how a man could do such a thing. It makes no sense to me, and I am trying my hardest to understand this world they live in. I really am.

"How about a name? Does he have a name? Should we call the police?" I ask.

"His name is Alfonzo. He likes to be called Fonzie though he said," Marcus replies.

I should have known he would get the kid's name out of him.

"Can't go to the police yet. Just can't. And so that's enough of that talk for now," he replies.

Marcus is bothered and rightfully so. I realize that I have

never asked Marcus about his family life. Does he have children of his own? How about a wife at home, where they sit on a couch at night watching something and laughing over a drink before heading to bed together? Maybe he lives alone in a small apartment, because his past has changed how he trusts people now.

The day wears on, and the people come and go at will. There are faces I have seen all the times I have been here, and new ones that I have yet to speak with. But for now, I am focused on Fonzie and his dire situation. What is this kid going to do? How is his life going to turn out if this is all he knows and expects of it?

Marcus begins to wrap up the afternoon and starts to say his round of goodbyes. He looks as if he is perplexed and seems to be fidgeting with his files more than I have seen.

"That boy," he begins.

"I don't have a clue to what to tell him. Shame it is. Damn shame," he says.

"Wait, so we just leave him here by himself? Marcus, we have to be able to do something," I ask.

Marcus looks to me with a look of frustration, but it's not directed towards me. He knows that I mean well and that I'm not trying to make leaving more difficult than it already is for him. But he can see I am struggling with leaving the 'Flaps while Fonzie stays here to fend for himself amongst who knows what.

"Ain't a damn lot we can do. What do you want me to do? Take him with me and have his father return and see he ain't here and call the cops on me? Or call the police myself and have him placed in care, where he may not ever be reunited with his family? You just don't get it yet, Michael," Marcus says.

He's right. I don't get it. I don't get any of this and it's pissing me off. These people act as if this is all normal and perfectly acceptable. It's not. None of this is normal and certainly it should not be acceptable to anyone outside of here. This makes little sense to me, and I am struggling hard.

"Well, see you next Saturday Marcus," I say.

"See me what? You don't need a ride back home? What are you going to do, sit here until it gets dark, and the camp grows restless with all these people? That what you are going to do?" Marcus says.

"I don't really know yet. Haven't thought that far out, but I do know this; I can't just leave and go home to a nice warm dinner and a clean home, while this young kid sits here with all these adults and cries to himself, scared out of his mind. I can't," I say.

Marcus tells me to sit down and to give him a moment. He places the files back in the front seat of his car, and walks back over with a brown duffel bag, places it on the picnic table in front of me and sits down.

"Michael, listen here. I know this is hard. I know this place can really get to you. Lord, more than you know, I know. There are things you don't know, and things you don't need to know, but I guess if you want to hang around for a while, nothing I can do about that. So take this bag.

There are some things inside that you may be able to use, and I have a few snacks tucked in as well, in case you get hungry. But son, don't let this take over. All of these people need us, not just the young ones."

I think to myself, am I really going to stay behind here again? Can I afford to do that? Hailey is going to be fuming, and rightfully so. She doesn't understand what I am trying to do, and nor should she just yet. And what about tomorrow? Just take the bus back home, shower, and then what? Who is going to watch Fonzie then?

I don't have the answers, and I wish Jitters was around tonight. He would keep me company, and maybe know more about what I need to do. Maybe Marcus knows where he went.

"Thanks Marcus. I'll be careful and just see that he is safe for a while. Then I will figure out what to do from there. Listen, there was a guy here last week when you all were away wherever. His name was Jitters, well, Aaron, but he said he goes by Jitters. Any chance he returns tonight? I feel like he could maybe keep an eye on this kid after I head out.

Marcus stops in his tracks. It's as if I told him his favorite Aunt died or something. He looks straight at me with a hard stare, but one more confused looking.

"You said Aaron was here last week, and that he told you he goes by Jitters. That what you just said? I hear you right?" Marcus asks.

Did I say something wrong? Was I not supposed to tell

him that Jitters was here last week? God, I hope I didn't get that kid in trouble. Man, I constantly feel like I am on thin ice and need to watch both what I do and what I ask around here.

"Forget it, never mind. Maybe I heard him wrong. Maybe that wasn't who he said he was. Just forget I asked."

Chapter 20

* * *

I was right. Hailey has apparently had enough and honestly, who could blame her? She comes from a good family. One that doesn't seem to find the wrong end of the law over and over, and one that has total respect for each other at least on the outside.

I texted her and told her that I was going to be late, and by late, that meant it could go into tomorrow morning again. I just couldn't leave this boy here alone tonight, and at the same time, I had to make a decision about my girlfriend wondering where my mind was at anymore.

Her text to me was short and to the point,

"Whatever Michael. I need some time."

When a woman says she needs some time, what she is really saying to you is that she is moving on from you. I've had girlfriends in the past that have used the exact same phrasing of "I need some time", and never once has any of them decided to try and work things out after that said time. It's the kiss of death for a relationship when they tell you they need some time.

I can't really think too much about that tonight though. Truth is, I have had a flood of emotions go through me all day today, and really for the past three weeks or so. My life hasn't made the sense I once thought it did and it's put me in a whirlwind of sorts.

Von hasn't been around at all today and I could sure use some of his preaching and positivity he spreads around like wildfire here. Maybe he moved on and had something else more important to deal with. Maybe he was arrested for begging from the wrong person and is too ashamed to come back for now. I have no idea, but wherever he is, I hope he is well.

"Hey Fonzie, you hungry buddy?" I ask.

He's back to sitting Indian style on the ground and has a stick and some pebbles spread out in the shape of what appears to be a baseball diamond. He's a smart kid and super creative, because if you leave me with some small rocks and twigs and dirt, I would want to give up on life. Not him. He knows this is a bump in the road for him that he needs to see his way through.

"Yes, I am, sir," he says.

"Whoa, listen buddy, you don't need to call me sir. Okay? Michael. Just call me Michael," I respond with a laugh.

I'm realizing something tonight that I did not see during the days I've been here. There are times when people bring donated food for the homeless to share in, and there are times when no one drops off a thing at all. I think to myself that there must be someone who can drop off a meal for them, like Marcus or Von, but then when you really see the sheer amount of people that are here and need assistance, you understand how impossible that is in reality.

"Let's go grab something. It's on me," I tell him.

He grabs a small bag he has in the tent, and tucks it under his arm.

"You can leave that here," I tell him.

But he grips it tighter and looks as if he may cry if I force him to do so. The fear on his little face is real.

I'm not going to of course, but he doesn't know that. It hits me that this is all he owns in this world, wrapped tightly in a small bag he now carries. If I had to take everything I owned with me to grab a bite to eat, I would need a moving truck, several friends to help me load it, and some way to tow my car.

He has so little and more than that, his father is now nowhere to be found. So, for him to leave this bag, which could be looted and removed from his life, is not an option.

"You know what buddy? It's okay. Take the bag with you. That way anytime you need something from it, you have it close by. Let's go grab something."

We walk through the crowd of ever-growing people coming in, and they look at me as if I am intruding on their land and wonder just what I am doing here. The feeling of acceptance is not here tonight, and I begin to wonder why things have changed suddenly from the daytime.

I can see why Fonzie is so scared, and why he feels the

need to keep all his possessions close to his body. On top of that, as we are walking out, I can see him carefully searching the faces at each person that goes by, more than likely scanning for his father so he doesn't miss him by chance.

It reminds me of the day I was removed from my home. All I had was in that house, and when I was told I needed to go, I was able to take a black trash bag of items with me and told I could go back for the rest at another point in time. But that later time never arrived for me. My foster family told me I needed to let go of the past, and that I needed to create a new life for myself without the distractions of times gone by. They told me they would provide for me all that I needed going forward. But that was a lie as it turns out.

Fonzie has probably done that several times over in his short existence. He's probably had more than he does now, and for whatever reasons has had to leave it behind. If I had to guess, it wasn't the first time and it won't be the last. Damn kid just can't catch a break.

"What are you hungry for? You like pizza? Burgers?" I ask.

He nods. I assume that means he doesn't care what it is, he's going to enjoy it.

We come to the edge of the 'Flaps and head down the winding gravel path leading out. I can hear the sound of the city bustling with life as we emerge and begin to wrestle with myself about what I am doing. But for now, I need to get this kid dinner, and then I can figure out what my next step will be.

We jump on a city bus and head a short distance to where we can grab some decent grub in a neighborhood I am familiar with. I want to be around comfortable surroundings so that I can relax some and figure out what to do with this kid.

We end up and Mama Nazzio's Pizzeria, a place where I eat at probably five or six times a month. It's by far my favorite spot to grab a quick bite. There are six tables outside and four chairs to each. It's a small joint, just perfect for Fonzie to not feel overwhelmed.

"Hey Bobby, let me get a pie and a side of mozz sticks, and two Cokes. Is Coke okay little guy?" I ask Fonzie.

He's distracted, looking out to the street that is slowly coming alive with people. It's a cooler evening and there are about a dozen or so couples walking back and forth, talking and laughing, and even one arguing. Pretty typical for Philly on a night like this, but I wonder if he's looking for his pops, or just people watching.

I decide not to bother him until the food comes, and tell the guy behind the counter, Bobby, that that will be all for now. Fonzie can look out and watch as each person goes by if he so chooses. I'm not going to tell him no. I'm actually just glad that I was able to get him out of there for a few hours and give him a sense of normalcy for a little that he probably desperately needs.

Once the pie comes out and the other food and drinks are ready, I place them on the table where we are to eat and pass him a paper plate to eat from. Fonzie looks down for a few moments, then back up and grabs a slice. I think he was praying. Funny that we find ourselves praying when things are tough, but I don't see many people praying over their food when times are good. But whatever he needs to do, is fine by me. God should hear his little prayer and help this kid out of this mess. Because I don't know how to, and nor does Marcus, who is much better accustomed to helping others.

He eats his food, but not at a pace you would think for someone who has had little to eat most days.

"Hey Fonzie, there is a lot here. I can't eat this all, so eat up. You can have as much as you like," I say.

He looks almost embarrassed, and I wonder what I said wrong. Did I just tell him he wasn't eating enough? Does he have a complex about this at such a young age?

"Thank you, sir, Michael. My belly hurts a little if I eat too fast."

Man. I had never even thought about it. When I was young and we had little to eat, it wasn't like how you would think it would be where you would get food and just eat your body weight in whatever you had. Your stomach shrinks and your appetite and eyes don't match up to each other. You cannot just eat nonstop to store it for later like hibernating animals do. You pace yourself and savor the flavor, but you get to the point where you are shocked with how little it takes to fill you up. I think that is what is happening here.

"So Fonzie, when you aren't at the Mudflaps, what is it

you like to do?" I begin.

He takes a bite, looks around for the hundredth time, and then opens up some to me.

"I like when I get to go to school. I like having friends and playing games."

Man, talk about a depressing situation. Most kids hate going to school, but this kid has lost that at times, and even though it's the end of Summer, he doesn't know if he is going to get to go to school this year, or where he is going to sleep, or if he will have any real friends his age.

"Where did you go to school last? Where is home, Fonzie?"

Fonzie takes a large sip of his Coke, and then a bite of his food, before placing the small piece of crust that is left onto the paper plate.

"I went to kindergarten last time. Saint Eliza. That's in New York. My dad told me that we were going to have a summer vacation and then he was going to get a job and I would get to go to another school. A better one, he said. But I was sad because I wanted to stay with my friends, but he said we didn't have no choice," Fonzie says.

"And your mom? What about her?" I ask curiously.

He doesn't answer that question. Instead, he asks me if we can bring the rest of the pizza back with us when we go home.

Home. He called the Mudflaps home for us. I am not sure he understands well enough that I do not reside there, and really, neither does he. It's a stop on the way to somewhere else for him, or at least it better be. He cannot live there and grow up in that place and learn that it's normal. He needs a proper place to call home and a school to attend with real friends. He needs this.

"Sure, let's take it with us. We can do that. Is there anything else you want to grab before we go back?" I ask him.

He wants another soda for his dad. His dad has been gone for several days now, leaving this kid here to take care of himself, and is being entirely selfish. And all this kid can think about is having something to give his dad. That is not his job. It's his father's job to give to him, but he's either strung up on drugs somewhere, or went back to New York to hopefully get this kid back eventually, or maybe even worse. God, what if his dad died and there is no way to contact Fonzie to tell him?

It reminds me of Terrance and his family. Did they ever find out he passed after being beating for singing? How can these people live like this day in and day out?

Chapter 21

* * *

The next week seems to go by at a snail's pace, and that kid Fonzie is on my mind more and more. So are some of the other people I have grown to know, like Von. What happened to Von?

I spent that Saturday evening talking with Fonzie about kindergarten, his favorite friends back home, and occasionally I asked him about his family back in New York. He would give me a shy response to most things, and occasionally a name or two of an aunt or cousin he remembered by name. But it certainly seems as if he's been bounced around more than just this time in his humble beginnings.

Jitters did not come back around, and I find myself hoping that he too is okay. When you witness something as terrible as I did with Terrance, you are imprinted with a horrible vision you cannot easily escape from.

It makes me think back to Marcus' thinking process of "ain't no one can occupy your thoughts without your say so," or something like that. I get his point a little more now that I am thinking about it. That boy, Terrance, Von, my girlfriend, even my own birth mother are all part of my thinking process, and it's mainly because they have captured a part of my memory that I refuse to let go of. Could I if I wanted to? I don't know that answer. I may need to revisit that with Marcus at some point.

But for now, I am dealing with some inner turmoil and trying to not let it get to me more than it already seems to be doing. I just want this kid to find his father and get back to New York and for things to be right by him. I want Von to show back up. I want to know he is coming back. This place does not seem the same without his presence. I want my girlfriend to, well, what do I want for her to do? Do I want her to understand that I am trying to change the person I am, and trying to help a few people that cannot seem to help themselves? Or do I want her to move on, because she clearly seems ready to, and the last thing I want is someone who cannot stick by my side through everything, even the bad times?

And what is happening to me? I despise everything those people at the 'Flaps represent. I detest how they beg and scrounge off others by making them feel terrible for having more than they do. I hate that each of them had a choice and simply chose wrong. I hate it. But maybe there is more to what they do and why, and I am learning all of that after spending time alone with them.

Like Fonzie. He isn't there because he wants to be there. He's there because he has no choice. Does that mean someone in their teens has a choice more than he? Or what about someone who hits their twenties and that life of paycheck-to-paycheck crashes down quickly without notice, and they have no family to turn to?

I think about the people who placed most of their money in the market or into buying properties when things were hot. They had trouble paying the loans back and life changed overnight. What about them? Maybe they get a pass.

I don't know the answers, but I am questioning things that I never did before and it's causing me to get more emotional than I have since I was a child.

It's now Wednesday and I have returned for three days to a home without Hailey, and no information on how Fonzie is doing. I need to figure things out, so I decide to first text Hailey to see where we stand.

"Hey. Just wanted to check in on you. Hope you are okay," I send.

Minutes go by. Then more and more time until it's getting late. Each time my phone chimes I quickly look, hoping it is her, but each time I am disappointed.

I place my phone on the nightstand that has been on my side of the bed since the moment we've slept next to each other. I am not sure how we came to pick the sides we did, but it seemed like we both got the right side down.

There have been days where we have slept apart; a bachelor party I attended awhile back in Atlantic City, the times she travels for work to the west coast, or sometimes down south to Atlanta. More recently, the times I have been placed in a cell overnight, or the two days I spent sleeping in a homeless community among the other people who had no other place to go.

But this hurts. Having someone purposefully ignore your attempts at communications seems unfair. I want to call it childish, but I'm sure I am overthinking it. I've sent her a message letting her know I am thinking of her and that I care. Plus, she left most of what she owns in our place, so she can't go for long. I have that at least.

I sit in my bed with my head on a pillow and my arm tucked neatly around another. My mind refuses to shut off and I am not liking how this is going. I have to work tomorrow and not getting sleep is only going to be a hindrance.

I roam my mind thinking about what I need to do in order to fix this, and what if my brother is right and I need to visit with my mother before I no longer have an opportunity to. I think back to the night I stayed at the 'Flaps with Fonzie, trying to give him some sense of comfort and security. And Jitters. I think about that kid who looked so lost, and just seemed to want Von to give him a second chance and some better direction.

As I begin to block one out of my mind, the next in line appears without a second of reprieve. Then as they run through the gamut of thoughts and I think I am finished, they repeat over again, as if they are teasing my body into thinking they will go away, but then they don't.

Damn it. I hate this night. I hate this feeling of unknowns and I hate how I am so mentally exhausted from not knowing what I need to do and where I need to start.

Eventually, at some point in the early a.m., I pass out into a deep sleep. My raging mind lets me out of its clutches and gives me a break from the aching I feel in my soul. But it won't be long before I am awake, and I have to relive each of these thoughts for another entire day. I will wake up alone, but a different alone than I do when she is not here normally. I will still need to eat something, start the coffee, get showered and dressed, and walk out the front door without having my person to say goodbye to.

That morning is exactly like that. I never make the bed because I am exhausted. The dish from the microwave breakfast sandwich I throw in sits on the counter where I ate and probably will for days. The coffee pot stands clean, because I never set it in the first place and figured there just isn't enough time to make any.

My mornings alone when I know she is coming back are normally better, but not being sure of where she stands makes this morning suck something awful. A pit in my stomach is driving me crazy, as I hate the thought of abandonment and just want to vomit it away. I felt this after my life was shattered years ago, and I still remember that feeling.

I love Hailey, but her not responding to me is not only making me miss her, it is also driving a rage through my body. Who does she think she is to leave me wondering? Haven't I been respectful enough of who she is to at least earn a response? I'm sure she's left for work by now and could have messaged me first thing this morning had she chosen to, but she did not.

Work goes by slowly, much like this week has, and I am feeling an array of emotions that are messing with my mind. I have to pull it together because I have a job to do, and in two more days, I will be back by the river for another full day. I do not want to go there all mentally confused and put myself in a bad spot where I snap on someone, or tell someone what I think about their lifestyle. I just don't.

By the end of the day, I cannot wait any longer. As I am heading out to the elevator, and quickly saying goodbye to everyone that seems to need one this particular afternoon, I message her again.

"Babe, what the hell are you doing? Can you just at least let me know you are okay? Can we just talk?" I send.

Down the elevator and out to the noisy street with tons of people walking quickly both left and right, and I can't keep my phone out of my hand. I am waiting for the buzz to let me know I have a message. Nothing. I head back home and place the key into the door lock and open the door so I can see if she's stopped back to grab more things.

As I stand there in my living room, I am frozen in disbelief.

Her small vases she had placed around the home to make it feel a little more feminine, are gone. I race to the bedroom and see that she has removed her throw pillows and the comforter she purchased as a gift for us. In the closet we share, she has cleared all of her belongings out.

This just can't be. Wait, this has to be some type of bad dream.

I race out to the living room again and look for a sign of anything of hers. She's left our photos but has removed anything that she brought into this relationship, and some of what we purchased together. Then I look over to the counter where we have shared breakfast together hundreds of times and see a white envelope with my name neatly written on the front.

I am paralyzed in my stance for a few moments, knowing a letter, after seeing all I have today thus far, cannot be anything good. I don't even have the stomach to open it yet, so I sit down on the sofa, push my hands through my hair, and throw my head back against the cushions.

As I do, I feel my phone go off. I, as quickly as possible, grab it out and beg for it to be her, apologizing for overreacting and asking to come home. I of course will say yes, I love you, let's figure this out.

But my short-lived excitement fades when I see it is not her. It's Marcus.

"Hello?" I answer.

"Michael. I know you aren't expected over to the Mudflaps until Saturday but thought you would like to know that Fonzie is no longer there. His father came back earlier today, and in a hasty fashion, grabbed him and took back off," he says.

I don't want to have this conversation now, but I am slightly worried about the boy. I want to drown in my sorrow using a bottle of cheap bourbon, but the reality of it is that I am going to be concerned for Fonzie regardless of what I ingest.

"Any idea where they were headed? Maybe back to New York?" I ask.

"Haven't a clue. That's what can happen 'round here. People come, and people go. Never really leaving a forwarding address," he responds.

"Yea, I guess not. That sucks for sure. Hope he's all right," I say.

Marcus, as Marcus always does, senses I am off. He can hear it in in the tone of my voice and how I am relaying my responses to him. It's his gift, and he hasn't lost it.

"You doing all right there Michael?"

"Me? Yea. I'm all right. Just dealing with some things. I'll be alright," I say.

"It's all right to not feel okay, Michael. It's part of this ride of ours. Anything you want to talk about?" Marcus asks.

Honestly, I want to get it off my chest so bad. I want to scream at him for letting me fall into the trap of wanting to help those people. I want to call my brother and tell him to never mention my mother to me again, because it throws me off into an emotional rollercoaster. I want to beg Hailey to just give me one more shot at us before calling it quits, but at the same time I want to yell at her for giving up so easily. Just give me one shot. Leaving without that seems truly unfair, but I don't think this is about fair. And I don't think this is about the 'Flaps. I think this is all about me, and I hate that.

Chapter 22

* * *

As Saturday arrives, I have still heard nothing from Hailey, and I am in a fog, trying to see my way through to a clearing that will allow me to relax. Because right now, I feel anything but relaxed. I want to feel like I did those weeks ago before choosing this community service. Sure, I was mad at myself for getting into this spot in the first place, but things were vastly different just a short time ago.

It makes me wonder about my future. Will there always be an end to something good in my life, and will those times trump the many great moments I had? Because if that's going to be the case, maybe I just refuse to care any longer. Maybe that will make it easier when things go south for me, and I can move forward without the pain and guilt that took over months or years of happiness.

There's an old saying that you don't know what you have until it's gone, and truer words have never been spoken. When we are happy, and life seems to be moving along well enough, we sometimes get complacent and forget to enjoy the small moments more. Then when that is pulled away from us, everything seems to be a letdown, and we wish we could just will those times back. That we could turn the clocks back just a few hours, or days, or weeks, or to a childhood the day before it was destroyed.

But we cannot. We have no say in how things went because they just went. That part of the process is behind us, and yet we will carry that loss for a time to come. Sometimes it's only a few weeks and we recover quickly. Sometimes it's a lifetime, and although we feel as if we recover, we never fully do.

Marcus is waiting for me outside of his building, sitting on the top steps with two coffees from Wawa next to him. I haven't had any coffee as of yet, because once again, I forgot to set the coffee pot up. Hailey usually remembered, so I need to remind myself that it's on me to do that now.

Thankfully, Marcus was kind enough to grab some. He is either growing on me, or I am growing on him. Either way, it's a nice change from four weeks ago when he barely said three words to me in the course of an entire day.

It's chilly this morning. More than it has been for the past several months of the summer. Things are changing. A light frost touches the small patches of grass on the city streets, and the air doesn't feel as gentle. Change is always coming, without your say and without you needing to give it permission. It's inevitable, and although I am not a fan of the cooler weather, it can bring a season of change much needed. Football in the city of Philly is massive. The playoffs, for a seemingly too long season of baseball begins. Fall jackets change the look and style you have had for the past three or four months. Change isn't always bad, but it always takes some adjusting to get in the groove of things.

"Michael," Marcus says as I walk over to where he is seated.

"Marcus," I reply, just as nonchalantly as he has.

He's back to his not looking my way, and I wonder if he's mad at me for something I may have done or not done, or if he's just having a rough morning like I am. God I hope it's neither of those. I cannot deal with two of me today.

"Have a seat, Michael. Drink your coffee," Marcus continues.

I sit down next to him, crack the top of the coffee cup, put it to my mouth, and take a sip. It's still warm, so I assume he picked it up just a short time ago.

Marcus has a pullover on, which is a first for me. I usually see this man in a blue, short sleeve t-shirt, his muscular arms bulging at the seams of the sleeves, and a barreled chest making me wonder if he purposely buys these in a size below what he should, just to be that much more intimidating.

"Seems the warm mornings are coming to an end, don't it now?" he says to me.

"Yup. It does indeed," I reply half-heartedly.

We sit in silence for a minute or two, and eventually Marcus opens up to me more.

"Listen, son. Change is a part of this all. We don't need to like it, but we need to accept it. If you challenge it constantly, you lose over and over for sure. You can't win that battle. Take it from me, you cannot keep fighting a losing battle and keep sane," he says.

I am wondering if he is referring to Fonzie and him leaving abruptly without us knowing where or how he is going to survive. Maybe he is feeling the effects of his friend's death a few weeks back at the hands of those senseless teens. He could be referring to what I am going through, or have gone through, despite him not knowing what the entails entirely.

"I know, Marcus," I reply.

Just two men sitting on an old, crumbling set of steps, having a hot cup of coffee, and pondering the change all around us. It's simple yet needed. I would think this is needed just as much for Marcus as it is for me.

"You ready to head out?" Marcus asks.

He never asks. He goes and I follow, or I am shit out of luck. It's different now, getting to know more about one and other and realizing we have our own set of reasons for wanting, or doing, or for needing. I don't know a hell of a lot about this man, but he reads me like a book. I wish I had that gift, but maybe, just maybe, he will share a glimpse into his soul and let me see what makes Marcus the man that he is. It could help me with the adjustments I need to make.

The ride is as it always is, heading to help out those

who may not seek us out, but those who in their own way, appreciate what it is we bring. I am hoping today is the day that Von returns. If he does not, I need to press Marcus for more on what happened to him. Perhaps he will, in light of him opening more to me, let me in on more of the truth.

But as we get to the outside, park the car, and walk down the path, I grow a little emotional. I sense he is here and that I am going to learn from him today. I sense that Marcus knows Von is here and for that, feels just a little better about how things are going to be for everyone.

I need something to carry me, or at the very least, push me through this stage of my life. Von hopefully can offer that help.

As we come to the clearing, I can see people waking to the morning sun, and preparing the fires used to make the coffee. The mood is very different from the night I spent here keeping Fonzie company, as there is a happiness in the air that was lacking that evening. Perhaps the mornings at the 'Flaps are far superior to the nights, whether it's because the people are less rowdy and anxious, or the people here are different from the ones that lurk late at night. Or maybe it has to do with the leadership that reigns here on different days.

Then I see him. Von is off in the distance helping an older couple with something. He catches Marcus and I entering the grounds through the opening and throws his hands up in the air as if he is the excited person here, when in reality, it is I that is filled with a strange sense of excitement.

Marcus spots him as well, and a warm smile fills that tough guy's face. Marcus, he needed to see Von just as much as I did for some reason. I think he senses his work here was that much harder without his friend to assist. People respect Marcus for a much different reason than they do Von. It's a great balance they have when they are both present.

Von continues to work with those two people, and Marcus and I tend to the coffee area to see what we can do. Really, we are just talking with the people here, which seems to be enough for them.

I've learned that when you give them the tools to live, most have a will to live. And at times, I see them find solutions to their problems without having to ask anyone for a second opinion. They are surprisingly resilient when you take the time to watch them make something from nothing. Why can't they turn that into a career of sorts? Why can't they just get up one day, use all that creative juice they have inside, and make a decent living out of it?

Eventually we see Von work his way over to where we are sitting around with others. It's still unusually cold this morning, and the fire gives a nice sense of relief, even if only for a short time.

"Gentlemen, what's the good word this morning?" Von asks.

Marcus shakes his head and laughs before saying back, "I'm here hoping you have those good words."

These two don't miss much. Even if it's just a chance to

tease each other playfully, or to finish each other's thoughts. They, for a broke homeless person and a low salaried worker, can be quite magnificent when together.

"Michael? Tell me. How are things for you? I've heard that you have been pretty busy around here, helping out. I do appreciate that more than you know," Von says.

It's nice to hear that he knows. That someone or a few people have told this man that I was useful for something other than a Saturday court-ordered chore. Because to me, that is all this was, until it wasn't any longer. It's become so much larger than that, and while I am here, I feel a strange sense of belonging, almost more than when I am out with the boys, or home with Hailey.

Hailey. It just hits me like a knife. She's gone. She's really gone, and that part sucks.

"I'm okay Von. Ready to help out where I can," I respond.

Von is looking at me. Deep into my eyes as if he is trying to see the path straight to my soul. He knows. Just as Marcus knows, Von does as well. He knows I am struggling fiercely, and he knows it's not just whatever happened recently. I can see he knows I have been pained for many years, and it hurts him to see this.

"My friend, Michael, it's going to be okay. That much I can promise you, as surely as I am sitting here today. I feel your struggle and I know you are hurting, and that's okay. Hurt isn't the terrible thing people make it out to be. Struggle is a necessity in life. Without pain and without struggle, we simple don't grow. We don't grow into the beautiful specimens we are destined to be," Von says.

And there it is. A plethora of words, mixed from all different directions, that somehow come together in beautiful harmony, and land directly onto the ears of a man who is dying for relief.

"Thank you, Von. I appreciate it. Yea, it's all going to be okay," I respond.

"Oh Michael, you can't fool me. No, it's not as easy as that. You need to let that struggle happen within and clear it out of your body so that the tip of the struggle can be felt by others. Let me feel that struggle and let me help. I want to help," Von says.

Now I am officially confused, and his words are going to take me some time to figure out. I do not know how to let the tip of my struggle out. I am built differently than that. I can either keep things in or let them out like a raging California wildfire. That's just the person I am.

Marcus is over there nodding as if he understands completely and who knows. Maybe that man does, or maybe he is just pretending to get it. I don't really know, but I am confused. That much I am sure of.

I just smile and nod at Von, and he smiles back warmly, but still does not remove his eyes from mine. It's a little uncomfortable, but not in a weird way. I just don't know how long he is going stare at me like that, or if he is waiting for a reaction from me first.

Then, Marcus pats me hard as anything on my shoulder, and he has to know just how much I felt that. But it's funny.

It snaps me out of the daze I am in, and makes me want to throw a left hook at him. But then I realize who the *him* is. Still, I feel like taking my chances for a second or two.

"You feel that? Pain is what happens when your body feels, and then your mind is disrupted, allowing itself to grow agitated. Then what happens with pain? It starts to go away. Not always quick, and certainly not always with ease and without some regret, but it eventually goes away, and your body goes back to being fine, and so then does that mind of yours" Marcus says.

"Yea, but what the hell? Why did you need me to feel pain just now?" I ask.

Marcus puts his bear of a hand, with less force this time, onto the same shoulder that he hurled a shot at moments ago.

"Because every time you experience something, it comes in different. A hard hit, or a soft hit. A big loss, or a small loss. Each can affect you differently, but they all have one thing in common. They all need you to heal from the blow," Marcus says.

That's it. These guys are messing with me. There is no way this wasn't rehearsed in advance. No way. This is like a skit where one person goes, and then the next starts where the first one left off, and then they follow the script and feed off each other as if they are at an intervention for me. This can't be real, what they are doing now.

"Von is going to take my car for a few hours. He has something he needs to do and asked if he could borrow your services. I told him you would have no problems with that. Right?" Marcus asks me, but really, he is letting me know that is what I am doing.

"Yea sure, whatever. As long as we can stop off for an ice pack for my broken shoulder blade," I respond.

They all laugh, including the few people sitting around within earshot. I am a source of amusement here for them, or for the ones that understand it anyway.

And off we head towards Marcus' car, to go where? I'm not really certain just yet.

Chapter 23

* * *

"To be honest, Von, I didn't even know you had a license. Don't you need a permanent residence of some sort to get one?" I ask confused.

Von starts up the car, and puts the heat on mid-range, because it doesn't seem as if it's going to warm up much at all today. The air just gives off that feel that it may get cooler before it gets warmer.

"Well Michael, you don't think the state counts the Mudflaps as a permanent residence? Seems pretty strange to me that wherever you lay your head at night isn't considered a residence," he says laughing.

Von has a strange sense of humor to couple with his quick wit.

"You know what I mean. How do you get mail, and get renewals for your license every few years? Wait, just how long have you been here anyway?" I ask.

"Well, Michael, you have a lot of curious questions in

you this morning. Next you will want to know where we are heading this fine morning. Am I right?" he replies.

He isn't wrong. I am filled with an unquenched sense of wonderment about everything I have witnessed in the last four weeks, and as I am beginning to search for answers, I find myself seeking understanding to more of life's questions that stretch back much further than just my time her at the 'Flaps. I don't just want to know the answers. I feel as if I have to know.

"Time," he says.

"What about time?" I ask.

Von is driving through the streets of Philly, and heading towards the Schuylkill Expressway, which runs for part of it along the river with the same name. When he gets there, he begins to head west, and once he gets on comfortably to the main stretch, he returns to our conversation.

"With time you will understand more. Having someone give you all the answers you are after doesn't help you much at all. Besides, what fun would it be if we had questions about our past, present, and future, and could access the answers at the snap of a finger? What would we have in life to work on and figure out and to grow from? Nothing much I suppose."

But how cool would it be to have a search engine for all of the answers that are not found anywhere else? You have a relationship issue? Here is the fix. You want to know why a person reacts to whatever it is you are doing to them? Click here. You want to know why something that happened to change your path in life roughly two decades ago still causes you pain and how can you stop that pain from returning? Just press this button.

But I know what he is saying. It's not going to happen, figuring out everything in life, so hoping for that doesn't change the fact we won't ever have it.

We head down the expressway, and within a half hour or so, I am able to see the suburbs outside the city limits. To my left and to my right, I am seeing a change from the last time I was out this way. New stores are being built, and apartments are shooting up at a pace quicker than they can probably be filled. It's crazy to me that they can build so many new residences, have them sit there for months and months unfilled, and yet there are places in the city that have people sleeping on metal grates, or parks, or homeless communities tucked away along the rivers, hidden from the public's eye.

But I get it. Why should someone who has built an empire give it away for nothing? What would be the advantage to a builder who had started off his career building that first house brick by brick, giving away his work that he earned through his own sweat and determination?

Von isn't saying a heck of a lot, but I don't mind. I am looking out the dirty windows of Marcus' car, first hoping this clunker doesn't break down and leave us stranded on the side of an unfamiliar road, and then just relishing the change of scenery. Life is so different in the city, and out here it just seems, I don't know. maybe easier.

People have larger homes and plenty of ground so their children can run around, tiring themselves out as they chase a dog or a sibling. The landscape is different as well. There are no massive skyscrapers blocking off views for home-owners. If you had one of these homes on the top of a hill, I would bet you could see from one end of the town, straight through the next.

My mom is in a rural place from what I was told. Even more so than this place. My brother said there are cows as far as the eye can see, and the roads out there wind and go on and on forever without a traffic light in sight. This area is much different than the city, but I can see that it is not anywhere as empty as where my mom lives. I mean is incarcerated.

Maybe Von had a point to the comment he made about where you lay your head being your residence. I never thought about that for my mom. Her life, while earned, is all she has to her name. Her cell is her bedroom, her bathroom, and her living area all in one. That is her home, even if no one on the outside of that situation would agree. It's where she lays her head at night and has for two decades now.

My home, while larger than a one room prison cell, is where I mostly lay my head at night, but without Hailey there, it doesn't have that same feeling of home. Funny now that I think about it. Both Von and my mother have more of a home than I do, and neither of them pays any rent or mortgage. What a kick in the ass that is.

"You doing some deep thinking over there, Michael? You look like you are. Nothing wrong with that," Von says.

"Huh? Oh. Yea, just going through a few things in my head. Where we heading Von?" I ask.

I know I asked him before and he had an answer that told me absolutely nothing about where we were heading, but I figured at some point he will need to tell me. I'm either going to hear it from him, or see it, even if I have no clue where we are heading.

"You've been patient enough. We are heading to a small town just to the other side of this bridge, along the same waters that the people of our community call home. I wanted to show you something," Von says.

As we cross the bridge, I can read the green and white metal sign just to the foot of the bridge's frame.

"City of Springs".

No clue what a place known for Springs is all about, but it sounds boring and old. I don't know a lot about what a spring is or does, but if it's the water type, we no longer use those. Everything, as far as I know anyway, comes from the public water system, straight from the cities or boroughs or towns that service that area. A spring was probably something they cared for a century or so ago.

Von wills that damn car steadily along the road that greets the river, and down to an area where there are some older factories that I'm sure made something of use back in their heyday. But now, they look as if they have been abandoned long ago, and all the workers of these buildings long buried beneath the surface of the earth. But they are interesting for sure.

"This is what you wanted to show me? Are we picking something up here or what?" I ask.

Von smiles and pulls into an abandoned gravel parking lot that has the macadam torn to small pieces from years of neglect.

"Here. We are here. Thank you for the company along our drive!" Von says.

We park and he exits the car, and I do the same. There is nothing around, other than this old brick building, a few more in the near distance, and two guys standing in the middle of it all with some birds chirping not too far off.

"Where? Von, where are we?" I ask confused.

He walks over to the front of the building, as if he never heard my question I just laid onto him. Then he reaches into his pockets, pulls out a large set of keys, and proceeds to open the front door to the building. What is he doing? How did he get these keys? Shit, are we about to break into this place and steal something? I have enough trouble on my record. I cannot and will not add to this. I already lost my girlfriend over this homeless nonsense, and now he wants me to participate in theft? Ain't happening.

"Von, I'm sorry, but I can't follow you in there. No way I am looking for any more trouble than I already have. Sorry, man. I really want to help, but can't this way," I say.

"Michael, I would never allow for that to happen on my time. We aren't committing any transgressions. I promise you, have some faith in me," he responds.

He opens the door, and stands back, extending his arms

as if to usher me past where he is, and into the building. I walk in, cautiously, not knowing what is actually going on.

The first thing I can see is that the building seems void of light, with the exception for what the sun allows through the broken windows surrounding the exterior. The floors are covered in years of dust and grime, and the ceilings filled with spider webs that long served their purpose. There are still machines here that resemble some type of manufacturing that was once probably state of the art.

This place looks mostly dead to me. As if it was being killed off by time, and should be left to die entirely an honorable, a quick death. There is absolutely no need for a place such as this to be anywhere. It's outlived its time and usefulness and there is no shame in that. But it's time to move on and to let much more advanced places do their job.

"Nice place here Von," I joke.

Von smiles. Not a lot seems to change this guy's demeanor. He is solid in that sense, and I do respect that. For someone with so little, he seems to feel as if he has more than most.

He walks around, moving a box from where it has sat for decades on end, and blows dust high into the air as he watches it leave the spot it called home for far too long. He looks at everything as if he is truly impressed by something I cannot seem to see. There is nothing here worth a second look, and besides, Marcus' car is small and filled with boxes of paper. We aren't bringing any scraps of metal back to the 'Flaps in that.

"This place, Michael. This place is filled with stories that have shaped generations of great people, tireless workers, and families that relied on it to give just as much as it took from them all. She still has a lot to give, Michael. She does, despite what you see," Von tells me.

I can imagine it was a decent place to work, although probably more of a sweatshop type of place where men and women worked more hours than they should have been required to, and the safety they had? Probably nonexistent compared to today's standards. He sees this as a place that gave to people as much as it took from them. I bet there are souls here that lost more than they ever wanted, and regret working in its thick walls and poor ventilation. We just see the world from different lenses I suppose.

"Here, imagine this. A Dining hall here in the center of this grand area, and off to the left there, rooms where people can sit and talk and feel warmth from the harsh winters, or a coolness from the most heated days of the year," he says.

Von has officially lost his marbles. Don't get me wrong. Yea, if someone had millions, and I mean millions of dollars to throw at this place, you could probably turn it into anything you desired, but I feel bad for Von. He isn't being realistic. No one is going to give him this building, and certainly no one is going to loan or gift him the piles of money it would take to transform this place into what it is not. Plus, can you imagine the people of The City of Springs? No way in hell they would let this place be giving to beggars and mentally ill people who can roam around as they like.

He continues to walk around, and I can see his wheels are spinning, and his heart is pumping at an excitable pace. He loves what he sees, and sadly he is going to be let down horribly. I feel for the old man, really. Such a waste of a passion for him, but you know what? If this little fairy tale gives him a sense of purpose for the day, then good for him. Let him own the day.

"Yea, sure would be a nice place for people to call home, Von. Shame it needs so much work. I bet this was something once," I say, trying to sound wistful without encouraging.

Von walks around for a few more moments, seemingly to breathe each dusty inch of this place into his soul, and then picks up a folded pile of papers from a desk drawer, closes the drawer, and takes them under his arms and out to the car.

I follow and wonder what those papers are he took from this place. I guess if those papers were there for decades, no one is going to miss those at all.

He walks back over, locks the front doors with the keys he somehow received, and proceeds to walk down to the river's edge, just to the rear of the building.

As he bends down to the water, Von reaches his hand out and allows it to run over the tips of his fingers. He watches his hands and smiles down as if he is expecting something back from her. Maybe he thinks this water will remember him from back home, or that he is expecting to somehow drive fast enough to beat the water back to Philly, so he can greet her again. I don't really know, but I just hope he isn't going to be too disappointed. Life is hard enough for the people there and adding senseless dreams can only make a man or woman want to quit, when those dreams cannot possibly come to fruition.

The ride back to the city is slow due to traffic, and we barely speak at all. Von is in a state of pure happiness, and while I have zero idea of why he needed me to go on this little adventure with him, I am happy I did.

Happy because I got to get out from the city for a while, happy that I got to see the burbs and the changes it brings, and most happy that I got to see my friend happy, if only for today.

I do feel that Von is a friend, and that too, makes me oddly happy.

Chapter 24

* * *

As the week passed by without any word from Hailey, I slowly began to understand that some people need to go on different journeys alone, and that is okay. I hate that she left and did not give me a chance to go over her concerns and see if there was something, anything, I could do to fix whatever it is that broke, but I have to accept it.

I know life is funny that way. You sit on an enormous high and get so routine that when it shifts, it can drain you of everything you have. Change is not always good or easy and can cause a lingering resentment if you let it.

I love Hailey, but I need someone who isn't frightened by the thought of adjustments needed in life and knows that the best part of that life can come from that change. We live in a world where so much is accessible right at our fingertips, with the exception of understanding. That seems to be the one piece that goes missing the most when a couple cannot communicate well, or simply refuses to.

But week five comes to the Mudflaps for me, and I am feeling a sense of eagerness and anticipation with each week I am a part of this process. I find myself looking forward to the time spent there, where before, I found myself dreading each second of its very existence.

But there is more to this week five than I had thought about until the day before. I was served with legal papers, at my place of work of all places, pertaining to my court appearance for the issue involving Terrance and those stupid kids. While I knew this was coming up, I hate that they embarrassed me where I make my living, instead of just sending them in the mail. I could have gone off so easily on the man serving me, but he was simply doing his job. I'm certain he gets people all day long crying and trying to explain their version of what really happened or going off on him and telling him to get the hell off their property. So, I decided to just let him do what he was going to do anyway, thanked him, and moved on with my day.

Who knows, maybe my job figured it was nothing big because I did not make a big commotion out of it. I went back to my desk, placed it in the bag I carry to work each morning, and went right back to work without opening it. I could not bring myself to do that at the office.

But when I returned home, I opened it and read the contents. The prosecution was subpoenaing several people to see how they were going to proceed with charges. I'm scared out of my mind, because I know that if anyone thinks I was also looking for trouble that night, or if someone thinks I was involved with getting those kids riled up, I could be facing serious charges.

The fact I was let out after a short time makes me feel a little better about my chances at escaping the more severe consequences, but at the end of the day, things can shift quickly for a number of reasons and that doesn't sit well with me at all. I understand how quickly life can shift without notice or my prior approval.

I try to keep my head up, but I am so off that it's going to show for sure. Marcus reads me well enough to know, and Von, well, Von just knows even when I don't show any emotions. It's weird but pretty marvelous at the same time.

"So, let's see. Week five for you, son," Marcus says.

"Yea, just three more to go and I can go back and figure out my life better," I respond.

Marcus scratches his head, and looks at me with piercing eyes, making it so that I have to turn away without giving out too much.

"Now the way I see it, your life is better just for these five weeks you have witnessed here. I don't see how you think it got worse, because for sure you learned a great deal more than you had known," he continues.

I think for a moment, and feel sheer confusion fall over me. For sure I have learned that just because someone is homeless, doesn't necessarily mean they are useless. Or that they are all beggars or need us to allow them to live. I have learned that for certain, they do not all need things. But I have lost my girlfriend, and have possibly lost my present freedom, depending on how this hearing coming up goes. I haven't really seen my boys much over these past several weeks, and my job? Feels as if that is suffering as well.

What does he mean I have seen a better life? He may not read me as well as I had thought.

"Better, yea. It's better," I respond mockingly.

Von is once again not there, and Marcus doesn't mention that at all. In fact, he tells me that today I am on my own. He has to go to city hall for something, but I know not to ask what. He would just not tell me and would probably use some wording to make it sound as if me being curious is holding me back from achieving, or something along those lines. It would probably just not make any sense at all.

But all is not lost, because as scared as I am to be here alone helping these people, the moment that Marcus exits the grounds, I see an old friend.

"Aaron? I mean, Jitters? How the hell are you, man?" I ask.

Jitters is off sitting alone, with a small bag of used, smoked butts in his hand. He doesn't look as jumpy as I remember seeing him, but maybe he is just coming down from whatever made him that anxious.

I walk over to where he is, excited that I at least know someone here who knows the ins and outs of this place. Otherwise, I remember what it was like the last time both Marcus and Von were gone. It was that night I took Fonzie out to grab dinner. The entire vibe of this place changed, and I am not trained for how to handle such a drastic change in circumstances here.

"Hey, dude. How are you? Is everything okay?" I ask as I get to where he is seated.

"Michael, hey brother. Yea, things are going okay. So much is changing and happening, that I am just amazed. I'm in a good state enjoying this part," he says.

I'm confused because I have no clue what he is referencing when he says that so much is changing and happening. It can't be this place he is talking about, because it looks the exact same to me. Could he mean that in his personal life things are rapidly adjusting either for better or worse? I'm curious as to how the shift in his mind as come in such a seemingly overpowering way.

"What do you mean, changing? You okay, man? Tell me what's been going on. I'll listen," I say.

Funny, as I say that, I realize that I am doing exactly what I was meant to do here from day one. To listen, and to offer help in any way I can. It took me more than half my time here to get the point that Marcus never needed to tell me what my job was. I just needed to find that for myself. He's a slick man, Marcus. He knew I would figure this part out myself, although he probably still had some doubts in his mind.

"Ah, you know. With so much happening all over, I am just happy. These people here are about to have their lives changed and they barely even know it. That's exciting, don't you think? It's as if a big surprise is coming for everyone, but they have no clue," Jitters says.

He's scaring me just a little, because I don't know what he is talking about, but more than that, I am concerned he is not in the right mind. Perhaps he is not off the drugs and hallucinating. He could have a case of schizophrenia that is raging inside, making him think that something great is about to take place, when there is absolutely no possibility of that. This is where I think Marcus and Von are at their best. They would both know exactly what to say in a situation such as this, but I am struggling. I have not a clue of how to deal with this.

I even start to wonder if Jitters is capable of hurting anyone, including himself. He doesn't appear to be violent, but with mind shifts and mood changes, for those people that have psychological and chemical imbalances, anything is possible. I need to be pretty cautious as I tiptoe into more in-depth conversations here.

"Yea, I hear you. Change is important for sure. Good change, anyway, Jitters. Good change is important. Sometimes what we think is good change, isn't really though. And other times, well, change is needed, even though we can't see it at the time. It's a balance for sure, man," I say.

Jitters is smiling at me, as if he either doesn't believe that I truly believe a word I am saying, or that he is on to me that I am trying to pull whatever he is referring to, out of his mouth. These homeless people are far from dumb, and that took me time to figure that part out as well. They know more about life than many of the people on the outside that have never had a need to learn from intense suffering and outright loss.

As we are sitting there talking, people are going about their day, mostly unnoticed, including Jitters and I. It's almost as if we are invisible to those I am here to help, and that is most probably due to the fact the most important people in this equation, the sheer leaders that have somehow rose in the ranks and garnered the respect of an entire community through just being the people they are, are not present.

But I know I have a job to do, and I feel this overwhelming sense to impress Marcus on his return, that I smile at Jitters, stand up, and let him know I have work to tend to.

He smiles. Jitters knows why I am here and knows that I want to do my very best at helping for the remaining time I am sentenced. He smiles as if to say, thank you for figuring this part out, because these people need you. But ultimately, what I will learn not now, but in time, is that it wasn't these people that needed me. It was I that needed them. I am just too blind at the moment to grasp that. But Jitters isn't. He can see clear as day, which makes him a pretty special individual.

Walking around this place, this commune of health hazards and filth and uncertainty, I begin to realize that I am seeing these people in a much different light. They are not the faceless scumbags I pass by on my way to or from work. They are not the waste of life souls that sit on warm metal grates in the coldest months of the year, as I am rushing in from my car to the bar, to fight off those few moments of cold that they are living in for days on end.

I begin to see stories develop in each of their faces, and

their eyes are telling me that I have misunderstood so much about their lives and mine. They are free to tell me their stories and I am free to decide on what I think of that all, but in the end, they have that. They have a past, they have a present, and they have a future, even if it does not line up with mine. What I think they don't have a right to, makes zero difference to them or the universe.

They are here to put their fingerprint upon this earth, and they will do so without hesitation. That mark may not be for me, and it may not be for Von or Marcus, or even their own family that is nowhere to be found. That print could be for a lost soul that just needs a day of peace and understanding. It may be for someone generations away who will stumble on to their story and wonder how they even found the will to carry on. That mark is real, whether I see it or not.

I stopped people who were walking along and minding their business, to see what it was I could offer to them in the way of help. Maybe they just needed someone to listen to them talk, or maybe they simply needed someone to see them. I offer that to as many of the people here today as I can, and I am proud today, as I have heard stories of love, loss, and bravery. I learned lessons in adaption, acceptance, and forgiveness.

There are those that cannot seem to place a solid thought together, but it doesn't matter. Their stories do not need to be told, for their shadows as they walk tell me more about who they are, than words could ever tell. I can almost see an entire lifetime in the wake of a lost past in those shadows. A past that most forgot existed, but that you can never run from entirely. No matter how fast you try.

All day I sit, talk, and listen. Each story I am hearing from these strangers is so different from the last one, and yet they all have tied these people to a common place in life. They all live for what they have, and not for what they wish they had. I cannot fathom accepting what I have as lucky, because I never seem to feel truly fulfilled. Instead, I struggle with feeling the need to have more and want more and I never accept the part about what I have been blessed with already.

I learn to ask questions that give me an ability to see these strangers as someone's family, friends, or people I run into in my normal daily life. I don't wish to see them as vagrants, leaches, or bums. I want to learn their given names, and the towns or cities where they were born and raised. I want to understand what they once did for work in their former lives, or where they studied school with children they enjoyed as peers. I ask about family they once had, or still possibly have somewhere out there. Brothers who may have giving up hope on them years gone, or a mother who tried with all she had in her heart, and felt failure at the very end because she could not pull them out.

Some are reluctant to talk much, and I completely understand their apprehension. Others, though, seem more eager to share memories they have kept locked in a vault, deep within their souls for more years than they can count. For those willing, I have created an opening they were waiting for. A time where someone wanted to know not what they wanted or needed, but who they were and are. How often do you go up to someone on a street corner who may be a bit dirty, smell different than you, and appear as if they have no hope, and ask them about who they are?

Jitters comes to me as the day winds down and lets me know that he will see me around. Maybe not next week or the week after, but that he will see me around.

I don't quite understand why he is telling me this, but I assume him that he is correct. I will see him around. Perhaps one day I will find a way to get him out of this life, and into a job where he can afford a small place to call his own, and he can find a life away from addiction, where he will shine. He has that in him, the shine part. I see it clear as day, and hope that he does one day as well.

As he walks away, I tell myself that I will find a way to help that kid one day. I will find a way for sure.

Chapter 25

* * *

Week six.

"Tell me something and be honest with me, Von. What exactly happened to you? I mean, why are you here, with all these other, well, you know. All these people that have nowhere else to go? What did you do that forced you to end up here, in this place where no man or woman, or child for that matter, should ever end up? You don't seem as if you belong here," I asked.

I knew I would eventually ask Von this question, and I can see the expression on his face, and the slight smile he cracks. He knew this question was coming, and I am sure he expected it a little sooner, but the truth is I was too busy with my own life's woes to concern myself with someone else's. Which, in hindsight, may have been the reason Hailey and I are no longer together.

Von sits down on the same log I have seen countless men and women use to pause while here in the 'Flaps. He stretches his legs out in front of him, and kicks away at a small gray rock that was in his path.

As I watch his face, studying his movements for a glimpse of something, anything, that tells me about his past, he gives me just a look. One that cautions me and gives me an option to pull the question back, before he answers. But I sit there, intent on learning more about this man and his past, which has led him into the path of my life and has changed me for the better.

"Michael, there was a time not long ago, but just long enough that it seems a world away, that I was a very different man. My mornings were set in a frantic scene of a much faster pace, and my days were rushed with a need that no man or woman should ever experience. The nights would come, and I would refuse to relent," he starts.

I can almost see this man back in that time, and I know, he is seeing himself there now. His eyes are no longer looking at the ground. They are now focused on the ghostly scene of his past, right in front of his own face. He is not only telling me his story, but also reliving it.

"I was filled with greed, and a desire that I never had quite enough. If there was a quota I wanted to reach and I did, then there was a terrible reason that it was set so low, and I raised it. Day in, and day out, my accomplishments and career were my life, and everything else suffered for that," he continued.

I want to ask him what suffered, and what career he had that he felt took so much from him. I have a million questions, but as impatient as I can be, I am struck with an awe for his storytelling, and I sit tight, anticipating each new word he throws to the air.

"You see this man before you, with dried, clay dirt under his brittle nails, and unkempt matted hair that has seen better days for sure. A man who has aged quicker than he should be for his natural age, and seemingly void of life's comforts without a say, but that is not the case, Michael. I have more of a say than most people here, and more of a say than most people out there in your world. Things sometimes aren't as they appear, but still, can be what they appear. I know it's a bit confusing for you," he says.

He's not lying. It's extremely confusing to me. Is this man, who lives entirely outside, in both extreme heat and brutal cold, capable of leaving this place at a moment's notice? No, it can't be. He has to mean something very different. Perhaps he means to say that he once had a good career but lost that as time went by him. That he had a life very different than he does now, but somehow was forced to leave that behind. I don't get it.

"It is, Von. I am trying to follow your story, but there are gaps that are not finishing it for me," I reply.

"Oh, there are gaps for sure. Years of senseless gaps and terrible regrets and unquestionable loss. Gaps so large, that can swallow a man's soul, and never let it emerge again the same. I have that all, but that is what has led me to this place of all places. It has giving me a second life that I would have never known, and for that, at least, I am truly thankful," he says.

"Tell me, if you would, about that loss. I am trying to understand how you can have loss as you say and be as happy as you are in a situation like this, Von. How is that possible?" I ask.

Von, for the first time since he began telling his story, moves his eyes from his past, and looks directly at me. He is back to smiling, as if he knows that he is exactly where he needs to be at this very moment in time. He accepts that he is sitting on an old worn-down log, with clothing that no longer fits a man such as he. He believes he is meant to be interacting with a man simply because that man could not control his rage after a night of drinking. He accepts this all more than someone accepts something much more suited for a human.

"Your loss, Michael, is not all that different from mine, but in your loss, you had no say until now. In my loss, I had a lot of say, but little now. Loss is something we have to come to terms with, because at some point, we all experience it. Oh, it can be a minor loss of time or a loss of a good friend after an argument over a girl, or it can be a loss that haunts your days and steals your nights from you. Those losses are terrible for someone to live with, but that doesn't mean we don't get that chance to live with them," Von says.

This man, I admire more now than I have the entire time I have been here. I have always known that he has read me like a newspaper from a week ago, but it's so much deeper than that. It goes beyond knowing my pain is real, and beyond knowing that I have things I am not able to let go of. He knows what is in me, and what makes me the guy I am today.

As Von continues, I am unaware that Marcus is standing nearby with an ear fixed on our conversation. He is refusing to interrupt, because he knows this moment means as much for me as it does for Von. This is probably a release Von has needed for some time. He has needed someone to listen to what his heart is aching from, instead of his time and energy that everyone here seems to need from him.

"Loss sucks for sure Von. I can agree with you there, but sometimes it is impossible to let go, you know?" I say, although I wish I had the eloquence that Von enjoys when he speaks.

"What is impossible is living without the memory of that loss, but what is in your control, is how you forgive that loss. It may be forgiving through a simple strand of words, or through much larger actions that you never felt possible. But either way, you have to come to terms with the loss or you cannot grow the way we are intended to grow. Michael, it's time. You have carried that loss for more years than you have needed to, and you have landed here in my home for a reason. I am here for you, and I am here to help you let go of that loss. Let me do that for you, my friend," Von says.

By now I am aware that not only does Marcus know

what happened to me as a child, but Von does as well. He seemingly knows the story of why I am the way I am, and beyond that story, he can see that I have never been able to properly heal from that past.

My eyes start to dampen, and as I sit there facing this man Von, I am feeling myself struggling to hold back my pain, and my years of heartache. I want to release for the first time since I was a young boy, but I am too afraid. I am embarrassed to openly cry out and beg for that relief I have wanted since that day. But by now, Marcus is sitting just to the other side of me, and he has that large hand on my shoulder, but this time more gently than before. He touches me as a father would touch his child, letting them know they are there for them.

Von tells me if I don't let go, I am never going to move past what is holding me in place.

In an instant, my eyes let go, and I am flooding my face with the salty tears I have not felt for decades. I am sobbing like a child that has lost his parents because I have. I am back to that day, and I am now begging my mother to give my dad the keys, and to sleep it off. I am screaming at my father to get the hell out of the way, before she does something she and he will never be able to live with.

Marcus is not speaking a word, but as I let go of this flood of emotions, both of his arms are on my shoulders, and he is willing me to let this out, while telling me he is not going to let anyone hurt me like this again.

I begin to see my mother's face clearly, and see that her

eyes are a scarlet red, and her face is filled with confusion. She does not appear angry or vengeful. She appears dazed and oblivious to what is truly happening.

I see my father slipping as he goes to the back of the car, just out of the view of my mother.

Then, without a second more notice, in one swift motion, she puts the car in reverse and hits the brake to back the car out.

My father, who was already lying on the ground, never saw it coming. But more than that, I can see in my mother's soft face, the absolute pain and fear of what may have just happened. She has no idea that in that very instance, it ended for them. As much as she fought with my father, he was her husband and she loved him.

She then exited the car, as my brother and I sit in the living room, well aware that something terrible just occurred. As she goes to the rear of the car, I can see my mother almost sober up in a simple moment. The gravity of what has just occurred is now very real, and her heart is shattered. She is aching throughout her body and knows not what to do.

My father, lifeless and now moved on from the life he lived, never saw, and possibly never felt for more than a second or two, the impact. He did not struggle for air that I can see. He did not speak his last words, telling his wife he forgives her and to let the kids know he will miss them, as you see in the movies. He simply died.

My mother rushes to him, and lays her body against

his, trying to will life back into his lungs, but it is too late. No amount of wishful thinking will change this. There are no do-overs and no second chances to fix what she has done. But the reality of it is, I never was able to see from where I was sitting inside. I was too young to know she was devastated, and probably so overwhelmed that I could not remember anything that day after seeing the extent of what the end result was.

She laid there until the police and paramedics arrived, sobbing incredibly. Not a sobbing that shared her fear of what was going to happen next to her, but a sobbing that her love was now gone forever. She didn't seem to fear the repercussions of her actions, as much as she feared a life without her spouse. She feared for her children, as I can see she was looking through the window, hoping they did not witness the tragedy they certainly had.

My mother was trying to die along with my father in that moment, but she did not. She begged of God to take her instead, but she knew that was not going to happen.

When questioned about what had happened, my mother could have made up a story of fearing for her life, and there may have been a chance that someone would have believed her. But she did not. She told the truth, and they did not believe her. They decided that she did not do this by accident as she had told the story, but that she was angry, knew he was there, and decided to end it.

The sad reality is that my mother has spent decades in a cell for telling the truth, and I have never once made that any easier on her. I have shunned her existence as if she destroyed a family for her pleasure. I have left her to die alone, and have never told her, "I know you didn't want for that day to go as it did, and I know that you love me. Mom, I love you. Mom! I love you!"

As I lift my head with a face drowned in tears, I am trying to see through the past. Von and Marcus have a tight grip onto my arms and are letting me go as I need to. Neither is talking or asking any questions. They can see I am on a journey to a past I tried to go around but ended up hitting head-on. They can tell that I am coming to terms with something so terrible but misunderstood.

I am wondering if what I just saw was true, or if I was simply imagining what I had hoped for. But either way, I am missing my parents like I have not in many years. I am willing the good memories of the two of them to come back into my mind. An obnoxious laugh at the dinner table because my father told a stupid joke. A night my mother was sober enough to head to work, and the kiss my father lovingly planted on the tip of her mouth, telling her to be careful. I can see the times when they tucked us into our beds and watched as my brother and I read a story from a book he picked out at the library not far from where we lived.

My parents were not all bad, but for some reason, those times were the memories I had lost or forgotten about. People easily quit, based on a moment in time that startled them. They could have a year and a half of amazing moments, followed by one seemingly insignificant issue that turns more important than it ought to, and give up completely and with ease.

I gave up on my mother because of what I assumed was correct, but looking back, was more than likely not the entire story. I created a scenario that suited my anger and frustration, and it changed the course of my life without a second notice. I allowed that to happen, as much as Von apparently did.

"Michael, it's going to be okay son. Look at me. It's going to be okay," Marcus says.

But how can it be okay?

Chapter 26

* * *

The thought of going to court and seeing that same judge who told me to never enter those halls again is haunting me more than I expected. If a mother who made a tragic mistake can end up losing the very freedom she was born with, so could I.

I've been meaning to reach out to my brother all week, but so far, I have been unable to find the words I need to say. I know I want to tell him more of what I remember now, but it's not as simple as that.

How will I look to him? Will he be able to forgive me for all the years I cost both he and I, with misinformed tales of what I swore happened on that dreadful day, even though he may have tried to remember it happening differently? Or will he see me as a miserable person, who harbored hatred in my bleeding heart and decided to drag him along for the ride, because I did not want to suffer in that alone?

And my mother. My God, what would I even begin to say to her, after banishing her to a troubled memory for two decades that she probably never deserved entirely? I want to reach out to her and collect a new set of memories that share a love that was clearly there, but unfortunately pushed away. I want to see the woman she has become and how quickly she has aged, but I know if I see that side of her, I will crumble under regret for not allowing that to take place over the time it was meant to take place.

Week seven is a few days away, but leaving last week was unsettling for me. My body felt completely released of all the hatred that I held so close, but as I found myself back at home, I began to realize that pain was not gone. It was simply brushed aside to allow me to see a clearer past than I was able to see on my own.

I walked along the narrow path that for six long weeks led me into a different world, where assumptions were invalid, and time stood still for just long enough to examine what was truly in front of me. For years I have made my way around this city, knowing I was unquestionably right, when in reality, I was anything but. And two men who I did not ask into my life, came and made an impact that will never be forgotten, because I allowed them to occupy space in my mind.

Maybe that is what Marcus was trying to tell me when he said that no one can occupy space in my head without my approval. I may not have realized it, but I was approving their place in my mind because deep enough inside of me, I wanted to hear what they had to offer. My curiosity for the knowledge they were sharing and have obtained over the course of great struggle and terrific loss, was strong enough to overcome the will I felt to end these eight weeks as quickly as possible.

My father was buried under a small granite marker with only his first initial and last name chiseled on the front, in a massive cemetery in Yeadon, Pennsylvania, but I had not visited with him over the years a single time. At first I thought it was senseless, as his spirit was never there and always somewhere else. For me, he is still lying in that driveway where his life was removed from his body, and I am still waiting for him to stand up, scream at my mother that she needs to give him those damn keys to the car he needs for work in the morning, and then he once again forgives her and tells her he loves her.

The house we lived in is a twelve-minute drive with slight traffic from where I now reside, but I have avoided that street for all this time. The last time I was there, my life was rattled like an earthquake, so I saw no need to ever cross that street for any reason. Bringing back the memories of all that loss and pain seemed senseless. I don't even know how I would react to seeing the same driveway, and the brick front home, with the large picture window my brother and I would peak out of.

I am not ready to deal with that just yet, because although I have opened a door that was locked tight for far too long, I need to pace myself through the epiphany I am experiencing with patience and care. It could cause me to spin out of control if I push too hard too soon, but

I am fully aware I need to allow this door to stay open a little, at least for now.

Friday night arrives, and I am wondering how Hailey is doing. Did she meet someone else, or is she just using this time as one of reflection, because moving on quickly seems impossible to me? She has not returned a single text, and the flowers I sent to her were marked as delivered, but no thank you was ever given in return.

I need a drink, but I have no idea if I want to head out with the boys, who for the last many weeks have been distant, or maybe I can just grab something on my own and head back, because early morning comes fast.

Instead, I decide I just need a walk through the streets around my place, just to clear my head some more. Way too much is going on up there, and for me to continue to carry this burden seems a little unfair and unrealistic. I haven't slept a full night in weeks, and not much seems to be satisfying my minds desire to work this out as quickly as I can.

It's cold, so I put on a heavier sweatshirt than I have in months. As I exit my house, I have no idea of where I am heading, or what I am really looking to find. But I feel a draw to walk and that is exactly what I do.

At first, I feel as if nothing is really doing much for me. I go left, and the scenery is the same. A few blocks up I turn right, and again, it's the same path I have crossed over many times when Hailey and I would go for walks at night. It's frustrating, trying to discover a new path in the city, as well as a new direction in my own life.

But each person I seem to encounter is different than before. In an instant, I look at them and see a past filled with happiness, sadness, excitement, and regret. Everyone seems to have a mixture of all of those feelings and emotions, just as I have been forced to accept in my own life.

But somehow, they seem to manage it on the outside well, and perhaps that was my excuse all along. I managed it well to the naked eye, but on the inside, it was a fire ragging through my soul, looking for the easiest way out. That struggle has caused me years of my life, the woman I love, and it has allowed me to look at people in a way I never should have.

"Michael, hey Michael, over here," comes a voice from out near the curb.

"Yea? Do I know you?" I ask back.

He comes into light, and in his hands I can see a baggie of half smoked cigarettes, and the tips of his fingers are forever stained with a yellow hue. It's Jitters.

"Hey man, yea you know me. I'm just out doing my searching, because man, listen, people throw away the best butts after work, and I can get a gold mine of them from here, all the way back to the Mudflaps," he says to me.

"Jitters, listen, let me buy you a carton to last you. No need to pick off other people's waste. Seriously, let me buy them for you," I say, trying not to embarrass him, but he needs to stop this.

He just smiles and keeps looking around the curb and

sidewalks for more. Something makes me think that even if I buy him a carton or even two, he's going to keep on picking up spent cigarettes discarded by others who know they are useless at some point. But to him, there is life left in them. There are drags to be had, and that feeling of relaxation he tells me it brings to his body.

What some see as having little to no value, others see as a treasured find. When you look at people who have seemingly wasted their lives away with decisions that do not line up with yours, perhaps they have a greater purpose behind them, that we cannot see as clear as someone else will.

"Hey, where are you headed? Wanna grab a bite or something?" I offer him.

"Nah, man. I'm good. Trust me, I'm good. Just going to hit a few more blocks north of here, and then it's back home for me," Jitter responds.

Back home to the Mudflaps. As the weather starts to cool, and the days grow darker earlier each night, I begin to wonder how they will survive the winter, but then I remind myself that they have survived winter for years, if not decades already. That still doesn't sit well with me. They have to be cold and praying for some simple warmth that I take for granted each night I turn up the thermostat.

Before he heads off, I begin to study his movements, his facial expressions, and his eyes. I am trying to see what I saw in the other people in the community, but I cannot seem to focus well enough to see much of anything. But he notices that I am watching him intently.

"Looking for something Michael?" He laughs.

"Sorry, Jitters. No, I was just, never mind," I respond embarrassed.

Jitters walks over to where I am, clearly aware that I am trying to learn more about what made him exactly who he is. He pulls down the hooded soft brown sweatshirt he is wearing, exposing a large red marking across the entire length of his neck. How I miss this when I first met him, after fishing all night long, I don't have a clue. But it is there, and I should have noticed it before. Even still, would I have had the balls to ask him what it was and why it was there? Most likely not.

But he knows that I was searching for something, and he offered that something to me without hesitation.

"Yea, brutal huh," he says.

"I wanted to get my parents attention, because they just never seemed to care. All my dad did was throw money at me, expecting whatever it was I was chasing, to be satisfied. It never was, man. I was looking for attention, and respect, and guidance, and all I found was a credit card with a set of rules on what I could use it for. I know for some people that sounds like a sweet deal, but it wasn't what I needed," Jitters says.

"So, what happened?" I ask.

Jitters looks out to the street he was just grabbing tossed butts from and stares off into the darkness.

"I got tired of having excuses for my behavior. Got tired

of daddy tossing his money around as if that should fix everything, because it can't. Michael, all the money in the world can't cure what you can't buy. You understand? There are things that require much more than money could ever buy, but my pops, yea, he could not see that. So, I went to the bridge to the north of the Mudflaps, tied a rope around the rusted trestle above, and placed the loop around my neck," he says.

I'm frozen in my stance, trying to figure out what would ever make someone get to that point, and how the hell he managed to survive such a stupid idea. Somehow though, he had, because here he is telling me a tale about a lesson he learned the hard way.

"Jitters, Aaron, listen, life is never bad enough to end that way. Never. You always have people that love you. So your dad couldn't see it then. Maybe he is changed now and can see what he was ignorant to before. Have you tried to find him since then?" I ask.

A million thoughts are dancing around in my head, like where he is from, and are his parents even still aware of where he is now. Have they tried to get him the mental help he desperately needs or are they washing their hands of this kid because technically, he is an adult.

"Yea, I can see that now, Michael. Seriously, I get it," he responds.

"And you don't feel the urge to try that again, right? You don't think you will ever get to that point in your life ever again?" I ask.

"Nah, man. I can promise you this. I will never get to the point where I try to take my own life again. That is a promise I can keep," he says laughing slightly.

We talk through the next twenty minutes or so, as he tells me about how he once resented his father, but now loves the man he has become. I ask if they have talked since that day, and he shakes his head to tell me no, but he does say he has seen his father and he's doing right by himself.

Aaron was born into a very well-to-do family, but never felt as if he belonged. It was incredibly hard trying to fit in with people who demanded a lot of themselves, and the same from their heirs. He did not have the same ability to retain information as his father, and always felt he was letting him down.

As time went on, his father seemed to give up on the idea that Aaron was going to follow in the same footsteps as he, and instead of fighting that battle any longer, he just figured he would always support Aaron, no matter what the cost.

It's a double-edged sword, Jitters would tell me. Having someone who needs, but the more you give him, the more he dies inside. He finally understood his father, as he told me, as a man who could not win with him. It was a lost cause, but he tried to give his son the world still.

At the time he tried to end his life, Aaron felt that he had no other options left. The money purchased drugs that both made him feel relaxed, but also took over control of who he was. They made him hate life and resent his parents. The more his father gave, the more his son purchased. The cycle was vicious and ended in Aaron dangling from a bridge.

I suspect that someone was close enough to witness what was going on, or Jitters would not be here before me to tell this sad story.

But when I ask about that, he, for the first time, shies away. I'm sure it's incredibly difficult to talk about being seconds away from death and having someone have to pull you from the literal bowels of hell, and feeling as if you failed at even that. But I for one am glad he failed. Not all failure is loss. That statement has never felt truer than now.

"Aaron, maybe we can talk more about this tomorrow. I will be back at the 'Flaps and will have an entire day to devote to learning more. I would be happy to reach out to your dad, with your permission first of course, and figure out how to get you two together. Think about it, Aaron. Just think about it," I say.

Jitters smiles warmly and nods his head up and down, but never fully commits. He starts to sing to himself as he walks away, and this time, I let him go. He has told me more than I expected to hear, and I no longer wish to bring up past wounds that he has tried to heal over time.

But looking at him, if you did not know this kid, you would never see just how strong of a person he really is. Strong enough to try to end his life, but stronger than that, he agreed to live it after, with no more thoughts of leaving this place anytime soon. That's strong for certain, even for someone as dense as I am at times, to understand.

I watch him walk away gently, vanishing into the ever

growing darkness, and then I hear no more music from his lips. He's gone, but tomorrow I promise myself, I am helping this kid learn more about his past, and I'm going to do whatever it takes to bring his father, mother, and him back as a family unit.

I may just have found my purpose in this project.

Chapter 27

* * *

"Erik, it's me. When you get this, call me back man. I need to talk to you."

That message I left on his cell phone could have been easily sent in a text, but I was hoping he would pick up. Only, he did not. I needed him to hear the urgency in my voice, and I needed to hear his immediate reply he always seems to have for me.

This is not easy for me, because I have to tell my brother that I have misunderstood the truth for so many years, and my heart is aching terribly. I need him, my younger brother, to assure me it's going to all be okay. That we are going to be able to find a way to help our mother free of her physical and mental chains and give her a life she so desperately deserves. She's paid any debt for her actions times four without question. It's time.

That night is so long and full of doubt for me. I am questioning everything in my life, wondering where else I have gone wrong, and trying to develop an understanding of the decisions I have made and the why. The why is so important, yet it's escaping me more than it's allowing me the answers.

I've used an entire community of truly remarkable people for my own ego, making it as if they are so far beneath me because I pushed through what they could not. But the reality of it is, they have pushed through more than I ever could have. They have let go of what was once such a massive burden in their own lives and learned that living doesn't revolve around what you have, it means knowing what you have to let go of.

There is a three-quarter full bottle of decent bourbon on the kitchen counter where it has been for many months, and more than once tonight I have walked by to grab it, to only leave it where it sits. I am trying to be a better person with a few less demons.

The night lingers on, and my brother has yet to return my call, which is unlike him. But it is a Friday and there is a time difference between the two cities we call home. He may just be busy with his life, and that's okay. I expect that he isn't sitting around awaiting word from his brother, as I have not reached out in far too long. That is my fault and I need to correct that. He has done nothing but love me, and I have kept him at a safe distance because I am scared to love back.

Somehow the morning comes without me remembering having even closed my eyes, and I am running late for my community service that is two weeks away from completion. It almost feels strange to call it that any longer. I am not serving anyone. I am there feeling as if I am almost a part of what they have created, and I find myself wanting more of what that city within a city offers to me and to all of those that enter through its narrow, brush-covered path.

I throw on whatever I can grab that seems halfway clean, pour old coffee from the day before into a travel mug, grab my keys, and run out the door. I decide it's best to drive to meet Marcus, because I am already running late by twenty minutes. But when I get to where I meet Marcus each Saturday morning, he has already left. Damn it. I hope with only two weeks left, this doesn't make an issue for me. I hope after last week, Marcus and Von see just how hard I am trying, at both this and within my own life.

Back in my car, I turn the engine on, and pause just for a moment. But that moment is all it takes to understand my purpose in life is shifting, and instead of dreading the days spent with these people, I am wondering how I can go beyond the eight weeks handed down to me. Eight weeks is simply not enough time to complete my lessons of my understanding of who I was and who I am becoming. My time of reflection is sacred now, and I cannot do so on my own without the help of a community that never existed, until it was planted directly in front of me.

With a soft smile, and a warmer heart, I head out to where the 'Flaps is located, park my car, and jump from the driver seat to head down to where Marcus hopefully is.

I see his car is not there, so perhaps he too was running

late this morning. I may be off the hook without them even knowing I was late to the meeting spot.

Von is there though, and he is up and tending to the people that look to him for inspiration and direction, or sometimes, just simple understanding. He does all of those things so well, effortlessly, without hesitation or regard for his own wellbeing. But maybe this is his penance in his mind for having lived a life once very different from the one he appreciates so differently now.

But Von has a much different look on his face this early Saturday morning. His eyes are lowered, and he is more focused than he usually is. Most times, he seems half focused and half willing to let the moment happen without his interference. It's a tremendous balance that I do not know he is even aware he possesses. I think it's in his DNA to be so good at whatever it is he does, and this is certainly no exception.

I also realize we never got to finish our talk about his life and how he officially ended up here with the acceptance of a prisoner accepting a sentence for a crime he fully acknowledges. But did Von commit a crime of sorts, or was it more of a misdirection of his personal life that caused him to slip away from the fruitfulness of one life, to the open challenges of another?

He sees me standing there, watching as he continues what he does. But he does not shoot that same wide smile he does each day, and he does not say my name at the beginning of his hello as he has done time and time again.

Instead, he nods with an almost forced smile, and goes about his business.

Something is off, and my desire to find out what it is and how I can help with that is intense, but I know Von by now. I know that I need to allow him to struggle with whatever it is, and to ensure him that I will give him that time. He knows he has Marcus for anything he needs, although Marcus is nowhere to be found yet. But I hope he also knows if he needs an ear, I will lend mine for the morning and afternoon to listen. I may not have any grand input that will change his day, or help him find a solution to whatever it is, but a listening person? That I can be.

There are people gathering tree branches, and others working on clearing brush away from the tents that line the grounds. A few are down by the edge of the river, washing off both utensils and clothing at the same time, ensuring that they are at least void of the dirt that covered them for who knows how long.

It's getting chillier out, and I am sure these people are prepping for the colder months in Philly that can be challenging for those with old brick and stone front houses, let alone those built from vinyl, cloth and cardboard.

I get busy walking the edge of the river for fallen branches, and good oak sticks that will serve as solid kindling. I hack away at overgrowth near the base of tents and recycle that brush on the banks of the water. For those that are carrying clothes to the edge, I offer my strength.

Today is not only hard work, but also purposeful work.

There is a difference that I seldom understood prior to today. Each day during the normal work week, I enter into an office building where many companies reside, with hundreds of employees working over and over on tasks that seem endless, but the point of those tasks is to help a company be profitable. There is nothing wrong with that of course, because without profit, there would be no wages to pay the employees, but purposeful? I don't know about that.

Sometimes we feel as if we are trapped in an endless cycle of a Monday through Friday, and of tasks sent to us in an email or through a zoom meeting by someone we've never met, and probably never will. But to see people working not for their wage, but essentially for their entire existence, is sobering.

Von has kept his distance throughout the morning, and as lunch approaches, I realize I have forgotten to pack mine. Usually, I pack something the night before, but I passed out before I had the chance. If I do forget, I pack the morning of, as I am generally an early riser. But that too, was not to be this morning. So, I can either push through and grab something on my way home, or I can run out and pick something up easily.

Easily. I can just use my bank card, or one of the four credit cards in my wallet to buy whatever I want to eat today. I can use the cash that lines my pockets from the boring work I do day after day and eat like a king.

These people? They do not have that luxury. It is not something they can do without a second thought, and I wonder how fair that really is. Should I be afforded the right to do as I please because of the position I have put myself in, and does that mean these people should suffer and wonder what tomorrow will bring for both them and their families because of the position they find themselves in?

If you asked me those same questions eight, seven, maybe even four weeks back, I would have answered without a single hesitation. Yes, I am afforded that because I earned this. I wanted more, and I pushed through a life that was steering towards a depression that was warranted, but not what I allowed. I worked hard on my career, and had a roadmap to success mapped out and all I needed to do was follow it.

But ask me now, and I don't know if that holds true any longer. Over the last several weeks here, I have heard stories that have touched me to the bone, and have shown me that just because we have a plan in front of us, does not mean there isn't a different plan in our future. It does not mean that we get to travel the path we wish for, without a detour that may or may not allow us back on the journey we had been told was ours to travel freely.

Things happen that are entirely outside of our control and no matter how much we bitch and beg for change, the change we get isn't always what we begged for. But maybe it's the change we needed, but still cannot accept.

I work harder today than I have any of the other weeks here. It's not that there is just more to do today, it's that I want there to be more to do today. Looking around, I know that eventually I will say goodbye to this place, and I am struggling to let go. These people that I loathed in my past, have become so much more to me than I would have ever imagined. I am having a difficult time coming to terms with what is going to naturally come for me after this is over and done.

I know that for these people, for Von, for Marcus, and for Aaron, or as my friend prefers I call him, Jitters, this life is going to go on pretty much as it has, until a time when their path is abruptly adjusted, if it ever is again.

My lunch was spent eating alongside other people who had nothing to eat moments ago, but somehow were able to find whatever they could to satisfy their hunger. I felt the need to question where they ended up getting half a hoagie but realized they did not need to give me that answer. I had a choice to accept what they offered, or to not. I chose to accept. Not because I could not purchase food of my own easily, but because I wanted to feel more a part of what these people live with day in and day out. I wanted them to know, I respect them more than I have, and that I no longer judge them as that drain on society that I once had. I see them as equals.

And Von? I need to make sure he is okay today. He's been in and out, walking around ensuring everyone is good, but he has yet to come and chat with me. I have to see what is off and wondering if maybe it was something I did to offend him or this community, is eating away at me.

"Von, hey, you have a second?" I ask.

He looks away from his task, up to where I am standing over him, and pushes his lips together to smile as best he can. He can already sense my apprehension and concern, as he always seems to do.

"Michael, I do. Here, sit. I wanted to talk with you about something, but I was unsure of how to bring it to your attention," he says.

Wait, this man who has the correct wording needed for any situation under the sun, now cannot put the words together to ask something of me? I don't get it. It makes no sense at all.

"Just ask. Whatever it is, just ask," I say confused.

He takes a deep breath in, closes his eyes for a second, and when he opens them, his question emerges with a sense of both concern and sheer curiosity.

"Tell me, Michael. This guy you told Marcus about here. The young man you met a few weeks back. Tell me his name again. Do you remember the one I am talking about?"

Of course, I remember. He is talking about the one with the yellowed fingertips and the Ziplock baggie filled with used butts. The kid I fished with for hours that night, and the one who woke me with an internal alarm clock that he swore would not disappoint. But why does he care about this kid? Did he do something wrong? Was he banished from ever coming back to this place and he broke that unwritten law? I could swear that he told me Von knew him and that he was there to let me know Von was busy for the day.

"Jitters? I mean, Aaron? What is it Von? Did I do something wrong?" I ask.

Chapter 28

* * *

The path that has lead Von here, to this dirt-covered, tent filled community that lays out of sight for the most part on the shores of the Schuylkill River, is remarkable for many reasons.

First, when I hear more about his past, I realize he has no business being in a place so full of desperation. And second, I also begin to realize he may be right in saying that he belongs here more than most of the people that live here.

"In a different time, that seems as if it were ages ago, but the reality of it is that it's more or less seven years of my life, I was a much different man, Michael. A very, very different man," he starts.

I am on each word he speaks. The people talking and laughing and moaning all around me are silent to my ears, because I have willed them to be. I cannot hear the many questions they ask of one another, or the slamming of hard wood as they throw another broken off branch onto the pile not far from where we are seated, nor can I hear my own thoughts that were on my mind just minutes ago. I am listening intently to each sound that exits this man's breath.

"For many years I was a successful businessman. A tremendously successful businessman. My family had all it could want, and then some. We ate at the best restaurants in the city, while enjoying the comforts of the suburbs in our large, private home with acres of free grounds for us to roam, all closed in and protected by the help of a large black metal fence that neatly lined the entire property. We lived that life most people dream of when they fall to sleep at night and pray to God for. And everything was perfect as could be, until I was forced to open my eyes to the truth, that nothing was as perfect as I had thought," he continues.

I can see the look on his face changes to a sadness, and he is no longer here. He is looking back on his life once again, and he's in that one moment where he realized his life was going to be forever different. I am on the edge, waiting to hear more from this man I have come to admire greatly, but he is so lost looking, that I wonder if he should even continue, but he does without my permission.

"I was away on a business trip, somewhere in Arizona if I remember correctly. Funny thing is, there was a time I could tell you the dates and destinations of all my trips away for business and assure you they were all spot on. Now, I couldn't tell you the hotel, city, or what I was there for to begin with. Time will do that for you, you know. Michael, don't let the unimportant cover what is truly important in your life, you hear me?" Von asks, but really, he is telling me.

"I won't Von. I won't," I respond.

My phone went off, but I was too busy entertaining people out at a restaurant known for attention to detail, so I let it go. I was more impressed with the presentation of what they were doing, to be concerned with my wife calling on the other end. She could wait, as I had made her wait time after time, and year after year. After all, her life style was determined by the number of hours I worked away from home, not in our home," he told me.

He's struggling something fierce, and I can see in his eyes, a sadness I have not seen for decades. A sadness that tells me he had a great loss, and still to this day, has that same loss. It feels the same, never truly subsiding as a loss should. He has not been able to grasp that time is supposed to heal old wounds, or maybe he knows that, but doesn't allow for it.

"Hours later, after she had called me a dozen or so times, and much after I turned my phone off to avoid her interruptions, I returned to my hotel suite with the large fancy bed, and the picturesque window facing the downtown area skyscrapers, to relax for the rest of the evening. My job was finished for the night, and I wanted to do nothing but unwind. It was then I realized I had not turned my phone back on and had forgotten to call my wife back. I had turned off my wife's ability to reach me, because I had more pressing things to tend to, Michael. And that changed my world forever," he says.

I am trying to stay composed, because he needs to see

that I am here to listen without judgement, and without inserting my advice. I am simply here for him to vent to, but it's tough because I can see his struggles are continuing to weigh on him, yet I know he needs this. He absolutely needs to get this all out.

"How did it change exactly, Von?" I ask back.

"How? Why? Those are the very questions I ask myself each and every morning I rise to meet the day, and each and every evening I lay my head down in acceptance of my penance. I have no answers for the how, but the why, I struggle with daily. When I turned my phone back on, it started to ping nonstop with messages that were left while it had been turned off. I had to wait for them all to finish going through, before I could even make the call back to my wife. Eventually, those messages did stop, and I was able to see the last text my wife sent. She messaged me to please, come home, please! I knew in my heart, something was horribly off, and I immediately dialed her number," Von said.

This man, for all his strengths, seems so lost in this moment. All his charm, and wit, and happiness, are drained in the minutes we have engaged in this conversation that to him was probably long overdue. I am not sure he felt the ability to talk with anyone else here as deep as this before, and I am unsure of why he chose me for this, but I am glad he did. I am happy he found a way to trust me with his deepest thoughts, and the incredibly confusing life he lived prior to coming here.

"Von, what did she say? What was it that was so urgent?" I ask.

"She...she wanted to inform me that my son, our son, was delivered to the hospital in the city, not too far from where I sit now," he said.

Delivered is such a strange word to use, even for someone as educated as Von is. I am not sure I am understanding it correctly, but I assume he means sent by ambulance or dropped off by someone, and not delivered. But when he continues, I begin to understand that his word was used correctly, unfortunately for him and those involved.

"He had hung himself hours earlier, and my wife, my loving, beautiful wife, was trying to get in touch with me to tell me that our son had passed. She needed me to comfort her, and to tell her no, it's not true. I will jump on a plane this moment, get back into town, go to where he is, throw money at the person in charge, and fix this. Because that is what I do. I throw money and people fix things," he said.

I'm feeling lightheaded as his story goes on, because for some strange reason, I feel as if I have heard this story in the past, and I am wondering how I know it to be true.

"But of course, I was unable to do any of that. I could not write a check to correct what he did that night. I could not comfort my wife and tell her it was all going to be okay. I could not even answer the phone, when she needed me most. I failed, and for that, I have accepted my fate entirely," Von says.

I place an arm on my friend and offer him what he so

needed back then. Although it's years later, I hope that my gesture gives him a small sense of comfort as well. But that is all I can do. I don't have anything to say that will make him feel as if this is all worth it. I don't know what to do that will eliminate a tenth of his pain, and I don't know how to tell him, it will eventually go away. Because I am still dealing with my trauma from decades back, and I don't believe those words myself.

"Michael, your mother. She needs you more than you need her. That I know. She is the one forever lost in time, and afraid of having nothing to look forward to, other than the end of that time. Don't let that be her reality, for she deserves so much more of you. She needs you to forgive her, and to forgive yourself, or she will die alone as she lives alone. We all die alone, but living alone? There is nothing sadder in the world than to feel as if you are truly, entirely, all alone. My son…" he starts to choke either from the strain of this all, or the weather is getting to him from being outside in the elements with no break.

"My son, he had so much in life, but he lived alone in his darkness, and I missed it. His mother, she missed it. We thought that we were decent parents, working to ensure he could buy whatever it is he needed. An education? We could provide Ivy League if he so wanted. A car? I had more cars over a five-year span than most people could accumulate in a lifetime. I offered my son the world at his fingers, but he didn't want or need the world. He just needed me. He needed me to love him in ways I did not, and for that, he lived alone," he tells me.

"Your son, Von. Did he ever get therapy? Was this something you could not help, no matter how you tried? Maybe some things aren't as easy to fix as we want, and nothing you would have done could have made any difference," I add.

Von, he just shakes his head, as if to tell me thank you for that, but no, I could have done better. I get it. In his state, he doesn't need to hear he couldn't have prevented it. He needs to hear that he could have done more, but that it's okay, because he did not know how to at the time. But he would counter that with something about how he deserved a chance to correct it, and never got that once his son decided he had had enough.

"My son lived in the largest, grandest house in the entire area, and yet he chose to mingle with people that had nothing near what he had. He found his way into addiction, as I am sure he hoped that would allow his body and mind to forget how lonely he really was. But the more he tried, the more he needed, and this went on for over a year. Once we found out, we got him into a rehab, but they were not able to help him. So many people are lost to addiction, and so many people need help that just isn't there. Mental illness, Michael, is so prevalent today, but the cure for it is sadly not. And so, my son saw only one way out, and he changed the direction of his path just like that," Von finishes.

With his son lost, I wonder more. Where is his wife? What is it she ended up doing with her life? Did he close his successful business, or did it ultimately collapse under the sadness he felt and could not close off? Did he have other children, or was his son the only child his wife bore to him?

I want to keep asking, but I see he needs time. He has given so much of himself just now, that he is drained of any desire to give more. He can't continue, even if he had the desire to. And so I give him that space he needs in his mind, and just sit there in silence like him. I have no wish to move from this spot, for as long as he will have me sit here. He needs me, and I am going to be there for my friend.

Minutes go by before he speaks another word, and the words he speaks will haunt me for as long as I shall have to endure my time here on earth.

"Michael. You never asked me my son's name, but I feel as if I need to tell you," he says.

"Yea, I did not, Von. I did not want to bring up more pain than you could handle right now, but please, what is, or was his name?" I ask.

He looks up to me, places his own arm around my shoulder, pulling me even closer to him, and whispers to me,

"His name was Aaron, but not to his friends, they did not call him by his given name. They only knew him as Jitters."

Chapter 29

* * *

I have a strange relationship with God and a strange understanding of the origin of, whatever he, or for that matter, she, really is.

When I was younger, my parents talked about God often. It was goddamn this and goddamn that, but on a few occasions, there were times when they were truly grateful for what little they had. My father would tell me,

"Michael? Be thankful your old man has a job, and a drink to come home to. Oh, and your mom. He has her to come home to at the end of a long day. For better or worse," he'd say.

My beliefs were adjusted over time as I grew older, questioned more, and challenged the notion that someone could sit high above us, on a jewel-covered golden throne that he built, while he watched as people suffered, starved, and laid in driveways on narrow streets in unforgiving cities.

The question for me was not was there a God, because someone, something had to ignite this all that we see. It was what type of jokester or twisted all-powerful being could allow so much struggle, and watch as desperation turned to grief, and life turned to death.

I've heard stories from church-going, bible-thumping souls that tried to assure me, there is a reason for it all. Oh, you don't need to see the reason, because he knows what's better for you on your journey than you do, after all. He will place you in situations that are so hard, and so strenuous, just so you can come out a better person than you were.

My response was always the same.

"Why then didn't he just create us better than we are?"

After speaking with Von, I stood up off the wood we sat on, and walked away with no final words. What was I going to say to this man who just told me the young guy I saw a few times, walking both the grounds of the 'Flaps and the city streets of Philly, was claiming to be his son? Did I want to describe him to see how closely he resembled the son he lost years back? Did I want to ask if others had seen this kid who tried to steal an identity of someone else, and for what purpose really?

This character calling himself Jitters, had raised markings across his neck, just like someone who had decided he had enough of this world, and placed a noose around his neck, hoping that it would solve all the problems he gained in his short time here. Someone who didn't just threaten to end their life but went ahead and tried his darndest to actually succeed, and came razor close.

I'm a little angered, but more confused. What I should have done was asked Von about specifics. What color hair did he have? Was it long or short? Did he have deep brown eyes that went back and forth, looking all around, as if someone was watching him more than he was watching for them? Maybe he was more on the short side than the kid claiming to be Jitters, or could he have been the same?

But there are other possibilities I have to explore. He could be a young man with a past of mental illness, that doesn't want to be that Jitters, but believes in his mind he is. I have a friend with a brother who swears he has lived many times before. He's convincing, too, when he talks about it. The stories are always the same, and the men and women he claims he was over a century ago, seem to have invaded his personal space for some strange reason. At least, that is what his mind is telling him.

My friend, Tony, doesn't know what to do with his brother, but the diagnosis the doctors have told his parents is schizophrenia. Tony loves him, but damn if he doesn't get pissed when his kid brother goes off about fighting in the Civil War on a battlefield in nearby Gettysburg, and losing a limb for his efforts, which he believes causes him severe pain in his leg even today.

The doctors have examined his left leg several times over the years when he cries out in sheer agony, but each time they do, they can find nothing. Not a muscle cramp, or a ruptured vein, and not a scratch from anything he did physically that day. A phantom pain that is surely made up in his sickened mind. But to see him grab at it out of nowhere? It's scary how real it seems. You would never think a human could make up a pain that intense and scream a blood-curdling curse to the heavens, just for attention.

The rest of that day is a blur to me. Von most likely went about his natural business, and I seemingly finished off the day, hopefully helping more than not.

When it was time to leave for the seventh week, I find myself searching the streets where I last saw this kid claiming to be the dead son of Von but have no luck. I want to ask him why he is a fraud, or maybe not. I have to tread lightly, because as I have learned over my time helping these people out, it's not always as it seems. He may just need help more than anyone there is capable of administering. He might just be mentally sick and has no control over what his mind tells his mouth to spit out.

But damn if I find this kid. I need to know who he really is and try to get him far away from Von before Von has a mental breakdown, or worse. Marcus seemed pissed when I told him at first, and the last thing Marcus, or this fraud needs, is for Marcus to lose his temper and go off. I can tell you how that would end. With this kid not wishing for death, but begging for it.

I am unaware if Marcus ever returned that day, but it doesn't make a difference. He's a grown-ass man who can clearly take care of himself and can do as he pleases. It's not his sentence he is serving there. It's his choice, well, his job, but he seems to have a lot of flexibility in when he comes and when he goes, unlike me. I have my predetermined day, and the hour for starting is set. The only difference for me is the time I am finished. That, I leave for Marcus to decide.

After driving around for thirty or so unfruitful minutes, I decide it's better to head home and let this go for the rest of the night. I have not been out with my boys in ages, and with me finally coming to terms with the fact that Hailey is not coming back, I need to let go some.

I'm reminding myself that there are court dates ahead, and even though I am about to complete my term at the Mudflaps, that doesn't guarantee me freedom from what comes next. I still need to be a better, more focused person, and I need to be more aware of my drinking, even with Hailey gone from my life.

The bar is packed and so my anxiety is soaring, much more so than it has been in recent memory. It could be that I am more aware of my surroundings than usual, trying desperately to avoid any and all confrontation that could quickly go south for this southpaw. It could be that Hailey hangs out at this very spot, and I have not seen her since she split on me. What would I even say, if anything at all?

The boys know something is off, but they are also aware that I have a lot of things going through my mind over the last few months. But still, they are ragging on me, which allows me to feel somewhat normal again. We do this as a sign of love and respect. I tease you about how you are dating a girl way above your rating, and you tease me about how I have a brother who is smart, and I am the other one. It's all done with respect behind it, but someone on the outside may never understand that.

Derrick is still dating Hailey's best friend, which I am sure is awkward for him, wondering if I will bring anything about her up. But as much as I would like to, and to know that she is aware I am still very much alive, I am not about to put him in a spot where he needs to decide between his loyalty to his girlfriend, and to his boy. I respect him enough to know it's not his time, and not his circus, so to speak.

My drink intake is down for a very good reason. One of the bartenders on tonight is a good dude. Mitch is his name, and Mitch knows some of my legal troubles, and certainly understands my quick temper. So, when I went over to grab the first round of drinks, he and I talked briefly, but with purpose for the few moments I was ordering.

"Hey, Michael. Good to see you bro. You good? Things going all right?" Mitch asks.

Just how much he is aware of, I am not certain, but I am not here to do what typically people do with their bartenders. I have little desire to go over my upcoming court case, my prior one, and certainly I have no desire to unload on him about the past seven weeks of what I have been quietly calling to myself, a time of losses and gains like no other.

"Yea, things are, you know. Things are moving along," I respond.

But he knows just a little more than that.

"Heard about Hailey, bro. Sorry man. I know that's tough. Anything I can do to help?" he says.

When people say things like "anything I can do," or "hey if you ever need anything, let me know," they do not always mean what they are saying. Your heart hears it that way, but you know it's not the intention of the words they use. They are really just saying that they get it. That you are having a rough time, but that it will get better over time and without their assistance. Just hang in there. But I do actually ask him for a small favor, regardless. One that may seem strange to most people, but somehow, he gets it.

"Mitch, listen. I need a favor tonight. Just a small one, but no judging me, okay?" I ask him.

Mitch leans in just over the curved side of the bar counter, as his curiosity is now setting in, and waits for me to explain what is on my mind.

"I am the only one ordering bourbon tonight. You know the boys all drink their IPA's, so listen. Whenever I or they come for another round, do me a favor, okay? More water than bourbon. It just needs to be that way. I'll pay for the full drink, but please, don't give that full bourbon drink to me," I say.

Mitch leans back, smiles as he is pouring the drinks for me to take back over, and nods. He gets it, and without a single judging eye, he knows what he needs to do.

Those aren't the people I enjoy in my life. Those that either judge me because of love, and those that don't judge me, out of respect. It's a great thing to have both in your life. One wants to mess with you because it's fun and they truly care, but they mean well regardless, and the other wants to see you do well, without the need to rib you all night.

The night goes on and we talk about work, or something that happened last week when they were all out prowling around the 'burbs, just to get a change of scenery. No one really mentions their girls or dating life though. They know I'm good, but they also know that because of how quickly things shut down, and without a moment's time to sit with Hailey to go over her concerns, that it's still fresh in my mind and still not easy for me.

All night I have one eye on them, and the other on the people coming and going in and out the front door, hoping either for a glimpse of Hailey, or maybe with better thought, no glimpse of her. I mean, yea I want to see her pretty face walk through the doors with her girlfriends by her side, all laughing and not paying attention to anything else around them. I want her to turn her head and catch my eyes as they are trained on her, willing her to come and say hi.

I want that all, but I know better. The way it happens in the movies, with all the romance shit and I miss you and let's never fight again, just isn't reality. Not for me, anyway. No. Hailey is gone, and if she did come through the doors, she would most likely ignore me, or walk back out to find another spot. It's just how it is.

"You all right, loser?" Derrick asks.

He's messing with me with that loser comment, but he's genuinely making sure that I am handling the night okay.

The truth is, I am not. And the further truth is, it's so much more than Hailey. I am concerned for Von, as we never got to finish our talk about his son, and that young guy claiming to be Aaron. We never were able to piece that together, and I am worried that Von was set back tonight because of it. I should have asked more questions. I could have assured Von that some people just aren't right, but he knows that already. He sees not right all day and night long.

But then, as I am glancing around once more, I see the shaved head of a man outside the bar window that faces the road, and it catches my attention. Everyone seems to have more hair than not now with the new trends and all, so why does this guy not?

In his hand I see the bag of butts, and quickly I know that it has to be that kid. There are a ton of people outside waiting to get in, as it is packed shoulder to shoulder here tonight, so I need to tell my boys to hang tight and save my seat, so I can go out and give this kid a talking to.

I don't even wait for a response from them, nor do I look their way. I am pushing my way through the oncoming crowd of new drinkers, or drinkers at least from the last spot they were at, and eventually with my eyes still on the prize so to speak, I am out the door.

There he is, wait, no he's on the move. For a second I swear he sees me and is now pushing his own way further up the street, trying to avoid me. He knows I know. He has to.

As I get through the larger groups, trying to not let anyone's harsh words sit on my ears for even a second, I see he is a good twenty feet up the street now, turning the corner. I race up, and as I come to the next corner where he had just been a second ago, he's gone. Vanished into the night as if someone picked him up into the air and just removed him from view.

I know he was here. I am not even just sure. I am positive. Damn it. This place is starting to drive me crazy, and I am allowing that to happen. I am allowing them all to occupy my space, because of who knows why.

I reluctantly turn and start to head back, when I hear someone call my name from the darkness of the one street light road behind me.

"Michael, bro. Hey, it's all cool, man. Don't worry. My dad knows. He knows the truth, Michael," someone says.

That someone is that damn kid, and he is now claiming for certain that Von is indeed his father. I could punch this kid if I didn't already have a hearing coming up for doing so. And, if I could see where he stands, because I still do not see him.

"Aaron, Jitters, whoever the hell you are, come here. Stop playing with me, I just want to talk. Just come out, and it'll all be good, I promise," I say back, hoping he will believe me.

Nothing. Not a word, nor a sighting of him. I take a few steps in the direction of the voice I heard, being careful to not allow those steps to make so much as a sound and listen with each one. It's as if the street died off, and so did whomever was with it tonight.

I need to just get back home and forget things for a

while. This is just becoming a little too much, and the last thing I need to do is to lose my own mind. Which, for the record, may be lost already.

Chapter 30

* * *

A simple text, from a brother on the opposite side of the country, has greeted me first thing in the morning. It's the kind of text you get that carries raw emotions with it, and a message far greater than the few words typed out. I knew something was up, but what exactly this meant, I was unsure.

"Michael, call me ASAP. About Mom, new news. We need to talk," read the text.

So, Seattle is approximately 2,800 miles from where I lay my head down on my pillow each night. If you walked out my front door to the city street, jumped in a car that was waiting for you and needed no warming up, and drove nonstop without food breaks, no stopping to refuel the car, and without needing a single break to use the bathroom, you would end up there in roughly 42 hours.

With a text, a message is sent that covers that 2,800-mile distance in the matter of a split second. Without a voice to carry it, I can still hear that my brother is anxious and full of news that is potentially life changing. Oddly I don't feel it's terrible news he needs to share, but more of news that could be beneficial to him, my mom, and ultimately to me.

I can't click his name quick enough on my phone because I need to hear what news he has, and despite the fact we are three hours difference, I can't think of things like that at this moment. The text came in at 4 am my time, so he was up late when he sent that to me. He's probably fast asleep and I may need to wait until much later in the day, but at least he will know my anxiousness as well.

It goes straight to his voicemail, which is odd to me. My brother never, and I mean never, turns off his phone. He lives and breathes for whatever is coming in from the other side, and because of his work, that can be at any hour on any day of the week.

"Hey Erik, it's me. Call me as soon as you get this. I'm around, so, anytime. Okay? Call me. I want to hear what new news you found and, we just need to talk. A lot going on as well on this end. I'll tell you all about it. But call me. Okay?"

I am sure I sounded like a mess and unable to sound intelligent, but in my defense, it is early on a Sunday morning, and I literally just woke up from a late night out. The only thing saving me this morning from difficulty is that Mitch, the bartender from last night, listened well to my instructions. He did exactly as I had asked of him, and that made for an easier night with no added legal troubles, and a break in the morning without needing three aspirin and a bottle of Gatorade just to get out of my own bed.

Coffee. I need to make the coffee. Damn it. This is one of those mornings where life gives you a perspective you thought was in the rearview mirror. Hailey was my favorite Sunday morning coffee companion. It was mostly due to the drinking we did the night before, and we both would feel as if we could not function without an entire pot between the two of us, but she is not here for that. I am not able to ask her if she can start the coffee while I take a piss. If I did ask this morning, I would be more disappointed than I already feel.

Those emotions that you feel when you experience a loss are brutal and couldn't care less if you want to move on from them or not. They don't concern themselves with the notion that you have pushed through weeks of torturing yourself over the what ifs and what should have beens. When you least expect it, and when things are swirling around your life like an untamed wind, about to create a storm that is going to take so much from your soul, there they come.

The only decent part that those emotions allow for is that the time between these episodes of loss get further and further apart. They don't hit you as they did when whatever changed in your life first started to bother you. At first, you hate each waking moment, begging for peace. Then when you are granted that peace, you feel as if you are over the hump and ready to move on, but your heart doesn't allow for that just yet. It's not finished teaching you from this loss. You are not just able to let go, move on, and live your life. You have to experience more, and usually so out of the blue, that you wonder why you even have the thoughts in your head at that exact moment.

Coffee. That is my moment of grief. The simplest moments that I took for granted turned out to be the biggest moments that I miss. Watching Hailey get out of bed, walk over to the kitchen in one of my t-shirts she wore the night before to go to sleep, and then waiting for that first scent from the aroma that wakes even the dead, was my favorite part. It wasn't about the coffee we shared on those mornings. It was about the time we shared. No rushing around, and no worry of being late for an appointment. Just her and I, sitting there within feet of each other, and God, what I would not give for that feeling here and now.

I sit there drinking my black coffee alone and without a sound around, other than the occasional car passing by my street. It's peaceful, but lonely. Makes me think of my mother's time away, and how her morning is at this same exact moment in time. Is she having coffee, and if so, with other inmates who have become friends, or does she fear for her life, year after year, from some of the more hardened criminals that are there for greater reason than hers?

I don't know that I have really given a lot of in-depth thought to the routine she's had to endure for two decades. I imagine she wakes early in the morning as instructed, waits for someone free to open her cage, letting her out into a hall filled with gray blocks and void of color, but still far from anything that resembles free. She probably lines up, follows those other women who have had to accept their new life, and heads down to a room where she is fed what they say she will eat. She probably cannot decide when to get seconds, or if she wants her eggs scrambled versus over easy with a side of Canadian bacon.

Life must be so bleak for her, and here I am on the outside, a free man (at least for now), able to eat whatever I like for breakfast and able to sit here for as long as I choose, sipping my coffee and not having to wait for someone in a blue uniform to tell me when I am finished. But yet, I am sad over losing a woman who refused to fight for me and refused to offer a chance for me to correct whatever it is she felt she needed me to do.

It shows me that loss is loss. There are always going to be levels to loss, but that doesn't mean one hurts less than the other at any given moment. Your body processes loss very much the same despite the level of that loss. It seems to need you to understand that losing money gambling, or a significant partner, or the death of a close family member or friend, is all going to be relative. Sure, some loss will take longer to heal from, depending on what it was and how massive it impacts your future, but that immediate shock of pain seems to all feel the same.

As I am sitting there thinking about what message my brother needs to get to me, my phone vibrates on the counter just behind me. I turn to pick it up and look at the screen to see the message. It's from my brother, Erik.

"Michael, just landed. At Philly airport, terminal B. Can you come grab me? Let me know."

Am I reading that right? Did he just text that he is here in Philly, waiting at the airport for me to come grab him? What the hell is he doing here, this early in the morning on a Sunday? Okay, something is up. This is not making any sense to me, but yea, of course I am going to grab him.

"Be there ASAP," is all I send back.

As quickly as I can, I get myself composed, walk out to where my car is, and jump in. It's cold again, and so I need to defrost the windows so that I can see clearly in front of me. As it defrosts, my mind starts to drift off about that fact. I need to see clearly in front of me, just as much as I am learning to see clearly behind me. It doesn't sound possible, but to be fair, not much makes much sense around here.

Von has taught me a great deal about my past, almost as if he were walking it side by side with me, willing me to understand, and then teaching me to move forward from it. Marcus has allowed me to understand that it's perfectly fine to let others into your space, no matter how long they decide to be a part of your world, as long as you want them to be there.

I've come to know so many previously unknown faces of people that I had never laid proper eyes on before and have been told many stories over the past two months of my service. Wonderful stories that were tucked away for only the few to know, but that didn't matter to those holding those tales. Those stories are true and important before they ever come to the surface for air.

We grow to believe that everyone has sorrows, struggles,

and that each person fights through them as best they are able to, but not all battles are fought the same, and not all people can clearly navigate the righteous path alone. Some need a set of directions laid out, and others, well, others need a broken path through brush and debris, just to find a clearing that has at least some of the answers.

My path, my intended trail through this journey of life, has lent me people that are here for one purpose or another, despite the time they are able to stay. I can will that time to move quickly, or beg for it to stay just a little longer, but the truth is, once the lesson has been dropped off before me, their task is complete and they move on down the road to whatever comes next. Even if the lesson is not meant to be shared at the time they go. Some lessons take flight immediately, while others, well, they linger awhile until a time when we are able to handle the truth.

The car is warm enough, and I see my brother is asking for an ETA. Normally, he's a pretty patient man. I guess to be an attorney, one needs to have a tremendous amount of patience. Listening to the same story, and the same scenarios and excuses over and over, has got to get annoying as hell, but he handles that well from what I can tell.

"Bro, 20 minutes. I'm coming, it's not right outside my door," I text back.

I'm nervous, but excited at the same time. I have not seen my brother in far too long, but I am concerned about the news he brings with him. Why he could not just share that with me over the phone from Seattle is baffling, but knowing my brother, it's big and he needs to share that with me one-on-one, in person, brother to brother.

The drive is an easy one, as traffic is light on Sunday mornings, even in the city. Normally as I drive, I look straight ahead and do not concern myself with anything else not in the path I am traveling. But today, I find that I am distracted by just about everything around me. A building I have passed a thousand times but have never touched, or a street that looks like you would only travel down if you had three people the looks and size of Marcus standing in front and behind you.

I also am seeing that the city has more homeless people laying on their cold walkways than I had remembered seeing in my entire life. I see newspapers blowing to the beat of the mysterious wind, and underneath, a body trying to keep warm. There are men and women sitting there, looking as if they are searching for something to do, but deep down, they know this to be all they have for today.

It's frustrating and sad at the same time. Watching a human suffer, seemingly all alone and without a way to move on, is defeating for me to see, but I can't imagine what it must feel like for them to actually live it. Not all these souls end up at the 'Flaps, and if they did, what then? Von and Marcus are but two men with limited resources to even begin a task like this. The facts are the facts, and it's pissing me off for some crazy reason.

I once imagined these people were invisible to me, pretending as I walked by that they had no feelings, and no past to remember. As if they were not real, and only created to allow me to feel better about myself, but I don't. I don't feel good at all about the person I am. I have a warm place to call home, and food delivered whenever I so choose. I can bathe ten times a day if I wish, with unlimited water at my disposal to waste as I see fit. I have no one chasing me from stoop to stoop, shouting words that no person should ever be forced to hear in two lifetimes. I have none of that, and yet, there are those that live this daily and are forced to accept the terms of their existence.

Why now, and why do I have to feel so emotional and helpless about people that are not my problem? I have my own problems, and I have my own set of hardships to face, and they aren't there to help me. So why should I care so much to help them? And not just why should I, but why do I? Because I do.

"Michael, hey. Thanks for picking me up. Sorry I did not call sooner, it's been crazy. How are you doing?" Erik asks.

"Not a problem, man. Good to see you. I was going to come visit you out there, but you know," I start.

"Yea, I know. You don't need to worry. I get it, Michael," Erik responds.

I'm driving him back to my place and waiting for the small talk to die down. The catching up is great, but there is something much more important to discuss, but as brothers often do, it's a chess match. It's as if he's waiting for me to ask, and I am waiting for him to tell me without having to ask. In his mind, I need to give a damn. In mine, by picking him up at the airport on short notice, I am giving a damn. Yea, it's safe to say, I am glad he's back in town.

Back home, we walk in, and I ask if he would like some coffee.

"Yea sure. I could use some. But first, let's talk. It's been a while," he responds.

"So, come all this way to do a little fishing with your brother?" I ask, being a smartass.

He smiles, rubs his eyes from what was probably a tough nap to have on a plane, and begins to explain.

"Yea a fishing trip with you is exactly why I am here. So, remember that parole hearing mom had a while back, where she was denied her freedom?" Erik asks.

"Yea, what about it?"

"Well, there was an issue with it. Not all the evidence that was to be presented, was. Mom has been counseling other women there for years, and those women wrote letter after letter about the truly remarkable work mom has done for them. Those letters never made it to the hearing, and so they are going to have essentially a do-over parole hearing. Michael, she's getting another chance to be free," he says.

Chapter 31

* * *

The news Erik carried with him all those miles, over all those states I've never visited that he flew past, was drawing out emotions that were unnatural for me. For the first time ever, I felt a sense of pride for my mother. I heard that instead of doing her time, quitting on a life that seemed to be over from the one she knew, she grew. She helped others who were lost and did so to probably feel human again.

My brother flew in to tell me because I think he felt I would not care, and he was going to ensure I saw the look of determination in his eyes to do whatever necessary to see this through. I did. I saw the look he had, and knew little would impact his energy, even if I tried my best to sap it dry.

But he need not worry. I am not of the same mindset I had been seven or so weeks ago. I am not that same thinker, that resentful human that was pissed off at how a human could change my direction without my approval. That man is gone now.

"So, what's the plan? Where do we go from here?" I ask him.

Erik is surprised to say the least. It's as if I pulled the chair he now sits in, right from under him and he slams to the floor without a chance to brace for impact.

"I'm here to speak to an attorney recommended by a colleague of mine. She's a pistol and has a great knowledge of what she can and can't do to help. I'm taking a few weeks off from the firm to see if something can be done to help. If you like, I could use you to help keep things in order for me. I have a lot of ground to cover, Michael. I need you brother," he says.

The morning is spent catching up on lost time, recanting stories that were lost for far too many years, and wishing for things to be different, if only for a moment. We talk about how we can't change what has already occurred, but that we can alter the direction for things to come, if we just try.

There are things I will need to put aside and store away for a later time if I am going to be of help to my brother. Funny, I am the older one, and he is in charge on this challenge we face. But I'm okay with that, and feel no resentment at all toward the different upbringings we were given. It shaped us into the people that sit here today, and I have come to terms with that. I love my brother, and I am damn proud of all he has accomplished in his life.

As the time passes and I put on a second pot of coffee, he is interested in learning about what I've been up to here in Philly. He knows all about my legal woes and tries to encourage me by telling me it would be incredibly hard for them to prosecute someone who was simply coming to the aid of a defenseless person. He reminds me that when I need him, he is only a text away and will not allow things to go as they did for our mother.

We talk about my time at the Mudflaps, and the impact that has had on my life and my outlook going forward. I find myself able to be entirely honest with him, and insanely open, when before, I would have stayed guarded with my emotions.

"Erik, these people there, they aren't who I thought they were. There is so much more to them and that place than you would think. It's sad but at the same time, a happy place if you look hard enough. It takes time, and man it took me a lot of letting go, to truly see what they are," I say.

"And what are they?" Erik asks.

"They are the same as you and I. People who deserve respect and a little understanding. It's not what I thought at all, but I am glad this was the one I chose to do when they presented me the options," I say.

Then I realize to myself, maybe I didn't choose this place at all. Maybe the Mudflaps chose me.

When the second pot is finished off, Erik lets me know that he needs to get to work but needs just a little rest. I tell him to crash wherever he likes, and quickly he parks himself down on my couch, and despite the amount of coffee he has just consumed, he finds himself fast asleep.

I throw a blanket that was thrown on the top of the couch over top of him and decide to head out for some air. I want to give him some space to rest and give myself some room to clear my thoughts.

I need to see when I can get out to see my mom, and I need to figure out what I want or need to say when I do. It's not as easy as saying,

"Nice to finally see you, how have you been?"

I have to somehow speak for two decades of emotions in one opening sentence, and that may be the toughest challenge ahead for me. And what if by some chance she does get paroled, and is able to come back to a life she no longer remembers, and one she has built a deep regret towards? What then? She is going to need to start over from literally nothing, and have to find a place to call home, and people to call friends. Will she end up as Von and the other residents of the 'Flaps have? I mean, I would not want that for her at all, but she has that choice to make for herself, I suppose.

I decide to jump in my car and head over to see if Von is around. I know it's technically my day off, but he doesn't get any of those, so maybe I will just sit with him and see if he feels like talking. We left things at an odd spot, and I would like to maybe revisit that, if just for my own sanity.

As I head over, I look at each person along the way. I swear I see Aaron, but then as I get closer, it's not him. But I do see other guests of the Mudflaps, and stop to just say hello, or to offer them a few dollars. Some are grateful, and others, well, maybe they are too but don't know how to convey that to me. And that's okay because I know they mean well.

Von is there, doing as he always does. Giving of himself, tirelessly at times, but always with that smile on his face. I watch him from a distance for a short time, trying to gauge how he is feeling today, so I know how to approach him, or if I even should.

What right do I have to be here today? Maybe he doesn't need that from me and would prefer to be left alone so he does not need to relive what his son did, and what that kid made him remember.

There's a man walking back and forth not far from where I stopped, and I watch him as he mumbles to himself about something or other. I can't really hear what he is saying, but the struggle he is living is real. What I have learned about people is that it's not always the words that get the message across best. Sometimes, it's what is not said, that has the biggest meaning.

When Hailey left, she never had spoken a word afterwards, and at first, that was incredibly hard to deal with. But as time went by, it showed me that her lack of words was more than enough said. We focus so much on what we want to hear, that we forget to listen to what we actually are being told.

I ask this man if I can do anything for him, and he smiles at me and shakes his head no. Then he wanders off out the same path I have walked each time I visit this place.

Maybe he just needed to be acknowledged for his existence and nothing more. And maybe I was able to give him that.

I start my walk over to where Von is working on one of the tents, I assume prepping for the cold that will come without warning and I try to stay out of sight. But the funny thing is, Von does not need to use his eyes to know, I am there.

"Michael, I see you are back. Is everything all right?" he says.

This man, who has never asked me to check on him, and has never asked me to do something to make his life better, is selfless. He is always so worried about how all those around him are doing, that I wonder if he ever has taken the time to evaluate how he is doing.

It's been years since his son passed away sadly, and I'm certain he could use some time away from here, if only to regroup. But he just seems hell-bent on pushing forward with his daily tasks, and the bigger picture his vision shares with him. That building in the City of Springs gives him a greater sense of purpose, and I just hope he knows what he is doing. I would hate for him to lose control of that mind of his.

"Everything is as right as it could be for now," I respond.

He laughs, still not looking in my direction because his focus is so important to him, but he knows I am struggling.

"Well, for now is important, but so is for later, Michael. What are you doing to ensure for later is right as well?" he says.

He always has a way of making me think deep. Much deeper than I could on my own, and I value that my friend has that gift. Because sometimes I see things as black and white, and nothing more. But he lends his wisdom long enough to remind me that there are many other colors and shades that need to be seen, even if I would rather not see them.

"I have some news about my mother that I just learned this morning. My brother flew in from Seattle this morning, early, and told me that she may have a new parole hearing coming up. Something about not admitting evidence of her good behavior, or something like that. Anyway, I think I am going to go and see her, and I don't know. See where that takes me," I say to Von.

Von doesn't say a word at first and gets up to tend to another of the tents. I walk over, almost shyly, wondering if he heard what I had said, and if so, does he care to even know?

"I am struggling with what I need to tell her, and after all these years, do I apologize or just move forward?" I say, again wondering what his advice will be.

But he just isn't looking my way at all. He's busy with tying things down, tidying up the areas around, and talking with the people who call these tents their homes. I know he can hear me, because he can hear them when they talk, but he's not addressing any of my conversation and I am growing confused. Maybe talking about his son and hearing about the kid I met has really taken a toll on him. Much more than I had seen the last time we chatted.

"I don't know, Von. Maybe I just need to see what comes out in the moment, and not rehearse it. You know, see how the moment goes and let whatever happens, happen. Maybe that is the best thing to do here," I say.

Von smiles, and now, looks up to me.

"Well, Michael, doesn't seem as if you need my input at all here. You seemed to have answered your own question, and may I add, it seems like a wise decision," he says.

And just like that, the whole less is more comes around full circle. He did not need to open his mouth and tell me what I needed. No, he just needed to listen, and allow me to find that for myself. Just as Hailey did. I found the answers myself, without needing their input. It makes me smile, and laugh just a little. And Von too. He laughs just a little with me.

"Whatever happens, Michael, remember this. Life is not always the way we plan it to be, and it doesn't always offer the forgiveness we seek when we seek it. But it ends up going the way it was meant to be, and that forgiveness? It comes with patience, time, and a lot of healing. But it does come," Von says.

"Von, I wanted to talk with you about something we didn't finish," I start.

But Von quickly cuts me off, and responds,

"I know you do, and for that, I am thankful that you care enough to want to. Michael, I dealt with my pain over the years, and I have come to accept that whatever happened to Aaron, was a lesson for me to grow from. These people here are better off because my son lost his battle. He did not die in vain, and nor did he die without a voice. I may not have been there for his final words, and perhaps when I needed to listen, well, I was too busy with my own life to listen, but now? I hear him. I hear him every morning as he wakes with me, and all day long as I help these truly amazing people. I hear him as I am so exhausted from the day and need to rest. His words travel from his soul, right to my ears. I hear him daily, Michael. And he is so grateful for all the help you are giving here."

Before I can follow up with anything, he adds one last thought,

"Next week, week eight for you, I want you to travel back to that old, abandoned factory we toured. I want your help with something that is terribly important, and I want you to share in that moment with me. Would you do that for me Michael? It'll be the last thing you need to do for these people, and one they will not forget."

Chapter 32

* * *

I have a mental list of the things I need to put together in my life, or at the very least, let go of.

Allow whatever time I had with Hailey to serve as a fond memory, but to let that go as she has willed it to die.

Prepare myself for what may come with this subpoena, but not let that distract me from everything else in my life. It's just going to be what it is going to be.

Bond with my brother. I have no idea how long he is back for, but I intend to use this time with him to my full advantage. It's been far too long.

My mother, and this one is probably the hardest one for me. I have to find a way to forgive her, and to forgive myself. Years have gone by without any time for finding true forgiveness, and it has weighed on me for much longer than I should have allowed it.

Week eight. I am not sure how I am going to prepare for my final day there, and the emotions I may have to face as the time winds down and the sun begins to set. I have a lot of letting go to do there as well but need to remind myself of all the lessons I have gained.

The rest of that Sunday my brother arrived is spent combing through his bag of papers now neatly piled in columns along the floor. He has everything in categories separated by color and timelines. It's impressive to watch as he talks himself through the stacks of papers he creates, ensuring he does not miss a single piece of information. They are all just as important as the next to him, and he's determined to get this right this time.

I ask my brother if he has been involved with the other parole hearings, because I just assumed he received a phone call saying it was denied, and he moved on. But that was not the case. He prepared for each one, and not only that, but he was also present in the buildings for each. I never knew he was in the same state as I, and why he decided not to inform me or tell me to meet up with him for a drink or two. But he had his reasons.

Being amazed is an understatement, but he is right. There is work to do, and so I get down on the floor with Erik and watch as he finishes up the piles.

"There, that all looks correct," he says.

I would have no idea, because to me, it's just a bunch of papers, both old and new, filled with scribbling and also neatly typed sentences with different color markers highlighting key phrases that I have never set eyes to before.

"What can I do, Erik?" I ask anxiously.

He hands me a stack and tells me,

"Read. I've looked through these papers so many times, nothing new seems to come from them, but a new set of eyes may see what I cannot. You have to familiarize yourself with this all, Michael. I know it's a lot, but so is her time away. Read. Let's bring mom home."

Home. Again, where will home be? Does he expect that she will walk out of those cages, hop into a car that will drive her back to the city she called home, and drop her off at her old place that is now owned by a different family? Or maybe he thinks because he is in Seattle that she can move in with me, until, you know, she can find her way? This, assuming she even wins her freedom. My brother is so intent on fighting for her, but I hope he is also willing to accept defeat if that should be what is handed down.

As I read, I keep seeing in the bag a stack of envelopes. I wonder if this is the stack that the women wrote to the board, telling them all about how my mom is a changed person, and gave them all a better reason to better themselves while a guest of the state. I figure he will get to those eventually, but I have to ask.

"How about those in there? Need me to read those too?" I ask.

He looks back at the bag, and then to me, and says,

"Those are yours. Those were to be read by you over a long stretch of time, but they remain unread, including by me. Those letters are the ones Mom wrote to you and sent to me to give to you. But you were never ready to receive them. I saved them, hoping that one day you might be at enough peace to see what she needed you to see."

I had forgotten all about those letters my mother wrote week after week, month after month, and eventually year after year. I knew she had, but I grew to a point where I no longer heard when my brother said he had another. It was just unimportant to me, and I blocked out the emotions that they once carried with them.

The pile is massive, and each is stamped and addressed to me, care of my brother by way of wherever he was living at the time. Now, it sits here in my living room, its intended target location for decades.

I put down the papers I have in my hands, and begin to reach for the bag, stopping only to gain permission from my brother. He nods, letting me know it's fine to grab what is rightfully mine.

The next few minutes seem like hours to me. I open the bag and run my hands across the front of each envelope. They are addressed as if someone took great care to ensure they were delivered properly. The handwriting is impeccable, and honestly the first time I can remember seeing my mother's writing. She probably signed a report card back years ago when I was young, but those are long gone. We took only what we absolutely needed, and they were not needed.

I want to open them but have no idea where to start. Do I start with the last, or with the first? How do I even know which one is first and then second and third? My eyes are feeling heavy, and I am fighting the urge to let go.

My brother can see I am struggling and puts down what he is doing as well.

"Hey man, it's okay. I get it. Take your time with this. You don't need to unwrap all these years in one sitting. Whenever you are ready, you open them," he says.

"But how? How do I know where to start?" I ask.

My brother turns over a few of the envelopes and shares the answer.

"Look to the center of each, where the seal mark is. You will find a small number there. Mom wrote a number for each letter, so that she knew which one she was on. She didn't want her thoughts to be confusing as much as she knew they already would, so she made that part just a little simpler for you."

I look to where he told me the numbers were and began to open the very first letter she wrote while incarcerated. The envelope is no longer a bright white as it would have been long ago. It has shades of yellows and browns, and the edges are no longer sharp, from years of being tucked away.

"Michael, what have I done? Please, don't ever hate me. I love you..."

"My dear boy, I cannot believe where I am now, and wish to God I knew where you were..."

They go on, as the time that passes does as well. With each letter I read, I slowly see her turn from a frightened, confused young woman in denial, to one of anger, and eventually, acceptance. What never changed through all those letters stuffed in all those envelopes, is how she begs for me to love her back, and to forgive her for removing so much from my youth.

As the years went by, her letters changed into stories. Not of a past she tried desperately to forget but could not, but of a lesson she learned while in a cage made for anyone but a mother. She told me of helping others cope with their sentences when they first arrived and were scared to death. She talked about the guards who become friendly enough that she knew some of their backgrounds. She mentioned how proud she was that she had two sons that were dealt a miserable poker-like hand of seven-two, but somehow, turned that into a winning set.

Her grammar improved tremendously, as did her storytelling. The letters went from a few sentences scribbled with pure regret, to pages of well thought out paragraphs that should be one day published in a book for others to read.

My mother, who needed me so badly all those years, never once gave up hope that one day I would come around, and she would see the man I had grown into.

Would she be proud that I pushed through all that trauma, or disappointed that I had never once allowed her some peace? I don't know, but it's time. Time to let go of what I can no longer see clearly, and to open my eyes to what I have now, even if it still feels lost for the moment. That will change with time I suppose.

I read and read and read, until there are no more letters to sift through. It was hours of emotions I never knew I had, spewed out along a trail of time that seemed to never end. But it finally ended with the letter marked seven hundred thirty-three. There were a few weeks in the beginning where she wrote a few a week, and then gaps where she mentions being sick and needing time off. Towards the end, she was fairly consistent, but there were weeks where she was so consumed with helping other inmates, she just did not have the time.

My brother had never opened a single one. He knew those words and thoughts were for me, and despite the fact I wanted to ask him what his letters were about, I knew those words and thoughts were just for him.

Erik smiles and comes over to where I am seated, mentally exhausted from the task I have finally completed in a single day, twenty years later. He places his arm around my shoulder, just as Von and Marcus have done in recent weeks, and says to me,

"Big brother, I know that was intense and so hard for you but know this. I am super proud of you for having the guts to go through that all just now. Mom will be so happy to know that her messages finally found your heart. I love you, man. I hope you know that. You are absolutely loved brother."

We sit there for a few minutes, and eventually, I need a break. I stand up and stretch my sore legs that have been in the same position for hours on end and let out a lion's roar. I am angry, hurt, frustrated, happy, confused, and whatever other emotions God has placed in this body of mine. I want to fight more than I ever have, and this time, without throwing a left jab. I want to do this legally now.

"Alright that's enough of the brotherly love speech. How do we get this done?" I say.

Chapter 33

* * *

Week 8.

All week I went to work as per usual, while Erik stayed back at my place using my car whenever he needed it to run around the city, searching for whatever he could that would help our mother's case.

But I have something to finish today and cannot be there to help him. This is my final week serving this community, and my final week with Von, and if Marcus is back, him as well.

When I arrive to where Marcus has met me so many times before, I see he is there sitting on the stoop, drinking his morning coffee, with another sitting just to the left of him.

"Morning, Michael," he says.

I sit down, first grabbing the hot coffee that seems to be the lifeline to my mornings more than I had realized and begin to do as he does. I look around to the city street just to the front of us. I gaze further out to where the tall buildings of the city's center shadow us from the morning sunrise. From where we sit, there isn't a lot to see. A few loose papers are tumbling around the gutters, caught in a wind that resembles the tiniest tornado. An empty liquor bottle from most likely the evening before that someone polished off. A weed, fighting for the last bit of summer through a crack in the sidewalk, before dying away for the season.

But I know what Marcus sees. He sees an entire community of people struggling, looking for their next meal and a place to lay their weary head for the night ahead. He sees the people holding up makeshift signs all throughout the shadows of those mighty buildings, hoping for something, anything, to get them through until the next day.

I see through this moment we share that just because I cannot see something with my eyes, does not mean it does not exist. How selfish I have been to dismiss so many lives because they were not in my line of sight.

"So, this is it. Your last day helping out those folks. Did you gain anything from this?" Marcus asks.

Man, where do I start. I gained so much from what seemed like nothing at all, and my entire perspective has shifted in a short time.

"Yea, I gained," I say, trying to sound like Marcus.

He laughs just enough to let me know he caught it.

"You ready?" he asks.

I don't need to answer, as he already knows, it does not matter if I am, because he is. I can, just as the very first week I arrived on these steps, follow him to his car or stay behind. I follow of course, not because I need him to sign off on whatever form it is after this last of eight weekends, but because I want to see what this place, and these people for that matter, have yet to teach me. My thirst to get everything I can from the confines of the 'Flaps is strong, and I intend to drink heavily today.

The ride is like any other, but then I see Marcus heads in a different direction from the one he usually takes. The last time he did this, we were heading to the hospital to see that old Terrance guy. But I don't feel as if we are heading that way this time. We get onto the Schuylkill Expressway once again and begin to head west, just as Von had done before.

"Heading back to that factory where Von took me last time, aren't we?" I say to Marcus.

He just mutters a "mmhmm," to me.

Sometimes I get Marcus to talk, while others, he tends to keep his deepest thoughts to himself. I've tried to figure out this man and what makes him do as he does, but he has a hard exterior that doesn't crack easily. But still, I know this is my last time here, and I need to know more about this man.

"Hey Marcus, let me ask you something if you don't mind. If you do, just say so, okay?" I begin.

Nothing. He just drives with his shades covering his dark brown eyes, blocking out that morning sun that chases us wherever we twist and turn.

"Who are you? What I mean is, what made you decide

to work here, and do you have family? I'm genuinely curious," I ask.

Marcus doesn't flinch, and I am thinking he is just going to enjoy this ride and forget that a question had even been lobbied in his direction, but then, he opens up.

"Yea I have a family. I have a wife, a son somewhere only he knows, and two tabby cats named Otis and Arthur," he responds.

Cats? This hulk of a man has a soft spot for kittens? I would never have guessed. And a son that he doesn't know where he lives?

"Why don't you know where your son lives, Marcus?"

"I never said he lives anywhere. I said that only he knows where he is. I haven't seen him in, let's see, maybe eleven years now. Going on twelve this winter," he responds.

I can see he is starting to feel somewhat uncomfortable, and don't want him to get upset on my account. I guess I don't really need him to go on if he can't. I feel kind of terrible now for having even opened this door to his past, just as I had done with Von.

"Sorry, man. We can talk about something else," I offer.

"No, it's okay to be curious. I have many curiosities and have a past that I too ran from. But I am here now correcting what I can and thanking the Lord for what I have and for what I have to come. You see, I had a bad habit long ago, and ended up on the streets. My wife and son were ashamed and although they tried to love me, I couldn't even love myself. So, they left me to my sorrows, and I had no choice but to accept that. I spent time in the filthiest of places and saw the most disheartening of lives all around. At one point I was resolved to let this be my life, but then someone came into my life. Someone promised me that if I wanted to get clean, and if I wanted to find my way again, that he would ensure I did," Marcus says.

"What happened? You obviously listened, but was it easy?" I ask curiously.

"Easy? No. Addiction is a terribly strong beast with an incredible grip, stronger than any man I know. I told that man I wanted to, but could not. But he would not let that go. He said he saw something in me that I could not see in myself, and he was making it his mission to correct my path. He said that if I wanted to, he would make sure I did," Marcus says.

We are now getting off of the expressway, and back on that same stretch of road that leads to those suburban views I witnessed a short time ago with Von. It's got me wondering if Von has more up his sleeve about that place we visited, with the broken windows and a century of dust choking the pieces of furniture that lay there, no longer needed. I figure if that is indeed where we are headed, I will know soon enough.

"Well, it worked, and is that man still helping, or is it that you took his place? Was he just like you, helping people turn what they once could not, around again?" I ask.

"Not much has changed for him. He's still there, doing for others what he did for me. Struggling to get folks to see that they are capable of so much more, despite the incredible setbacks they have faced. He doesn't quit, and neither should you, Michael. Setbacks are a part of life, and if we don't push forward, those setbacks become who we are," he says.

Wait, is he? He's speaking about Von. Von was the voice of reason and Von was the man who saw a clearing in the path that Marcus could not find on his own. He is the one who turned Marcus' life around. It has to be him.

"Von. Right Marcus?" I ask, but I already know.

"Mmhmm," Marcus responds.

I see that same bridge with that same weathered sign, just over the northern stretch of the Schuylkill River, telling us we have once again arrived in the City of Springs.

Down a road here, and around a bend there, we arrive to where I can see men and women walking into the building, and out with whatever their hands can carry. They are walking things over to large storage containers and placing them inside. Some in an orderly fashion, while others not so careful.

Marcus parks his car, and we walk out, heading towards the entrance that seems to be like a revolving door of people. Some I recognize from the 'Flaps, and others, I have never set eyes on before. But everyone seems to be helping just the same. There does not seem to be anyone standing around barking directions, but more a team of people all coming together for one cause. I just don't know what the cause is.

"Michael! I am so glad you decided to join us this

glorious morning. Welcome, Michael. Come in," Von says as he sees me enter.

I'm clearly confused but do as he says.

"You ready for your final task? I see you brought Marcus along for the ride," he laughs.

Marcus smiles too, and you can now see that this bond between these two men was forged over struggle, pain, suffering, and triumph. When Von told me that it was a tale filled with triumphs before sadness and of great loss before a new, impossible gain, he was talking about not only him, but his friend Marcus. He has watched people fall far from the highest peak, suffering deep down to the very depths of rock bottom, and then somehow, almost impossibly, regain some of their life back.

As I lend a hand to help the other workers, I feel my own sense of accomplishment come across my body. I have come to the final stages of my community service handed down by the city courts and learned more about myself than I ever expected to. I am not a terrible man, and although I clearly have issues with both my uncontrolled temper and selfish ego, and an inability to let go of a troubles past, I have time to change that.

My mother, who was once the most hated person in my existence, is now someone I am gaining an inquisitive respect for. I have so much I need to tell her, but I wish to listen to her even more so. I want to hear all about her time away and relearn the person she was before that horrible day. She's not that young senseless woman with the alcohol dependency problem that acted totally irrationally, changing the entire course of time for me and for her. She's a grown woman who has found herself first hating her life and wanting to forget it existed, to now wanting to live it more than she ever could.

I work hard, carrying each item I find in front of me to those containers out in the parking area. Occasionally I find myself looking out to the banks of the river, wondering what the 'Flaps community is up against today miles downstream from here. Without Marcus and Von there to help support, it's an entirely different place. But when they are there within the unseen walls that surround its unknown borders, it's not so bad.

There is a blanketed covered sign to the top of the entranceway that I do not recall from the first time I was here, but I pay it no mind. There seems to be a lot of commotion around this old factory, and I have little time to question much at all.

My last day. I am amazed I made it this far. From a young man who could not see human decency in any of these people, to a man filled with a yearning to learn each of their tales, I have come a long way in just eight weeks. Without them, I would probably end up living the remainder of my life never reconnecting with my mother and having a terrible hatred towards anyone that did not see life through my eyes.

As the day runs out of hours, I find myself anxious to slow down the time. I am not ready for this to end, but I know in life, all good things do come to a final end.

"Michael, it's getting to be that time. Let's say we wrap this up, head back to the office, and I will get those papers to you. You have done your time," Marcus says.

Chapter 34

* * *

"Mrs. Kelley, they are ready for you, are you ready?" the tall, slender guard asks her. Several of the guards at North Oakmont have developed a respect for my mother, which really tells me about the person she has become. They probably don't take the time to see just who someone truly is unless they can't help but to take notice.

She was told that there was an error in her last hearing and that she was heading back to go over things once again. But what she was not told, was that I would be there for this as well. The truth is, I wasn't entirely sure I could find it within myself to attend, having not seen her face or heard a single word she has uttered since I was a young kid. Why get her emotions knotted up if I decided it was going to be too much for me to attend? That would not be fair to her, and Erik knew that for certain.

As she walks into the room, there are guards to either side of her, and people seated across from where she is to sit. My brother is there, standing now to greet her, and she smiles warmly at her son. He has seen her many more times than I have, both in person and through photos they have sent back and forth. But still, it's emotional for him. But he is her hope here, and he knows that as well. It's his job to ensure she has a proper hearing this time with all items presented and also to fight within the parameters of the law, so he can free this woman after so many years tucked away from society.

She is not facing me just yet, and so I can only see a small piece of her. But then she comes into a clearer line of sight.

She's much older than I remember of course, and if I ran into her on the streets of Philly on any given Saturday, I would most likely walk right by her, unaware that I came from the same bloodline. She just does not look like the same person I knew and loved as a boy, but still, I can tell it is her.

Her hair is turning a light shade of gray, but she has done her best to keep it presentable for today. Her eyes are the same light green as always, but you can tell they have seen several years of lives passed by, for they have a sorrow that they carry with them wherever she looks around the room.

Her hands are fidgeting and seem uncontrolled, as she is understandably nervous. I guess in her shoes I would be as nervous as she. She's either going to head back to the only home she has known for two decades with less hope than she came here with, or she is going to be set free to find a home she has yet to know. Either one of those options has got to make her a little uneasy for sure.

There is a time allowed for her to speak with my brother, and then they will get on with the hearing. She reaches over to give Erik a hug, and for the first time, she has made eye contact with me. At first, she is unsure, but she knows there is something about me that is all too familiar, like an uncle at a family reunion that you know is family, but not exactly sure how they fit in. But then it hits her. Her stare becomes too hard to hold steady, and she plants her head into Erik's chest, and begins to sob.

I look to Erik to see if it would be okay if I go over to where they are, and he motions for me to join them.

My legs feel as if they are weighed down by lead shackles, but I find a way to break them free from their restraints, and head over to where she is hiding behind her youngest son.

"Mom, it's okay, mom. Don't cry," I begin, with tears in my own eyes.

I pictured this moment for a while now. How it would be when we first got together, and what the emotions would feel like, but it's not at all what I expected.

In the movies, this moment is filled with conversations about lost time and forgiveness beyond any imaginable measure, with the cameras focused on the two of us, while the courts wait patiently. But they do not. They would like to get on with the hearing, and back to wherever they call home.

We don't get a lot of time to talk, but I don't need it now. I can save that for later, because twenty years is a lot of time to overcome in a few-minute meeting. I will need more time to convey my thoughts, and even more than that, time to listen to what it is she has held in her heart for me. I'm sure those letters do not explain all of her feelings, so that will all just need to happen when it does.

As the hearing proceeds, the woman in charge of the board before us speaks up. She informs my mother that the reason they are back here, is because thirty-two letters were never entered at her last hearing, and the board felt that needed to be addressed. They don't seem as if they have made any decisions based on the letters, so I am nervous. But we are here to right a wrong, so at least if she is taken back to her housing at the prison, she will know what those ladies did for her, and she can at least hold onto that piece of happiness.

The woman speaks of other items first, including my mother's good behavior over the years, and the wardens remarks about how she has stood out for her willingness to help others whenever called upon. All items that did not grant her a release the last time, so I doubt they make any change this time.

The letters are next, and now another board member starts to explain those to the rest of the board.

"Mrs. Kelley, Board, and those here present to witness this hearing, I have here a stack of letters that were omitted from our last hearing, as was previously mentioned. These letters were read in their entirety by each member seated here, and so we would like to discuss these if you will," he says.

My brother is whispering to my mother, and she just

nods ever so slightly to let him know she understands.

"There are, as mentioned, thirty-two or so letters, each written from the perspective of a unique inmate who has come into contact with you, Mrs. Kelley, while you have been incarcerated here by the State. In these letters, I myself have read not just words, but true testimonies of your generosity, and ability to touch the lives of those who may not believe they have much to give. But somehow, you were able to extract a little hope, for lack of a better word, from each. I will say that letters are something we read often. But rarely are they enough to make a difference," he says.

Is he telling us that even though they have pulled us in here, and given my mother a hope for a second chance in a short amount of time, that it was for nothing? That all she has done to alter the existence of thirty-two unique women, as they have said, is not enough to show she is deserving of a release from that place of little hope? Is that what this guy is saying? I can feel my blood boiling within me, and I want to stand up and let loose on this entire proceeding, and Erik can sense it. He motions to me, trying not to get the boards attention that he is doing so, for me to stay cool.

I do as he wishes, but I want to scream and curse and throw hands at people right now.

Another member speaks up as well and she begins,

"These letters I too have read. It happens a lot when people come to us for parole, and honestly, it's not that hard to get people to write letters for you in prison, many times because a favor was owed, or will be owed. But I did read them all and have allowed them to be a part of my decision as well."

This is feeling like horseshit right about now, and my mother senses it. She has her head hung low, and is nodding softly to herself, probably realizing that her hopes are drifting away like the wind carrying one of those letters to somewhere far from here. Her mind has got to be close to cutting off the words these people are saying, as I know mine would be.

I watch my mother shifting around in the chair, and I want to grab her and take her from this shitty hearing, and seriously, who is going to stand in my way? None of these people put any fear in me. They aren't Marcus, and if he were here, he would talk sense into them and tell them everyone deserves a second shot, and even a third, at life. It's too short to allow one's soul to die off for the actions of one drunken day two decades ago.

Each of the panel members speaks about what they have been told and what they have read. But none of them have actually witnessed her with those women. None of these people are able to see deep inside of that older woman to truly understand here apology for her actions, and her will to make amends with both society and her children.

They see a woman who decades ago was sentenced to a term that took not only her freedom away, but the life her children were supposed to have. Sure, we were poorer than dirt at times, but I had my family intact, and even if we needed to walk the tracks early in the morning here and there to collect cans with magnets in our hands, so be it. I love those memories more than they know, and that made us truly rich.

They finish and ask if there is anyone else who wishes to give a testimony. Erik stands up and declares that he has words to add if it will please the board.

"Respectful people of the Pennsylvania Parole Board, I am Erik Kelley, Attorney, and youngest child to Bridgett Kelley, who is seated to my left. I would only like to ask that this board take a deeper look into the actions of Mrs. Kelley. We, of course, cannot change the outcome of that horrible morning, and Bridgett is not asking for that. She is asking that the time she has served be penalty enough for the fact that not only did she alter her life and the life of her husband that day, but of her two sons' as well. The years spent trying to forgive herself for her actions are second only to the desire she has to spend her remaining days with her children. She is aware that gaining those lost years back is impossible but building a new life into what years are to come is imperative to finishing her legacy as a mother," he says.

He is looking at mom now, smiling down on her while trying to keep the stern composure he must have learned doing legal work. I've never seen him in action so this is all new to me.

"Please, consider this woman to have been rehabilitated, and no longer a danger to anyone on the outside. She is a fraction of what she was, sober for twenty some odd years, and ready to be productive. It's time," he says looking at mom.

"It's time."

The board sits still, waits a moment, and then without much else, asks if there is anyone else that would like to speak on her behalf.

I am sitting in that lead again, frozen by emotions that I did not know existed. A trail of them is running rampant throughout my veins, telling me to go left and right and up and down. I have no idea of what I should be doing, but somehow, I know I need to do something. So, I force myself to stand, and without much warning, I slam my hand down onto the desk in front of me, and speak,

"I am not sure how to address this group of men and women, as that is more of my brother's strength. He was raised by people better than I was and learned to love with a heart of gold. Me? Not so much. I am angry at times with my life that was not the one I asked for. My anger has caused me problems in life, both legal and personal. But I know this to be true. I have been granted a second chance for the mistakes I have made many times over, and those second chances have changed not only who I am, but how I view society as a whole. Sometimes we learn the most from that which hurts others the most," I start.

I take a deep breath as I am now understanding that my words, my statements here now, have a greater weight to them than any words I have spoken in my entire life. These words that will and are being spoken can literally place a woman back into a metal cage surrounded by people that probably deserve their sentence more than she, or best case, I am able to convince these people to set her free, finally, and rightfully.

"Look, this woman is my mom. She was my mom then when she decided to place the keys in that car, and even though I never cared to admit it, she has been my mom for the last twenty years while locked up. She didn't just receive a life sentence. She received something far worse. The loss of her husband, the loss of her ability to raise her young sons, and more than that, the sentence that I handed to her. I quit on her, but as my life has shown me, not everything is always as I remember it, and sometimes forgiveness is not just about forgiving the person you felt wronged you, it's about forgiving yourself," I continue.

Now I am getting emotional and my eyes are watering, which makes my own mother do the same. Instead of speaking to the board, I finish speaking to my mother.

"Mom, I forgive you. I forgive you. I forgive you. I know you did not mean for that day to happen, and I know each and every day since that tragedy, you have wanted forgiveness. Not from this state who unfortunately has control over you, but from your children, who are a part of you. I held that forgiveness from you because I was selfish, not because you didn't deserve it. And I don't care what these people here think or say, because they cannot speak for me. I love you, mom. And I promise you, I will be here no matter how long you have to fight this. Damnit, I miss you mom," I cry.

Chapter 35

* * *

It's unusually cold for a spring morning, and I just wish that they would get on with it, but I know they want this moment to be just right.

Von is perched on the top of the stairs just to the front of the entry doors of his dream that he not only set out to do, but actually accomplished. He's proud, and I can see it in his facial expressions from his clean-shaven face that I have never once seen in the past. His beaming from ear to ear and looking over the people who have gathered here for his presentation. Before he starts, he motions for Marcus to go up and stand beside him. Marcus declines, but Von won't let that be it. Eventually, Marcus realized that Von is not going to start until he goes up. It's clear he does not relish the attention as much as Von, and that's okay.

I am standing about fifteen or so feet away from where they both are, and anxiously awaiting the unveiling. I look over to the river and can see a morning steam rise off its mirror finish.

Von looks down to the watch I gave to him months back when I completed my eight weeks, sees that it is time, and begins to speak.

"Ladies and gentlemen, I have always wanted to start a speech that way."

The crowd starts to laugh, and Von is at pure ease. All eyes are on the man most of these people have known as a leader of their community, although he has never wanted that title.

"We are all here not because of me, but because of everyone here, for those that cannot be here, and for one very special young man, that no matter where he is, is always here by my side. Several years ago, I decided it was time to move on to a different path in life, and because of that one decision, I am truly a better man. What I have learned in this experiment of life is that when you believe you have everything, you don't. When you believe you have nothing, you don't. It's all about balancing the wants and needs of your inner self and appreciating what you have trouble seeing with your eyes at times," he says.

I am following as best I can, but Von of course is a deep meaning man. Much deeper than I could possibly ever be, but I appreciate his poetic way of seeing the world even after the most difficult of circumstances that would bring another human to rock bottom and never let them back. As the saying goes, he can make lemonade out of any old lemon thrown at him, and that makes him a special, special person.

"For many great people, the world can be a place of

misunderstanding, terrible assumptions, and views that would be better served unseen. There is good in the hearts of those that maybe cannot express it the way you would like, but that makes little difference, for it's still there. I want to not keep you all waiting for what we have come here to see, but I need to thank a few individuals who have made this more possible than I could on my own," he says.

I can see Marcus is trying to slouch down in his stance, knowing that he does not favor attention of any kind, but to hide his massive frame is futile at best.

"I don't want to put anyone in order of importance here, so please know that I am simply going off of how they are placed in my humble mind, not out of contribution, but of how I have remembered a particular moment in time that sticks with me right now," he continues.

As he speaks those words that only he can speak, he wishes to thank people that I have never heard of, but that have a clear space in Vons' heart. Some of them have most likely contributed money, while others have lent a hand from higher places than I could ever hope to be. I notice that as he thanks those he feels he needs to, none of them are waving up their hands looking for any attention. This place we stand at is not craving for attention at all, but instead is hoping to be a place of no one man, woman, or child having more importance than the next.

Then after a few moments, he starts to thank those I have known, or heard of, during my time at the 'Flaps.

"My dear friend, who has risen above more than one

man should ever need to. A man who has devoted his time and energy into helping those around him, despite their willingness or lack thereof to accept. I have seen him hold in rage when things do not go as he is willing them to. Instead, he smiles through each day, painful as it may be at times, knowing that tomorrow he will simply do more to ensure he reaches everyone in his path. Marcus? I have come to respect you more than I could ever possibly express in a lifetime. My words conveyed to you will never show you the true gratitude I share for the man you are. And for that, I am blessed to be in your shadow."

Marcus tries to keep his composure that he seems to have perfected so well, but he cannot. I've seen him walk the toughest streets of Philly without allowing anyone to read how he feels, or if there is a splatter of fear in his eyes. I've watched as he has helped, or tried to help, countless others. Some of whom, no matter how hard he tries, cannot figure it out on their own. But he has never stopped trying, even for a second. I've even watched as he visited with a man who was struggling for his life, and probably knew his time was upon him, and Marcus gave him comfort when no one else could.

Now, he is standing in front of a large gathering of people from all different walks of life, all heading in very different directions after today's ceremonies are finished, and he is sobbing as quietly as possible to himself, but it's noticeable just enough. His life as I have learned over the past several months, was much harder than mine, and while he stumbled around with excuses, ultimately, he never allowed those to become permanent setbacks. He accepted, forgave, and pushed on. He may just be the strongest man, outside of his imposing physique, that I have ever had the pleasure to meet.

"I would also like to thank a man who was by the grace of God, placed into our lives for a short time, but a valuable time. A young man who came to me with such apprehension but learned that just because you see with your eyes, does not mean you know how to see with your heart. He had to open up to things he never imagined he would or ever could, and for that, I am proud to know him. Michael, thank you. I am also proud to call you friend, more than you will ever know," he says to me.

It's a touching moment, and one I did not expect to be part of. For those first eight weeks I encountered there along the river, changed not only my perception of the people who inhabited that tent city, but my perception of myself as well. I learned much more about who I was than I had in all the years of my life prior. I learned something I could never have learned on my own. I learned absolute forgiveness.

"Lastly, I need to be thankful for those that knew me best, even if I did not know them the same. My wife, who to this day, I will always cherish as the single most beautiful soul on the face of the earth. She knew that despite my flaws, my intentions were honest and pure. And when I came to a part in my life where I took her for granted, life blindsided me into a humbleness I never knew, reminding me that I am to treasure each morning as if it were my last. I simply did not," Von says softly.

When Aaron passed, his wife went into a depression that was to be expected, and although they were extremely wealthy and could afford the best of anything, there was not enough will in his wife or money in any account to carry on. She passed not long after their son died, of what he once told me was the saddest of hearts that he knew would never be able to heal. He talked to me about his wife with such pride, and while he missed her immensely, he never regretted not having more time with her. When I asked him why, he said that she gave him the best years of her life, and that it could never be topped. He knew she was called home to be with their son, and to Von, that loss for him was a bigger gain for Aaron, who needed her more than he did.

"My boy. Nothing will ever make up for the void left in my heart, but I know you are here with me today, as you have been for each step along this improbable journey of mine. Not a single morning goes by that I do not wish I had seen more with these old eyes, but alas, I have finally been healed enough to see what you did. I made a promise to you after you passed, that I would search the ends of the earth for you in the hearts of others and do whatever I could to help them see life is worth the battles we all face within," he concludes.

The only sound as he stops speaking, is the sound of

birds calling to one and other along the banks behind this building. This goes on for a long minute, and then Von looks up, and reveals to the crowd the name of this place of hope and acceptance.

He motions to a man holding a rope that is tied to the blanket covering the sign, and in a quick moment, the sign underneath is revealed.

The Aaron Jitters Community Center.

He knew his son as Aaron for his entire life, but those that accepted him for what Von could not knew him only as Jitters. Von was able to embrace this after years of frustration and loss, and now, he would like everyone to know that the name of his son was not as important as the heart of his son.

The sun is starting to add just a gentle warmth to the cooler air, and I lift my head up to greet its growing rays. My now closed eyes are filled with a magnitude of colors dancing through them, and I smile to the sky. When I look around to all the people here today, I swear I can see that man who called himself Jitters, but I know it's the effects of the sun and my mind allowing him to occupy that space that I have granted him permission to. As quickly as I thought he was there, smiling towards where his father is standing proud, he is gone.

They open the doors and for the first time, everyone gets a chance to see the months of hard work and dedication that went into creating this place from a useless abandoned factory. A place that seemed to have lost its purpose for decades on end, has shown that it still has a lot left to give if you just ask of her.

That reminds me of my own mother. She seemed lost and useless to me, but as I learned over the past year, she is anything but worthless. Her decades of sitting dormant in my mind were just that. In my mind. She had lent her life to others so that they may learn from her mistakes, and like this building, she has found a new renewed purpose in life.

That day in the parole hearing, a board of members who seemed entirely uninterested in what they were there to do, proved me wrong. They were looking at not what they could see, but what they could not. In the end, to my surprise, and my mother's and Erik's, she was granted her release.

It was not as you may think that very day. They did not smile at her and demand she be released immediately from their custody and turned over to us. It took time. Time that was important because she needed to figure out so much about a future she did not expect. But still, she was being released, and I could not be more excited. She also needed time to say her goodbyes to the people she had come to know as her family, because as she learned, family isn't always about blood. It's about loving and caring for others for no other reason than to want it.

Erik stayed for another week after to help me understand what was coming next, to fish for a night that was long overdue, and then he had to return to his job on the west coast. But he was content.

But my mother, who now stands beside me at this

opening ceremony, is ready to get this next chapter of her life started. She and Von have talked several times in the last few weeks and come to a conclusion that she should, at least for now, stay at the Aaron Jitters Community Center and assist in the transition of those who will call this place home for the time so they choose.

My issues within the city I call home are now mostly behind me. Marcus signed off on my service, and the judge thanked me for following through with my sentence. When he did, I told him it was me who wanted to thank him. He looked confused, and I never said more. I just smiled, letting him know without words, that it was a blessing in disguise, that had changed my entire outlook.

That other issue with Terrance? An entire community of people came to my aid and reminded those in power that what I did was not out of anger, but out of love and respect for a complete stranger who deserved both. It was a chaotic scene, but it doesn't seem as if it was about me being in danger of serving time. I think it was just about learning more of the truth, just as those letters the inmates had done for my mother. The trial is not over, and I will have to head back to serve as a witness, but with much less weight on my shoulders. I feel bad for Terrance having to give his life up, and those boys who made stupid life-altering mistakes that may require them to lose the same, but as my mother learned, we all have to serve our penance in life for each bad decision we make.

This place is going to allow for some true healing, and

I can feel that it is helping others already on the very first day, although there is still a lot of work to be done.

Von is much wealthier than I ever knew, but in his mind, his only wealth comes from what he has learned in the second phase of his life. His money, while important to those he serves, has never truly made him as complete as he thought it would. He was always chasing something that he already had, and he missed it. Now he spends his days and nights reminding others that what they have is more important than what they do not.

When Terrance passed, Von decided that the people he loved and cared for, needed much more than the Mud-flaps had provided for them. He knew that the homeless community was much larger than people expected, and so that time when the 'Flaps was empty, he summoned buses to pick up the community, and drove them all to The City of Springs, to ensure them they would have a safe place to call home always, for as long as they should need. That was his vision, and what he not only dreamed, but what his mind and his money did.

My job is no longer as it was. Von has found a way to keep me on, so that I can spend more of my hours helping these people I have learned to respect greatly. I counsel them, help them with accomplishing any goals I can, and in the end, simply listen. I have never felt more needed in my entire life.

The 'Flaps will go on as long as Von has a fight in him. He has spent more money on keeping that community where it is than I could ever imagine. But he has no intentions of letting that place go.

I once asked him where it got its name from. I mean the Mudflaps seemed to make little sense.

He told me that back in the 1920's, a group of women from a local dance club had used the grounds to practice their dancing under the warmth of the sun. When it rained, they refused to allow that be an excuse and continued on, laughing and splashing away through the wet clay muddy ground as if nothing could change their happiness. Not even a little rain. The city owned the land but had never made plans for its final purpose. Eventually the women would visit more and more, and some would even stay late into the night, enjoying themselves immensely. When the Great Depression hit, those same women who came to call this place their home away from home, ended up needing it more than they realized.

Since that time, it had become known as the Mudflaps. There have always been stories about the cities fight to close it down, but for reasons unknown, they never could officially get it entirely cleared. They either gave up fighting, figuring it was tucked out of the way enough that it did not matter, or maybe, just maybe, there has always been men and women like Von to ensure that no matter how much they wanted to empty that lot, they would never truly be able to break those spirits enough to accomplish any such thing.

I heard awhile back that Hailey had moved out west

somewhere, and although I never heard from her again, I learned to accept what life had in store for me, because I'll be damned if I knew on my own.

As Marcus once told me,

"Ain't no man or woman able to occupy that space without your say-so. You hear me?"

I heard you, Marcus. I heard you.

The End

If you enjoyed this story, be sure to check out the Authors other novels, available on eBook, paperback, and hardback.

When the Dandelions Sing

"When The Dandelions Sing," is a warm, heartfelt story about a young boy named Ronnie Jefferson McFarland Jr., who is trying to understand the meaning of the word "purpose", and what his purpose is in life.

His grammy, who nicknames him Jasper for some reason known only to her, and his grandad, give him valuable lessons through their own eyes, and a window to the past that sometimes gets overshadowed by bigger things in life, but never truly forgotten.

While Ronnie's momma struggles with her life, he leans on others around him to gain perspective and a sense of understanding. He learns that even after people leave his world, their impact remains, and he never stops learning from them. As it turns out, some of the best lessons in life come from those who seemingly have nothing left to give.

Ronnie learns that a family is not always conventional, but oftentimes made up of the people you choose for yourself, and who choose you in return. He discovers that joy can be found in the smallest of things and the simplest of moments...for even among a field of perfect flowers, the simple dandelion can sing.

"Everything has purpose, and everything, a meaning beyond what we are even meant to understand. That's just the way it is. Purpose is not what we want it to be. It's simply what is meant to be."

Phoebe's Heart of Stone

In 1919, an unthinkable tragedy struck the blue-collar town of Alliance Ohio, and one particular family, the Bradway family, found themselves at the center of its terrible wrath. In the wake of disaster, Carl, a father of six, was forced to make a decision that would affect both himself and those he loved for the rest of their lives.

Carl and his beloved wife, Phoebe, had worked tirelessly to build a life of love and contentment for themselves and their six young children. Though determined and deeply in love, the young family could not escape the horrible black cloud that haunted their family, seemingly hell-bent on taking all they had built together.

This story follows the shocking true-life events of a family who wished for the simple things in life, but instead faced a path riddled with misfortune that altered the course of each of their lives forever.

The Gift of Life, Plus One

Agnes is a young, unconventional little girl, who wants to be exactly who she is. Her father, Jon, struggles with the balance of raising his children the way he sees fit, while still allowing them to grow into the people they are destined to become.

When Agnes suddenly falls ill, her life and the lives of those around her are altered forever, in ways they never imagined. Both her father and mother, Amanda, are faced with challenges that will either break them, or save them.

Jon finds that when he drifts off to sleep, his mind often travels to a unique place where he is mostly alone with his thoughts, while discovering that accepting life is not always easy, but important to moving on to the next season of life.

"The Gift of Life, Plus One," provides the perspective that just because life doesn't necessarily go as we planned, it's exactly the way it was intended to go.

Made in United States
North Haven, CT
11 February 2024

48627626R00225